FRONTIER MILITARY SERIES
XVII

REGULARS
IN THE
REDWOODS

The U.S. Army
in Northern California
1852–1861

by
WILLIAM F. STROBRIDGE

THE ARTHUR H. CLARK COMPANY
Spokane, Washington
1994

LIBRARY OF CONGRESS CATALOG CARD NUMBER 94–71442
ISBN 0–87062–214–5

THE ARTHUR H. CLARK COMPANY
P.O. Box 14707, Spokane, WA 99214

Part of chapter three appeared
previously in *Journal of the West*,
October 1981, pages 20–25, and
is reprinted with permission.

Contents

Illustrations

Preface

Some years ago, I came across a series of letters, still in 1850s brown War Department wrappers, written in 1858 by a post commander in northern California. The explicit views of this lieutenant varied from those I recalled from history classes about California pioneers and contrasted with the stereotype of the so-called Indian-fighting Army. Further research in these letters and others in Record Group 393, Records of United States Army Continental Commands at the National Archives in Washington, D.C., revealed documents written by more than fifty Army officers in northern counties of California. They set the tone for better understanding of the Regular Army in northern California during the years 1852–1861, a period generally overlooked by historians.

The purpose of this book is to show how the U.S. Army operated in the difficult civil-military atmosphere of northern California in the decade preceding the Civil War and to show how the stereotypical myth of the Indian-fighting Army is inadequate to describe the attempts of the officers and men of the Regulars to maintain the peace between Indians and whites. In their letters and in their actions, these men were different from those in the local volunteer units. These volunteer units were composed of whites who, much of the time, were bent on destroying any Indian they could find.

For simplicity I have used modern county boundaries wherever possible and cited military officers by their brevet grades. When names or descriptions of Indian groups were vague in letters and reports, I have used published names where possible. I should warn the reader that the Department of the Pacific was called the Pacific Division from 1848 to 1853.

Sources are cited in full the first time they appear. In subsequent references, shortened forms are used for convenience. In addition, the notes include the following abbreviations: *ARSW = Annual Report of the Secretary of War; CHQ = California Historical Society Quarterly;* LR = Letters Received; LS = Letters Sent; M = National Archives, microcopy number; n.d. = no date; *OR = The Official Records of the Union and Confederate Armies,* volume L; PR = Post Return; R = roll; RG = Record Group in National Archives.

Valuable assistance was provided to me at the National Archives by Richard F. Cox, Jr.; Elaine Everly; Dale Floyd; Sara Dunlap Jackson; Timothy K. Nenninger and at the Smithsonian Institution by William A. Deiss and James S. Hutchins; also Mrs. Jane T. Hillard and Davis Walters of North Carolina. In California a number of helpful persons shared local lore, particularly Lieutenant Colonel Benjamin L. Booth, USA (Retired); Patricia H.

Byrne; Robert J. Chandler; Nancy Egeline; Charles G. Ellington; Colonel M. B. Halsey, Jr., USA (Retired); Irene Nelson; Colonel Norman A. Rial, USAR (Retired); Nita R. Spangler; George R. Stammerjohan; Anne and John Steven; the late Norris A. Bleyhl; and the late Father John B. McGloin, S.J. Successful searches for obscure archival material were made for me by Edie Bultler, Humboldt County Historical Society; Hazel McKim, Shasta Historical Society; Wayne C. Moore, Tennessee State Library and Archives; Dorothy Rapp, U.S. Military Academy Archives; and Michael J. Winey, U.S. Army Military History Institute. Daniel Salcedo, skillfully interpreting several historical sources, designed a map for this book.

I appreciate all the suggestions from Joanne W. Lafler, Jane S. Altman, and Robert J. Chandler, who gave generously of their time to read the manuscript. John Wilson of the U.S. Army Center of Military History added valuable comments on the manuscript. Editorial assistance and manuscript preparation was provided by Toni Murray and Alice Kuklok. At the Arthur H. Clark Company, David Leeth helped me clarify a number of points. Robert Clark showed understanding during a traumatic year. Any errors or omissions are my own.

Lois Strobridge gave unstinting encouragement, research assistance, support, and grace throughout the years spent on this book. I am grateful to all.

WILLIAM F. STROBRIDGE
San Francisco
May 1989

Introduction

The existence of Spanish California probably mattered little to Yankee or Tidewater families at the time of the American Revolution. Instead, frontier Indians were on the minds of many American colonists when the United States began its fight for freedom in 1775. Congress appointed three prominent patriots to deal with the Indians: Benjamin Franklin, Patrick Henry, and James Wilson. These three commissioners hoped to neutralize the Indians during the thirteen colonies' clash with England. During the Revolution a few northeastern Indian groups went so far as to aid the colonists. For the most part, though, Indians sided with the British and against those whites who offered them no trade and had crowded onto Indian lands.

Wartime acts by Indians bore little weight on the outcome of the Revolution, but the legacy of hostility carried over to the years of American independence. The Constitution retained governmental relations with Indians at the federal level rather than give responsibility to the individual states. Under the Constitution, the president's cabinet included a new position, secretary of war. Henry Knox, a successful Continental Army officer, assumed the new office in 1789. Congress gave Knox responsibility for Indian affairs and allowed him two civilian superintendents to help fulfill War Department obligations. Knox considered it a matter of national honor to treat Indians decently.

Successive civilian incumbents of the War Department post found that the Indian situation required more and more attention. Settler seizures of Indian lands, supervision of Indian trade and education, plus interminable conflict, all made demands on the secretary of war. For better control of this administrative burden, the tiny War Department staff created a Bureau of Indian Affairs in 1824. The bureau consisted of three civilians at the Washington, D.C., level.

In 1832 the War Department gained a new desk, that of the commissioner of Indian affairs. By then the government had decided to move Indians from five southern states to federally reserved lands across the Mississippi River. Between 1830 and 1835, use of uniformed soldiers in this forced migration of some forty-seven thousand Indian residents made military men reluctant witnesses to untold suffering. Lieutenant Erasmus D. Keyes, an aide to the Army's senior commander during the removal, regarded himself as "one of a gang of robbers."[1]

Congress eventually transferred the Bureau of Indian Affairs from the War Department to the Department of Interior, then a new branch of the federal government. Among those who supported the idea of making the Department of Interior responsible for dealing with the nation's Indian population was Senator Jefferson Davis, a former

[1] E. D. Keyes, *Fifty Years' Observation of Men and Events* (New York: Charles Scribner's Sons, 1884), p. 133.

secretary of war. The War Department's tenure with Indian affairs ended in 1849.

The War Department had more than enough responsibility without Indian affairs. Administering a peacetime army on a limited budget caused War Department leaders to keep the army smaller than requirements. The army's few regiments consisted of 550 to 800 soldiers. Regiments were further subdivided into field commands called companies, which were designated by sequential letters.

Companies on the frontier were often parceled out across the landscape to conduct operations individually. Purse strings held tight by Congress further limited field operations. Economy drives caused frontier army posts to be rustic at best.

That there was any army at all ran counter to Revolutionary thought. Americans knew that a standing army was "always dangerous to the Liberties of the People."[2] However, as the population of the United States expanded westward, settlers and Indians fought all along the country's boundary, causing civilians to modify their opinions on the need for an army. People were killed on the new republic's frontier. Federal intervention became necessary, and the United States raised a frontier military force.

Wearing hats crested with bearskin, the frontier troops won victories and became, in effect, the Regular Army. Even with military success, President John Adams worried over the expense of a professional army and thought that "Regiments are costly articles."[3] Still, the United

---

[2] Samuel Adams, quoted in Richard H. Kohn, *Eagle and Sword* (New York: The Free Press, 1975), p. 2.

[3] Russel F. Weigly, *History of the United States Army* (New York: Macmillan, 1967), p. 103.

States continued to maintain a full-time army of several thousand men.

The U.S. Army experienced some of the frustrations of frontier operations. Year after year, difficulties brought soldiers to the scene in various regions of the country. American squatters moved onto Indian lands in the Southeast. Commanders of U.S. troops refused to defend these illegal settlers. On the Missouri, traders and trappers tangled with Indians and then looked to the federal government's army for help. During the Black Hawk War, Regulars and state volunteers skirmished with Indians in Wisconsin and Illinois.

Between 1835 and 1842, Florida's uninviting climate and Seminole inhabitants wore down the Army in a debilitating contest. The Seminole War cast a shadow on the Regular Army's reputation. The Army's use of bloodhounds and violation of flags of truce offended republican values. Major General Thomas S. Jesup complained that finding the enemy, not fighting him, was the problem in Florida. On the other hand, Major Ethan Allen Hitchcock observed that the Seminoles were perfectly right in defending their homes. Ultimately, Florida fed Regular Army disdain for local, armed citizen volunteers and fostered sympathy for Indians.

By 1831 the Regular Army had garrisoned a dozen forts on or across the Mississippi. One of these posts, Fort Snelling, provided material for both infantry Captain Seth Eastman's later paintings of Native Americans and his wife Mary's book on Indians.

No railroads or turnpikes traversed these vast plains. Once across the Mississippi, the Army found that cavalry units were necessary for successful operations. Two regiments of dragoons were formed in the 1830s. The horse soldiers were authorized to use red and white guidons, and the troops went on lengthy mounted marches to impress Indians with the strength of federal forces. The cavalry expeditions covered much of what would later be Wyoming, Colorado, and Oklahoma. Waiting to inspect the bivouac guard on one such western march, Lieutenant J. Henry Carleton recorded that "Gentlemen in civil life . . . have no idea of the sleepless nights in storm and tempest" experienced by soldiers on service.[4] In 1846 the Army organized a third horse unit, a regiment of mounted riflemen, specifically to protect Americans on the Oregon Trail.

Beyond cavalry operations, the Army made geographical surveys of western America. Military men — including Stephen H. Long, Zebulon M. Pike, Stephen Watts Kearny, and John C. Fremont — collected a wealth of topographical and scientific information about the trans–Mississippi region. At South Pass, the great gateway on the Oregon Trail to the Pacific, Fremont calculated the elevation at seven thousand feet above sea level. The fact that the Army had invested in engineer schooling contributed to the success of government explorations.

The Army sought professionalism based on a European style of education. Dozens of Army officers went to Europe, where they studied at military academies and observed foreign army practices. Towering Brigadier General Winfield Scott and studious Captain Henry W. Halleck translated French military texts into English.

A host of army tasks, including the fortification of American harbors, called for engineering skills. Seeking

---

4 J. Henry Carleton, *The Prairie Logbooks* (Lincoln: Univ. of Nebraska Press, 1983), p. 111.

help, a French military officer, Simon Bernard, was placed on the American payroll and headed a board convened to plan the seacoast defenses of the United States. Bernard's study resulted in huge granite-and-brick forts that gradually took shape on the water's edge from Maine to Florida and, ultimately, San Francisco. Situated to level direct fire at enemy ships, such forts were armed with cannons, numbering from a few dozen to more than four hundred. American manufacturers cast the cannon. Artillery regiments of the Regular Army occupied the seacoast forts.

In the United States, informal schools of practice for artillery, held at Fortress Monroe, helped prepare cannoneers for war with foreign powers. Likewise, schools of practice for infantry, organized at Jefferson Barracks, readied ground forces for conventional warfare. The Army's commitment to military education and training allowed it to meet the challenge for war inside Mexico.

The Army showed its professional competence against Mexico in 1846–1847. Fighting an opponent that stood its ground, American forces employed successful and often innovative tactics and techniques. Bravery was added to skill. Major General Winfield Scott "played for the big stakes" and aimed his command for the Mexican capital.[5] In the final advance on Mexico City, American forces made a spectacular, two-hour assault on the castle of Chapultepec. The affair with Mexico seemed to prove the value of military education and training. Regulars may have expected a life of greater professionalism, more military schooling, and simple soldiering. Instead, the peace

---

[5] Winfield Scott, *Memoirs of Lieutenant General Scott* (New York: Sheldon & Co., Pub., 1864), p. 454.

treaty of Guadalupe Hidalgo pushed the Army into a complex role on an expanded frontier.

In the spacious, underpopulated territory acquired at Mexico's expense, many of the tactical ideas and wartime administrative procedures fell short of Army requirements in the Far West. Even the uniforms of the Mexican War came to be regarded as next to useless in forests of trees 350 feet high or on semiarid slopes of tough chaparral. Ironically, U.S. soldiers, who after the Mexican War ended up supervising civilian politicians, served under a general in chief, Winfield Scott, who prided himself on never having gone to the polls. The end of hostilities found the U.S. Army performing civil government functions in parts of the country's new lands, including California.

California and New Mexico had been objectives of an Army column sent out from Fort Leavenworth, Kansas, at the start of the Mexican War. Brigadier General Stephen W. Kearny, whose force eventually numbered two thousand men, took New Mexico without a fight. Solidifying his control, the American commander attended Sunday mass in Santa Fe. Kearny sat in the former Mexican governor's crimson chair at the cathedral. His accompanying officers distractedly counted some fifty images of the cross and listened to the music.

Kearny eventually continued on to California, with only a small portion of his command, the 1st Dragoons. He left New Mexico under a civil government headed by an American citizen. Native-born New Mexicans held some of the administrative and judicial positions under the American flag. Kearny reached southeastern California in December of 1846, with men and animals exhausted. He supposed that naval forces and American irregulars had already cleared the territory. Readying for a march across interior California to the ocean, Kearny's column got off to an inauspicious start.

A Marine Corps lieutenant met Kearny to guide the dragoons to San Diego. Kearny was informed that a Mexican force was nearby. Overconfident, Kearny attacked. Eighteen Americans were killed, and Kearny was wounded. The Americans, bloodied by the Mexicans and suffering from their mistake, reached San Diego six days later. Linked up with naval landing parties, the 1st Dragoons headed for Los Angeles. By March 1847, the combined American units had captured all of upper California. Kearny became one of a series of officers to hold the joint positions of commander of U.S. Army forces on the Pacific Coast and military governor of California.

Army officers governed U.S. citizens in California and administered customs houses. They changed the name of the busiest port from Yerba Buena to San Francisco. Conducting civil government functions included responsibility for a fast-growing American population of several thousand plus a well-established Indian population of 125,000. American and Mexican legal precedents complicated the decision process of Army officers when they tried to perform governmental duties. Soldiers worked to continue traditional Hispanic procedures. Captain Edward R. S. Canby managed to preserve the provincial archives of California. Captain Henry Halleck helped translate laws previously promulgated by Mexico. The Army in California received no extra staff assistants for the delicate duties of government. Instead, military government evolved into an additional duty for the troop commander and his staff, already loaded with the recurring task of submitting administrative reports to the War Department.

Moving more troops to California cost time and money. The only Regular Army reinforcement unit conveniently available for California duty was one company of the 3d Artillery, numbering just 118 men. They reached Monterey near the end of January 1847, after a 198-day voyage from New York via Cape Horn. Another long year passed before a full regiment, the 2d Infantry, prepared for California. Ordered to the faraway Pacific Coast after the Mexican War, the men of the 2d were unenthusiastic at the thought of separation from family and friends. The 2d Infantry also sailed via Cape Horn, a route that had advantages: Army units arrived cohesive and in good health. Yet, the voyage took five months—unproductive time for an entire unit destined for full service. The War Department paid dearly to charter civilian ships.

On land, the Regiment of Mounted Riflemen, delayed by action in Mexico, finally set out for Oregon, its original destination before the war. Marching from Fort Leavenworth in 1849, most of the regiment's seven hundred horses were lost or became disabled before reaching Oregon. War Department planners would look to a route across Panama for speed and economy the next time it moved troops to the Pacific Coast.

The Army deployed companies of combat troops through central and southern California. Soldiers at their new stations saw that, compared to local Indians, miners and settlers held different views of daily life. Ignorant of Indian claims, American civilians proceeded on the ill-founded assumption that the land was theirs for the taking. Indians, conversely, looked to the land for traditional and perpetual sustenance. Sometimes, troops attacked Indians. The soldiers thought they were defending innocent settlers from savage outbursts. On other occasions, military governors punished whites who, without provocation, had killed Indians. It was a puzzling scenario. Officers and men quickly perceived injustices to California Indians from American citizens but never found a way to cope effectively with such civil-military relations.

Gold further complicated the existing situation between newcomers and Indians. Colonel Richard B. Mason had succeeded Kearny as military governor and troop commander. Mason confirmed the presence of gold in California's hinterland. His unbiased findings were announced to Congress by President Polk on December 5, 1848.

Triggered by news of gold, thousands of Americans and foreigners determined to strike it rich. They rushed into California's hills and streams. Excluding the luckless Indians, California's population grew between 1849 and 1850 from an estimated twenty six thousand to about one hundred thousand. Most seemed wild with the idea that they would quickly find gold and return home with a fortune. Affairs reached such a state that Army officers were "quite bewildered" by fabulous stories of gold discoveries.[6] Enlisted soldiers were less bewildered and knew what to do: they deserted ranks. Soldiers headed for the gold fields, taking their chances and violating military law, to obtain wealth for a lifetime. Deserted by his troops, disturbed over the thankless duties of military governor, Mason asked to be sent home.

---

[6] William T. Sherman, *Memoirs* (Bloomington: Indiana Univ. Press, 1957), p. 54.

Unlike Colonel Mason, argonauts held high expectations for success. Many arrived in California from worldwide ports of origin. Others came by wagon train. Indians lived among the grasslands, rivers, and forests of northeastern California. In 1850 these native dwellers might have seen some of the 45,000 migrants who chose the California–Oregon overland trail to the gold fields.

Congress relented in its opposition to California statehood. Although Oregon was authorized a territorial government in 1848 and New Mexico waited until 1851 for similar status, California bypassed the territorial system. In California the military governor convened a state constitutional convention. Captain Halleck represented the Army and played an active role in drafting a California constitution. Major General Bennet Riley yielded authority to elected governor Peter H. Burnett. The new state was admitted to the Union on September 9, 1850.

Governor Burnett perceived an Indian problem in California's five original northern counties. An extended area near the headwaters of the Sacramento, far northern California, had yielded gold after the original strikes farther south in 1848. The discovery broke the area's tranquility and brought miners to the scene. Inland towns at Shasta and Yreka grew to supply miners' needs. Over the mountains from Shasta and on the Pacific Ocean, settlers founded Crescent City. Around Humboldt Bay, Americans made homes in several hamlets. Burnett and his successors in Sacramento expected the Regular Army to do something about Northern California's Indians. The Indians failed to comprehend why the strangers stayed on land instead of moving on.

California's Indian population suffered certain disadvantages. The state's one hundred thousand Indians spoke more than sixty languages. Each language was distinct and unintelligible to speakers of others. Such a communications gap prevented exchange of information and unification of effort. The fragmented Indians were technologically deficient. They lacked the tools or practice of agriculture, placing them at the whims of nature for food. More prohibitively, the Indians never adapted to firearms to match the incoming Americans, making Indians defenseless against mob violence.

American officials added to the confusion by inconsistent policies, particularly in the matter of treaties with Indians. In 1850 the U.S. Senate authorized treaties between the federal government and California Indians. The government would furnish these Native Americans with reserved acreage, protection, material support, and education in exchange for ceding Indian lands to the United States. Between March 1851 and January 1852, three federal commissioners entered into eighteen different treaties with various California Indian groups. Buttressed by opposition from the legislature in Sacramento, California's two U.S. senators pressured Washington to refuse treaty ratification. The Senate quietly shelved the documents in July 1852. Nobody explained the situation to the Indians.

The Army, meanwhile, surveyed California's shoreline for coastal defense sites, an action that had nothing to do with Indians. Moving slowly to a frontier-style mission, the War Department eventually garrisoned the northern counties, too. Arriving after settlement had begun in most cases, the Regulars manned nine forts in northern California. One line of posts girded the Sacramento Valley and a second line ran from Humboldt Bay up the Klamath River and its tributaries. In addition to the forts, temporary military camps appeared in mining districts, stock-raising valleys, and new settlements when necessary. For the next ten years isolated post complements operated contrary to the expectations of California's civilian governors. Regular Army commanders in the field and obscure Mexican War veterans named Wright, Buchanan, Adams, Johnson, and Lovell adopted a paternalistic attitude toward local Indians near their forts. While accepting federal policy that Indians were Department of Interior responsibility, Army officers stepped in when, in their opinion, occasion demanded. Army officers used their high status to fashion a truce between the California electorate and the unenfranchised Indians. Such efforts were partially successful in containing problems between the native and newly arrived Californians.

These years of Regular Army intervention were important ones for California's Indian population. Native American groups were caught in a conflict of cultures. Different institutional goals of the federal and state governments exacerbated problems. Bitterness sometimes existed between Army officers and Indian reservation officials. Settlers distrusted both. Hunger took its toll on Indian reservations and rancherias. When the Regular Army marched off to the Civil War in 1861, events combined to make Northern California Indians the losers. During the years between statehood and the Civil War, the best the Army could claim for ten years in northern California was a moral victory.[7]

---

[7] Robert Chandler, "The Failure of Reform: White Attitudes and Indian Response in California During the Civil War Era," *The Pacific Historian*, vol. 24, no. 3 (Fall 1980), pp. 284–94.

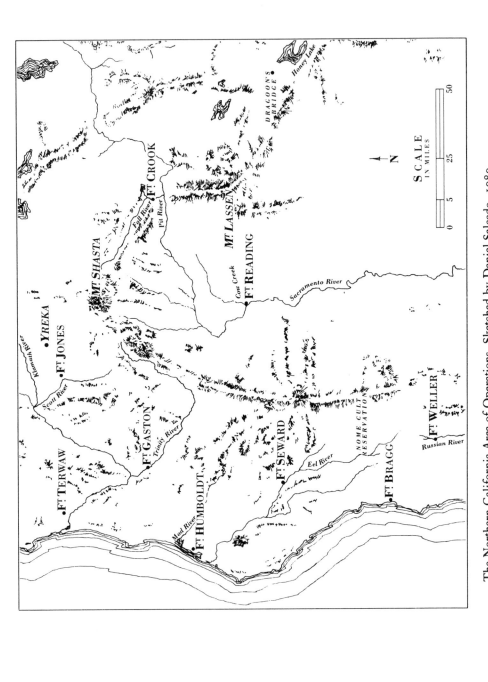

The Northern California Area of Operations. Sketched by Daniel Salcedo, 1989

Chapter 1
1852

Into the Redwoods

*. . . policy and humanity both require that we should employ
some other means of putting a stop to these [Indian] depredations than the terror of our arms. . .*
Annual Report of the Secretary of War (1851)

Where are the soldiers? So wondered many of the American settlers in the new state of California. When California became part of the Union in 1850, the adventurous
citizens of the state presumed many tasks for the federal
government—military defense was one of them. They
expected protection and retribution for continued theft of
stock and supplies across the northern quarter of the state.
Any violence was usually attributed to Indians.

North of Sacramento on Bear Creek, Fort Far West
housed the only Regular Army garrison north of the foggy
waters of San Francisco Bay. The site, judged by some as
not far enough west or north, held a vastly understrength
company of the 2d Infantry. In 1852 the unit was down to a
mere two dozen men, who made futile attempts at protecting routes to California's bursting gold-mine country.

Employed as the professional "Sword of the Republic" for several previous decades on the American frontier, the U.S. Army policy for protection of civilians had been roughly to keep ahead of them on the frontier by continually jumping units westward ahead of the emigrants, traders, and roughnecks. Each expedition sought to gain information about unknown lands, to awe the local inhabitants into law-abiding attitudes, and to chase unruly groups —usually Indians—until they acted peaceably.

In most cases this policy had worked, but now in California the situation had changed. The Army, situated only a little north of San Francisco, had to decide if it was going to continue to try and stay ahead of the hordes of gold seekers moving into northern California lands. By 1852, four years after the initial strikes, gold seekers had swollen California's population and covered her inland river valleys and mountain slopes.

Army policy for the coastline differed from its interior policy, and now that the Army had reached the coast in its westward movement, it seemed unable to decide which policy it should use. Coastline defense policy in most cases had the Army concentrated in traditional massive forts at the entrance to important harbors. Already in northern California the Army had begun this by establishing artillery at Monterey and San Francisco and supporting them with foot and horse soldiers at Sonoma and Benicia. But what should it do now? Move farther up the coast and establish a traditional coastal fort? Or move rapidly inland, establishing strings of crude forts and staying ahead of the 49ers and emigrants from the eastern states?

The Army simply did not have enough men to perform

all functions. In fact, in its entire Pacific Division, stretching from Puget Sound to San Diego, it could muster only 736 men.

Events forced action before the Army could decide. Secretary of War Charles M. Conrad acted to turn the Regular Army in northern California away from the coast and into the interior. Conrad disputed California Governor John McDougal's version of the situation.[1]

Governor McDougal claimed that the state contained one hundred thousand Indian warriors, "all animated by a spirit of bitter hostility." He may have overstated the case. The Native American population offered little armed resistance to the arriving emigrants.[2]

The governor warned President Millard Fillmore that people in the Golden State felt cheated by the capitol in Washington. They paid duties to the federal government but were not being defended by it. The citizens saw protection from violence as a clear constitutional right.

Washington, D.C., could point to recent treaties between federal agents and California Indians as factors that discounted the "bitter hostility" described by McDougal. Unimpressed by the governor's claims, Secretary of War Conrad charged that California Indians were goaded into militancy by the outrageous conduct of the settlers and miners.

---

[1] *ARSW* (1851) (Washington, D.C.), p. 209; Francis Paul Prucha, *The Sword of the Republic: The United States Army on the Frontier, 1783–1846* (New York: Macmillan, 1969). Camp Far West's manpower was drawn from the 2d Infantry, which was constituted in the Regular Army on April 12, 1808.

[2] *ARSW* (1851), pp. 138, 209; Emanuel Raymond Lewis, *Seacoast Fortifications of the United States* (Annapolis, Md.: Leeward Pub., 1979), pp. 38–39; Francis Paul Prucha, *Guide to the Military Posts of the United States* (Milwaukee: The State Hist. Soc. of Wisc., 1964), pp. 16–21; Robert M. Utley, *Frontiersmen in Blue* (New York: Macmillan, 1967), pp. 92–93.

Governor McDougal offered the secretary a simple solution to the Indian problem: permit McDougal to deploy state-organized troops to the troubled areas and let the federal government pay the bill. To this suggestion one Army general wryly commented that California's citizens, who were already killing Indians on the slightest pretext, could hardly be expected to transform themselves into saviors and protectors by sudden placement on a federal payroll.

Without publicly doubting that Governor McDougal would prevent physical abuse if given a free hand to deal with Indians, Secretary of War Conrad vetoed the idea of state-controlled troops. Despite McDougal's claim that the standing Army was "unfit" for Indian campaigns in the rough, mountainous landscape of California, Conrad decided that the job belonged to the Regular Army.

The secretary of war acted to turn the Regular Army in northern California away from the coast. In May 1851 Conrad directed Brevet Brigadier General Ethan Allen Hitchcock to take command of the Pacific Division and revise the whole system of administration and defense on the westernmost shores.

The War Department expected action in California. Secretary Conrad counseled General Hitchcock that the Army's priority in California was protecting American citizens against Indian marauders. Every facility of Hichcock's command should be afforded, with Conrad's blessing, to Indian agents of the Interior Department.[3]

The secretary recognized that slow, unreliable communication prevailed between the District of Columbia and

---

3 *ARSW* (1851), pp. 108, 137–42, 209: James J. Rawls, *Indians of California* (Norman: Univ. of Oklahoma Press, 1984), p. 144; Prucha, *Sword of the Republic*, p. 273. Hitchcock held a decade-long sympathy for Indian rights.

San Francisco Bay. As a result, he personally granted
Hitchcock an unusually large measure of discretion in
the command of the Pacific Division. Hitchcock could
exercise his own judgment in reorganizing the Army on
the Pacific Coast. He need not await approval from
Washington. Paradoxically, Conrad warned the new Pacific
Division commander to be prudent with government
money. Every penny counted.[4]

Hitchcock shifted inland what few troops were available.
The staff at Pacific Division headquarters obtained a
recently drawn map of northern California to help them
plan troop movements into the region. Heartening to
Hitchcock was the news that a major Regular Army unit,
the 4th Infantry, would shift from the Great Lakes to
California. The 4th Infantry would add some seven hundred troops to Pacific Coast garrisons.

Hitchcock's first move was to close Fort Far West in
1852 and to move the garrison north to a tributary of the
Sacramento River. From that locale the Regulars would
stand slightly in advance of settlements edging north from
Sacramento. The troops could shield miners and stock
owners from raids laid to Cow Creek Indians. Placed in
charge of the relocation of the 2d Infantry's move was 1st
Lieutenant Nelson H. Davis. Davis had served for six
years as a Regular Army officer and had been cited for
gallantry in the Mexican War.[5]

Displacing the Fort Far West garrison to a new northern

---

4 *ARSW* (1851), pp. 108, 137–42, 209. Conrad assured Hitchcock that he would
be supplied with seeds to allow troops to raise gardens and thereby cut expenses.

5 Lt. R. S. Williamson to Maj. Edward D. Townsend, Feb. 20, 1852, Pacific
Div., LR, RG393; Hitchcock to Brig. Gen. Roger Jones, June 7, 1852, Pacific
Div., LS, RG393; T. F. Rodenbough and W. L. Haskins, eds., *The Army of the
United States* (New York: Maynard, Merrill & Co., 1896), p. 460.

site little mollified the settlers. Writing to Hitchcock from Sacramento, newly elected Governor John Bigler, who replaced McDougal, stated flatly that "adequate protection has not been extended by the Government at Washington to American citizens residing in the State of California." To prove his point, the governor attached a letter from senators and representatives of the four northernmost California counties. The letter complained of bloodthirsty Indian attacks. From Weaverville in Trinity County another petition signed by 129 inhabitants demanded protection so that citizens might travel freely and keep unguarded livestock.

In addition to the settlements in the Sacramento Valley, a second group in northern California still needed protection. These hamlets lay beyond a hilly forty-mile stretch north of the Sacramento Valley in a region known as Shasta. Shasta was an area where not everybody blushed at murder. The Army might not have known that a lawless group of Americans, disguised as Indians, had attacked miners only the year before. In the spring of 1852, citizens lynched an innocent Shasta Indian for murder. Clashes between gold seekers and Karok Indians along the Salmon River caused more deaths.

Remembering the warning about conserving dollars, Hitchcock determined to hold down transportation costs. Instead of stationing troops in the Shasta area, the Army thought it could control troublesome Indians by forays from the garrison to be established by Lieutenant Davis. But where was Lieutenant Davis?[6]

---

[6] Bigler to Hitchcock, Apr. 8 and 30, 1852; and Hitchcock to Jones, June 7, 1852, RG393; Robert F. Heizer, ed., *Handbook of North American Indians: California* (Washington, D.C.: Smithsonian Inst., 1978), p. 188; Rosena A. Giles, *Shasta County, California: A History* (Oakland: Biobooks, 1949), p. 37; Keith A. Murray, *The Modocs and Their War* (Norman: Univ. of Oklahoma Press, 1984), pp. 21–22.

The move from Fort Far West was proving painfully slow. A site was selected after reconnoitering the Cow Creek area. Authorized to move by riverboat when practicable, the garrison should have reached the new site by mid May.

The Regular Army's shift north had bogged down due to poor logistical support; Davis was left to his own devices. By May 15, 1852, Davis was still struggling near Tehama, some fifty miles short of Cow Creek. The government mule teams were wild and footsore. Recruits pressed into service as untrained teamsters proved no match for the mules.[7]

Boat service ended at Tehama. Other transportation problems came to light. Davis had recognized that he needed a ferry to cross Cow Creek and set up the fort at the selected site. He requested delivery of rope from Pacific Division headquarters, and he sent an officer ahead to purchase a flat-bottomed boat. The officer obtained the boat for five hundred dollars, but 2d Infantry officers discovered to their mortification that no Army rope awaited them.

Davis persevered without the rope and reached the site on May 26. A mile upstream from Reading's ranch and on the west bank of Cow Creek, the new post nested in a grove of oak trees. Davis named it Fort Reading in honor of the pioneer American settler of the region, Pierson B. Reading.[8]

Weary from a twenty-two–day journey by foot and riverboat, Company E, 2d Infantry, set to work. Army policy

[7] Hitchcock to Oliver M. Wozencraft, Apr. 17, 1852; and Davis to Townsend, May 15, 1852, RG393; *ARSW* (1852), pp. 88, 91. Recognizing the heavy expense for hiring civilian teamsters, the secretary of war tried unsuccessfully to obtain congressional authority for recruiting soldier-teamsters. See also *ARSW* (1851), p. 112.

[8] Davis to Townsend, May 15, 1852, RG393; PR, Ft. Reading, May 1852, M617, R993.

called for troops to construct their own frontier posts whenever possible. Commanders faced the dilemma of building shelter for survival in the wilderness or initiating field operations. Construction usually took precedence over marching in these circumstances. Using their muscle power and what tools were available, the troops cut hay for the mules and began erecting buildings. Until quarters were finished, Company E moved into tents.

Davis's plans for the fort called for an open space to be used as a parade ground. He wanted the officers' quarters to be near the riverbank and across the parade from the enlisted mens' barracks. Davis deemed the creek a fine stream in which the men could bathe. North of the troop area, Davis situated the bakery and the guardhouse. Completing the square of the fort's layout would be the post hospital and the rations storehouse.

Under the system in effect, a penny-pinching War Department held officers personally responsible for loss of rations and animals and damage to supplies. Aware of the system, Davis ordered a stable, a corral, and other storehouses built down-stream to protect Army property. Fort Reading's commander gave priority to getting men, animals, and supplies under cover before winter.[9]

An inspector general's visit reinforced the emphasis that Davis placed on administration instead of scouting. The stay of War Department Inspector Major George A. McCall in July surely tried Davis's patience. With the barracks walls up and the hospital roofed, Davis halted construction while Major McCall checked muskets, audited commissary accounts, and looked at woolen uniforms.

9 *ARSW* (1852), p. 88; Robert W. Frazer, *Mansfield on the Condition of the Western Forts* (Norman: Univ. of Oklahoma Press, 1963), pp. 159–62, sketch 20.

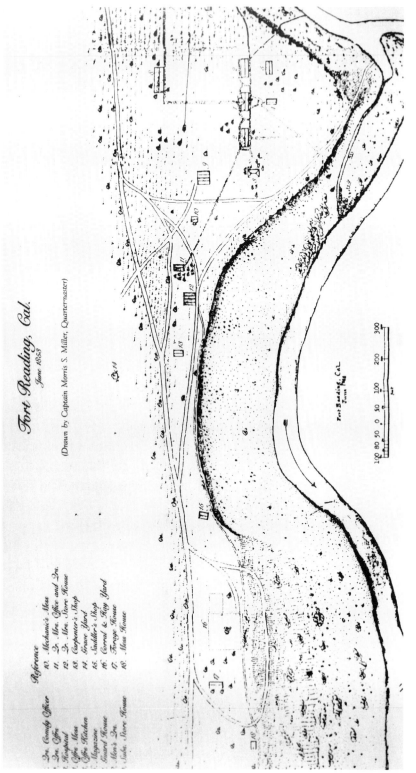

Fort Reading, Cal.
June 1853

(Drawn by Captain Morris S. Miller, Quartermaster)

Reference

1. Gen. Guard Office
2. Gen. Office
3. Hospital
4. Office Mess
5. Office Kitchen
6. Magazine
7. Guard House
8. Men's Den
9. Subs. Store House
10. Mechanic's Mess
11. Q. Mas. Office and Den.
12. Q. Mas. Store House
13. Carpenter's Shop
14. Grave Yard
15. Saddler's Shop
16. Corral & Hay Yard
17. Forage House
18. Mess House

Fort Reading, Cal.
June 1853

A Sketch of Fort Reading, 1858. Courtesy of Shasta Historical Society

McCall noted that due to lack of training, the troops drilled poorly on parade. He found six of the eleven mule-team harnesses worn beyond satisfactory condition. McCall recognized that Davis had little time to organize Fort Reading and many obstacles to surmount. He commended Davis for "industry and zeal."[10]

Fort Reading had only two other officers in addition to Davis. Second Lieutenant Ferdinand Paine of Company F handled supplies and rations. Like Davis, he hailed from New England. An experienced Army doctor, Assistant Surgeon John Campbell, looked to Fort Reading's medical problems.

In addition to other administrative problems, mail was not getting through to the fort. Davis advised the Army to solve the problem by using Cottonwood Post Office to communicate with Fort Reading. Davis also notified his superiors of a startling development: instead of swarms of Indians lurking about Cow Creek, the garrison saw groups of worn, hungry American emigrants appearing over the mountains from the older states. Migration from the eastern seaboard to California topped fifty thousand in 1852.

Using Nobles Cut Off, a new bypass on the California–Oregon Trail, a portion of the emigrants now filed by Fort Reading. The greenhorn settlers were often low on provisions after crossing the Sierra. Recognizing the military post as a friendly symbol, they asked the Army for food to tide them over until they could reach the town of Shasta.

Sensitive to the sufferings of these new Californians and unsure of Army policy, in August Davis issued Army rations to a group of sixty settlers who were "all destitute of

---

[10] LR, Office of the Adjutant General, Nov. 15, 1852 (main series), M567, R485. McCall inspected Fort Reading on July 20, 1852.

provisions and asking for them." Receiving reports that many more emigrants had taken Nobles Cut Off, Davis warned General Hitchcock of a potential disaster if large numbers of hungry Americans appeared at Fort Reading. He also worried that, if headquarters disapproved of his giving food to empty-bellied emigrants, he could be ordered to reimburse the War Department for costs.[11]

Allowing that "the claims of humanity are every where paramount," Pacific Division conceded that Davis had acted properly in feeding the emigrants. Elaborate instructions for him followed. In future cases at Fort Reading, Davis was to dispassionately judge the actual needs of wagon trains and settler parties who requested Army relief. To preclude War Department retribution for expenditures, headquarters warned Davis to issue commissary supplies only when necessary to prevent suffering and limit them to foodstuffs unavailable from local suppliers. Fort Reading's commander was told to at least try to collect payment for items furnished. Finally, when Davis decided that emergency issue of rations seemed absolutely necessary, other officers of the post were to execute written statements as further proof that the gesture was humanitarian.

The War Department assured the Pacific Division that the Army would hold no officer financially responsible for an act of humanity. The secretary of war went a step further by adding in his annual report to Congress that medical supplies would also be expended for emigrants taken sick en route to California and Oregon.[12]

---

[11] Davis to Townsend, Aug. 11, 1852, RG393; PR, Ft. Reading, May 1852, M617, R993; George R. Stewart, *The California Trail* (New York: McGraw-Hill, 1971), pp. 303–06.

[12] Townsend to Davis, Aug. 14, 1852, Colonel Samuel Cooper to Hitchcock, Sept. 29, 1852, RG393; *ARSW* (1852), p. 136.

Impatient California officials wanted the Army to attack Indians. Constructing a military post and helping hungry emigrants had left Lieutenant Davis little time for expeditions. Reports of Indians attacking gold miners on the Klamath River prompted Governor Bigler to approach General Hitchcock again. The Army maintained that roving expeditions from Fort Reading could control trouble at the northern mines. Bigler disagreed. He thought there should be forts on the Klamath and Trinity rivers. Bigler and Hitchcock met to discuss matters.

Hitchcock assured Bigler that the only cavalry available, two companies of the 1st Dragoons at Sonoma, would go north as a show of force to the gold-mining area. Bigler showed Hitchcock an irate letter from Yreka inhabitants. He expressed his hope that the dragoons would visit Yreka —and with little delay. [13]

In addition to Bigler, James W. Denver of the California Senate criticized the Army's lack of action. Describing the location of Fort Reading as "folly," he complained that the Cow Creek area already was heavily populated with Americans. By contrast, no soldiers protected settlers and miners on the Trinity River. Fellow legislator Royal T. Sprague joined Denver in demanding military protection. [14]

To protect the region north of Fort Reading, a provisional squadron of the 1st Dragoons followed Captain and Brevet Major Edward H. Fitzgerald to Siskiyou County. Breveted for bravery at Chapultepec, Fitzgerald

---

[13] Bigler to Hitchcock, July 3 and 31, 1852; and Hitchcock to Bigler, July 23, 1852, RG393; A. J. Bledsoe, *Indian Wars of the Northwest* (Oakland: Biobooks, 1956), pp. 83–84.

[14] James W. Denver to Hitchcock, May 23, 1852; and Hitchcock to Jones, July 30, 1852, RG393; Chad L. Hoopes, "Redick McKee and the Humboldt Bay Region 1851–1852," *CHQ*, vol. 59, no. 3 (Sept. 1970), p. 211.

commanded Companies A and E in the trek north. One of the two dragoon regiments in the Army, the 1st had served all over territories acquired by the United States after the Mexican War.

Instructed to range throughout California north of Fort Reading, Fitzgerald was told that he could depend on supplies from that post. Headquarters expected the 1st Dragoons to give settlers a sense of security and to somehow avoid an Indian war. Fitzgerald was to tell Indian leaders that thievery and similar disturbing moves caused trouble with settlers. Fitzgerald was also to confer with the "best citizens" to ascertain the true state of affairs, particularly in the Yreka area.

Because of their ability to move with speed over rough terrain, the 1st Dragoons appeared to be ideal for the job assigned them. Siskiyou County citizens, however, remained unimpressed by promises that the cavalry was on the way. In a mass meeting they passed a resolution calling on the governor of California for protection. Bigler also received ominous intimations to the effect that the same group intended to seize the state tax collector's funds to finance a private expedition against Indians.[15]

Bigler advised the Army of the new, heightened tension in the northern counties. Violent tempers and deep animosity resulted in more killings. Settlers accused Indians of further disturbances. Still the Army harbored doubts that frustrated the Californians. To many military officers, the obvious question was whether California Indians were entitled to legal protection similar to that which they

[15] Townsend to Fitzgerald, July 27 and Sept. 16, 1852; and Hitchcock to Bigler, Aug. 2, 1852; and Hitchcock to Cooper, Sept. 27, 1852, RG393.

received "in the older states." They doubted California's intention to afford Indians any rights whatsoever.

In the Army view, California's majority wanted Indians out of the way, even if they had to be removed east of the Sierra. Without the slightest attempt at negotiation, California settlers arbitrarily grabbed Indian lands for gold mining and agriculture. This unwarranted, extrajudicial squatting on traditional tribal lands provoked Indians. The settlers then called on the Army for protection.

By first irritating the Indians and then complaining if troops failed to appear quickly, Californians made matters endlessly worse. The Pacific Division commander held that his men were "placed in a most delicate and awkward position" by the loose legalities of their fellow citizens.

As the settlers and the Army argued, the situation for the Indians seemed to worsen. American disrespect for aboriginal land continued. Other new miseries, measles among the Karok and smallpox in Modoc families, further sapped a weakening family life. The Indians' resentment was magnified when they found that the soldiers often upheld the miners' acts against their people and lands.

Riled Indians attacked emigrants in the northern counties. The Modoc in particular hit wagon trains with regularity near California's northeastern boundary with Oregon. Fort Reading lacked sufficient soldiers and horses to send out expeditions. Whatever the justification for hostility, the Army concluded that, in light of the attacks, the Indians "must be compelled to keep the peace."[16]

In consequence, Major Fitzgerald received modified instructions for his 1st Dragoons. The original plan had

[16] *Ibid.; ARSW* (1852), p. 30; Heizer, *Indians*, p. 108; Murray, *Modocs*, pp. 17, 22–28.

been to return to the Bay Area after his show of force above the Sacramento Valley. Instead, Fitzgerald was ordered to keep his cavalry command in northern California throughout the coming winter. Fitzgerald's only injunction was to hold his horsemen anywhere within one hundred miles of Yreka.

In addition to changing Fitzgerald's orders, the Army sought to institute more stringent command measures to bring security to the inflamed area north of the state capital once and for all. To this end, Pacific Division organized a special military command area called the Northern District of California. The new command was under the supervision of Major and Brevet Lieutenant Colonel George Wright, who was senior to both Fitzgerald and Davis. General Hitchcock designated Fort Reading as district headquarters.

Wright's new command embraced the mountainous, scantily populated region from Fort Reading all the way to the Rogue River in Oregon, an area of roughly four thousand square miles. In addition to Company E, 2d Infantry (already at Fort Reading) and Fitzgerald's two companies of the 1st Dragoons, the Army added Company D, 4th Infantry, to Wright's California forces.

Newly arrived on the Pacific Coast, the 4th Infantry sustained over a hundred deaths to cholera before reaching San Francisco. Despite the losses, however, the regiment represented a significant reinforcement to the Pacific Division. With Wright on his way to Fort Reading and more troops deploying, Hitchcock apprised Bigler of the latest Army maneuvers in northern California.[17]

---

[17] Townsend to Fitzgerald, Sept. 16, 1852; and Townsend to Wright, Sept. 17, 1852; and Hitchcock to Bigler, Sept. 20, 1852, RG393.

Colonel Wright took the reins in northern California on September 25, 1852, and simultaneously succeeded Davis in command of Fort Reading. Energetic in Florida's Indian wars and wounded at Molino del Rey in the Mexican War, Wright needed no introduction to field campaigning.

At the beginning of October, Company D, 4th Infantry, marched into Fort Reading under 1st Lieutenant Edmund Russell and 2d Lieutenant Francis H. Bates. After the long journey from the Great Lakes, down the Atlantic Ocean routes, across Panama, and up the Pacific Coast, Company D numbered only forty-six soldiers, of which nine were ill.

Colonel Wright, aware of Russell's versatility and battlefield gallantry in Mexico, appointed him chief commissary for the Northern District of California in addition to his duties as company commander. Thus Russell inherited the demanding duty of procuring rations, a task that was hampered by toilsome communication.

When Wright came to Fort Reading, he brought two staff officers with him. Captain Morris S. Miller, a quartermaster officer, took over the district supply and transport problems. Brevet 2d Lieutenant and Topographical Engineer Robert S. Williamson planned to chart the region in detail. With Captain Miller in charge of quartermaster affairs and Lieutenant Russell in charge of the commissariate, logistical support in the northern military district seemed safe. Wright re-exerted efforts to protect everything from weather before winter rains hit Fort Reading.[18]

Fitzgerald's 1st Dragoons refreshed themselves at Fort

---

[18] Wright to Townsend, Sept. 25, 1852; Headquarters of the Northern Dist. of Calif., Order No. 7, Oct. 13, 1852, RG393; PR, Ft. Reading, Oct. 1852, M617, R993.

Reading on their way north. They moved out of the Shasta County post on October 5 after receiving explicit orders from Wright. Once in the area of settlements, Wright wanted Fitzgerald to establish an Army post either in Scott Valley or the vicinity of Yreka and extend military protection over the surrounding country. The plans of the dragoons had changed again.

Wright expected Fitzgerald to pick a fort site that offered good water, forage, and wood. Resupply for the dragoons' post would be accomplished by mule trail from Fort Reading, 120 miles away. Lieutenant Williamson accompanied the dragoons to gain an appreciation of the terrain.

Riding north through Shasta City, Fitzgerald marched his men over dirt trails to Scott Valley. He found the adjacent mountaintops already covered with snow, an unmistakable sign that winters could be cold in Siskiyou County. The dragoon commander reported to Wright that, "we have ice in our buckets every morning." On the optimistic side, the Indians seemed peaceful except in two areas. Near the headwaters of the Pit River, Indians had attacked emigrants and along the Trinity River, others had supposedly stolen some animals.

Fitzgerald delayed investigation of Indian matters while he searched for a suitable location to establish the military post that Wright wanted. He chose some six hundred acres in Scott Valley along the east side of Scott River. Yreka, a center for miners, ranchers, and traders, was fifteen miles away—close enough for the dragoons to protect but far enough to keep enlisted men out of mischief.

The dragoons occupied the post on October 16, 1852. With little ceremony Fitzgerald named the post Fort Jones in honor of the Army's adjutant general, Colonel Roger Jones, who died the previous summer. Eyeing the excellent grass for his mounts and noting sufficient timber to build shelter for his men, the dragoons' leader thought the resources of Fort Jones to be quite ample for the winter.

A total of ninety enlisted men garrisoned Fort Jones and an additional eleven performed detached service. Three of their 102 government steeds were rated as unserviceable after the march from Sonoma to Siskiyou County. At Fort Jones, Fitzgerald kept personal command of Company E, 1st Dragoons. First Lieutenant Thomas F. Castor, also a Mexican War veteran, commanded Company A. Medical help for the squadron rested in the competent hands of Assistant Surgeon Charles H. Crane, an "Army brat" with degrees from Harvard and Yale.[19]

Fitzgerald planned a quick expedition to the northernmost lakes. He selected fifty dragoons to aid him in at last making the Army's presence felt above the 40th parallel. Fifteen months had elapsed since Hitchcock had taken over the Pacific Division.

Fitzgerald left Castor and newly arrived 2d Lieutenant Charles H. Ogle to wrestle a supply packtrain back to Fort Reading and to start rudimentary construction of an Army post. He headed for Yreka. Yreka–area citizens had responded to reports that late-arriving emigrant parties were short of food by collecting provisions for the travelers' aid. Fitzgerald offered a military escort for the donated food.

Riding to the shore of Lake Rhett, Fitzgerald trans-

---

[19] Wright to Townsend, Oct. 5, 1852; and Fitzgerald to Davis, Oct. 12, 1852; and Fitzgerald to Wright, Nov. 6, 1852, RG393; PR, Ft. Jones, Oct. 1852, M617, R560.

ferred the foodstuffs to an approaching wagon train. A couple of dozen armed Yreka volunteers guarded the emigrants. Local volunteers and horse soldiers sized up one another. Neither side was overly impressed.

Composed of citizens of a particular settlement or county, volunteers were not part of an organized militia. They carried personal arms. Volunteer companies attacked Indians in California on their own volition. Sometimes the state government approved their actions, but the federal government certainly never favored them. Once their immediate aims were met, the volunteers disbanded. They expected to be paid for their exertions. By contrast, Fitzgerald's soldiers served five-year enlistments. Three quarters of the line officers in California were West Point graduates. Discipline was harsh in the federal ranks. A modern writer's description of Yreka's leading volunteer, Ben Wright, as "lawless, reckless, and violent" probably would have seemed apt to the Regular Army.

After finding the bodies of four emigrants, one of them a woman, near Lake Rhett, Fitzgerald decided to sweep the area for the killers. When the volunteers received a pair of boats from Yreka, Fitzgerald saw some advantage to adding the boats and the volunteers to his force. Twenty-five men took the boats out on the lake while another fifty waded into the tule marshes. The combined soldier-civilian force saw a few Modoc Indians, who escaped easily in canoes. Meeting no opposition, Fitzgerald's improvised command burned fourteen Indian rancherias. Somebody killed an Indian. The volunteers took three Indian women and a child captive to complete the sweep. Discovery of emigrant artifacts, clothes, and money erased any doubt from Fitzgerald's mind about who had been attacking emigrants

for the preceding three months. Fitzgerald went back to Fort
Jones. Ben Wright remained and killed forty Modocs.[20]

While Fitzgerald made his excursion on the traditional
emigrant route, Colonel Wright took to the saddle farther
south. Forming an improvised field detachment from the
infantry companies at Fort Reading, Wright reconnoitered
Cow Creek all the way to the headwaters. Like Fitzgerald,
Wright saw few Indians, all of whom seemed peaceably
inclined. The foray was the soldiers' introduction to conditions in northern California. They found their progress
through the mountains markedly impeded by heavy,
cold rain.[21]

Wright returned to Fort Reading before mid-November
1852. He discovered that despite Surgeon Campbell's best
efforts, the number of feverish and shivering men confined
to the post hospital had risen. Lack of sufficient heat in
quarters at Fort Reading had counteracted Campbell's
work. Skimping to save money, the Pacific Division
quartermaster had sent small, government-issue stoves
for use instead of larger, commercial models. There
had been no increase in the fuel allowance to make up for
the smaller stoves.

One of the four sick cavalrymen left at Fort Reading
when the 1st Dragoons trotted north died. Winter also
took a toll among Company D, 4th Infantry, and Company E, 2d Infantry. Five infantrymen of the garrison
died. By February the number of sick rose to nineteen. The
original commander of the post, Lieutenant Davis, was
also taken ill. He proved more fortunate than some of his
men and recovered.[22]

---

[20] Fitzgerald to Wright, Nov. 6, 1852; and Wright to Townsend, Nov. 19, 1852,
RG393; Utley, *Frontiersmen*, pp. 36, 39; Murray, *Modocs*, pp. 25–28.

Seven officers and eighty-six enlisted men greeted the new year of 1853 at Fort Reading. Prospects for them were not as grim as those of their comrades at Fort Jones. Although a packtrain from Fort Reading had come through the mountains to replenish Fort Jones the previous November, by the end of January 1853 Fitzgerald admitted that the rations had plainly "given out."

The four officers at Fort Jones discussed the situation. They decided that a full winter at the hastily established post would severely debilitate the command. To prevent the cruelty of reduced rations to soldiers and horses alike, Fitzgerald opted for a winter march to Fort Reading, where he expected provisions to be in greater abundance. He detailed Lieutenant Ogle and twenty-one soldiers to stay and watch over Fort Jones. Dr. Crane remained with Ogle to care for the sick.[23]

Fitzgerald started south with the horse squadron on the last day of January in a winter marked by deep snow. Reaching Fort Reading on February 9, the dragoons dispersed into available quarters. They swelled the number of soldiers on post to over 150. Fitzgerald turned himself in sick to Surgeon Campbell. Four months in northern California had been physically unkind to the dragoon officer. Professionally, he had been forced to abandon his mission.

At the same time that the officers of the 1st Dragoons had discussed plans to temporarily abandon Fort Jones, the

[21] Wright to Townsend, Nov. 11, 1852, RG393.

[22] Miller to Maj. Osborn Cross, Oct. 28, 1853, RG393; PR, Ft. Reading, Nov. and Dec. 1852 and Feb. 1853, M617, R993.

[23] Fitzgerald to Wright, Nov. 6, 1852, RG393; PR, Ft. Jones, Jan. 1853, M617, R560. Crane attained the highest rank possible for an Army medical officer, surgeon general, in 1882.

Army undertook to establish a third fort in northern California on the coast some 150 miles west of Scott Valley. Designed to protect a rapidly expanding population against alleged Indian hostility, the new post was to be in the Humboldt Bay region, the gateway to gold mines on the Klamath, Trinity, and Salmon rivers.

To establish the new post, the Army chose two companies of the 4th Infantry under the command of Captain and Brevet Lieutenant Colonel Robert C. Buchanan. The companies were temporarily encamped near Benicia after a hard voyage from the eastern seaboard. At first, plans had called for just one company of the 4th Infantry to go to Humboldt Bay. Due to the reduced strength of the 4th Infantry companies, however, and to mollify Buchanan in regard to his brevet grade, Pacific Division headquarters added a second company to the northbound military group. After serving twenty-two years in the Army, Buchanan had the option of picking the exact site for the Humboldt Bay post.[24]

Buchanan marched Companies B and F of the 4th Infantry to the Benicia wharf near the end of January 1853. There were no roads to Humboldt Bay, let alone railroads, so Buchanan planned to transport his two-company force by ship. The infantrymen were unenthusiastic about yet another sea voyage after the discomforts of their move to California, but they were herded aboard an old steamer whose seaworthiness some of the officers questioned.[25]

Enduring a rainy, windy, cold voyage, Buchanan's men

---

[24] Townsend to Buchanan, Jan. 11, 1853, RG393; PR, Ft. Reading, Feb. 1853, M617, R993; Heizer, *Indians*, p. 162.

[25] PR, Ft. Humboldt, Jan. 1853, M617, R497; Martin F. Schmitt, ed., *General George Crook: His Autobiography* (Norman: Univ. of Oklahoma Press, 1946), pp. 8–10.

put into Humboldt Bay after some difficulty. Sunshine and redwood forest greeted their eyes. In the background lofty Bald Mountain looked down on the four little settlements that lined the shore.

Buchanan decided to land at Bucksport and build his fort on high ground to the rear of the town. From those heights he could command a good view of the harbor entrance three miles away. Disembarking troops and tons of government supplies on January 30, Buchanan supervised the hauling of baggage to the chosen acres. In keeping with General Hitchcock's personal desire that forts be named after some local, well-known geographic point, Colonel Buchanan named the new post Fort Humboldt.

After establishing the first Army post on the rugged California coast north of San Francisco, Buchanan made no dash into the redwood forests. Fort Humboldt's complement set to work building quarters and roadways just as fellow soldiers had done at Fort Reading and Fort Jones. All three posts met the criteria ascribed to the locations of Army posts by an officer in 1853: "extremely inaccessible, [and] singularly uncomfortable."

Fortunately, most of the ground around Fort Humboldt consisted of grassland. Only brushwood needed clearing. Fort Humboldt was woefully short of soldiers; the three officers supervised ninety-one enlisted men, including a drummer and a bugler—the sum total of Companies B and F.

Separated from the upper Sacramento Valley by deep redwood forests and steep mountain ranges, Buchanan held an independent command at Fort Humboldt. Headquarters excluded him from Wright's Northern District of California. In addition to Buchanan, who commanded the post and the 4th Infantry detachment, Company B included 1st Lieutenant William H. Scott and 2d Lieutenant John C. Bonnycastle, both Virginia born. Company F had a more northern hue—it was headed by a Pennsylvanian, 2d Lieutenant Edmund Underwood, who was assisted by an Ohioan, Brevet 2d Lieutenant George Crook.

In addition to their company duties, Underwood performed as the local quartermaster and commissary officer, and Crook became post adjutant. Other than Buchanan, Crook was the only West Pointer at the newly established post. Assistant Surgeon Charles P. Deyerle provided medical support at Fort Humboldt.[26]

Buchanan's position on Humboldt Bay represented the completion of a painstakingly slow reorientation of the Regular Army in northern California. Three experienced commanders now supervised tactical operations and military administration in the region, something administrators in San Francisco or Benicia would not have been able to do. (See Appendix A for a list of post commanders.)

Commanders' wishes governed a typical day in one of the new posts. Calls from drum and bugle set day-to-day routine. As a result, a musician held a significant position. Buchanan prescribed his post calls three days after landing at Humboldt Bay. After reveille at sunrise, he scheduled breakfast at 7:00 A.M., followed by assembly of work details at 7:30, and guard mount at 9:00. Following the main meal at 1:00 P.M., work resumed at 1:30 and lasted until a half hour before sundown. Retreat blew at sundown. By 8:30 all enlisted men were expected to be in barracks.[27]

---

[26] Townsend to Wright, Nov. 27, 1852, RG393; PR, Ft. Humboldt, Jan. 1853, M617, R497; Schmitt, *Crook*, pp. 8–70; George R. Stewart, *John Phoenix, Esq.* (New York: De Capo Press, 1969), p. 72.

Failure to comply with calls and orders brought harsh Army discipline. Articles of War prescribed by Congress governed every facet of Army life pertinent to good order and discipline. Directions from an officer to an enlisted man were law. Confinement to the guardhouse required no lengthy legal process. Attachment of a heavy ball and chain to a guardhouse prisoner was not unusual. For the military crime of desertion, a plague on the Army in California, whipping of the deserter in front of the assembled garrison provided an example to others who might have contemplated skipping post before their enlistment expired.[28]

Desertion remained a durable problem at Fort Humboldt; the men seemed little deterred by punishment. Encouraged by word of gold strikes and discouraged by poor living conditions, soldiers left their posts with alarming frequency. Regardless of the fact that the fort was 220 miles north of San Francisco, five men deserted in March, and another half dozen followed in April. Buchanan jailed men in the guardhouse with alacrity. By April 1853, only three months after the first post returns were mailed to headquarters, ten men at Fort Humboldt were under arrest or confinement.[29]

The 2d Infantry also had a history of losing soldiers to the gold fields, and Lieutenant Davis's Company E at Fort Reading lacked no immunity to the attraction of riches.

[27] Headquarters Detachment, 4th Infantry, Order No. 1, Feb. 2, 1853, RG393; Utley, *Frontiersmen*, pp. 18, 44–45.

[28] Grant to Townsend, Mar. 5, 1854, RG393; Thomas W. Sweeney, "Military Occupation of California," *Journal of the Military Service Institution of the United States*, vol. 44 (1909), p. 117.

[29] PR, Ft. Humboldt, Jan. and Apr. 1853, M617, R497; Schmitt, *Crook*, pp. 9–10. Buchanan later gained some notoriety as Captain U. S. Grant's commander when Grant resigned from the Army before the Civil War.

Four men deserted in July 1852. After Wright took command he convened a court-martial to clean up disciplinary problems. During his first few months of command, he kept from six to eleven soldiers confined for breaches of military rules. Even these stiff measures failed. Desertion proved more tempting. To cut desertion, Congress granted extra pay for the Regular Army in California and Oregon. Additional money was not enough to kindle enthusiasm through a chilling winter at Fort Reading, however. Thirteen men deserted during the next summer.[30]

Another factor leading to dissatisfaction was a growing uneasiness concerning constabulary functions among northern California Indians. Sending a column to intercede in civilian-Indian standoffs seemed inconclusive. One Fort Humboldt officer, sensing civilian contempt for Indian abilities, warned that Indians of the interior could be "bold and daring." In his estimation only a paucity of firearms prevented the Native American dwellers by the Klamath and Trinity rivers and at the headwaters of the Eel and Mad rivers from being formidable opponents. Northern California Indians were as "hostile to the extent they dare to be."[31]

Surely a "humane policy" offered the only hope for ending the succession of attacks and counterattacks between settlers and Indians. Edward F. Beale, superintendent of Indian affairs for California (a federal position), proposed such a policy. Writing from San Francisco, he outlined a system of military reservations to be organized as self-supporting Indian colonies. Beale would invite Indians to

---

[30] Hitchcock to William M. Gwin, Jan. 14, 1853, RG393; PR, Ft. Reading, July and Nov. 1852 and Apr.-June 1853, M617, R993.

[31] Hunt to Cross, June 30, 1853, RG393.

collect on these reservations. His plans included the instruction of Indians in agriculture and industry by civilian agents. Regular Army garrisons would protect the reservations from outside disruption. The Pacific Division command strongly concurred with Beale's plan. Although Governor Bigler wanted all Indians moved outside the state, General Hitchcock termed Beale's concept as perhaps the only one "calculated to prevent the extermination of the Indians."

Many of Hitchcock's field officers reached similar conclusions about the wisdom of new policies designed to bring to an end the interminable killings. They judged that small parties of Regular Army troops should frequent northern California trails to intensify contacts with various Indian groups. Observation patrols would increase understanding between soldier and Indian, a comprehension that they hoped would produce the "happiest effects." Regular Army patrols on limited missions would, in addition, ensure better protection for packtrains and travelers. From the professional standpoint, the patrols would also serve as "an excellent school for the men" in campaign marching and field craftsmanship.[32]

To increase friendly contacts with Humboldt County Indians, Colonel Buchanan requisitioned a supply of gifts of the type commonly used in frontier parleys. Superintendent Beale had none and neither did Hitchcock. For the time being, Hitchcock authorized Buchanan to proffer standard Army rations to Indians who might visit Fort

[32] *Ibid.*; Beale to Superintendent of Indian Affairs, Oct. 29, 1852, RG393; Robert M. Krasnicka and Herman J. Viola, *The Commissioners of Indian Affairs* (Lincoln: Univ. of Nebraska Press, 1979), pp. 50, 53; Francis Paul Prucha, *The Great White Father* (Lincoln: Univ. of Nebraska Press, 1984), vol. 1, pp. 387–88; Hoopes, "McKee."

Humboldt. However, the division staff stayed the coastal commander's hand by warning him to discourage such visits lest the post transform itself into a tribal feeding station.[33]

Colonel Wright organized talks with Indians at Fort Reading. His diplomacy brought commendation from Pacific Division headquarters. Division staff was also pleased when Wright reacted quickly to the killing of a settler by bringing in the perpetrators to Fort Reading. Wright calmed the settlers and headed off the habitual, indiscriminate massacre of Indians.[34]

Congratulations quickly turned to condolences. After reports arrived of cattle thefts, Lieutenant Edmund Russell led a small party of soldiers beyond the post. On March 24, 1853, they encountered what he suspected to be marauding Indians. Often "brave and reckless," Russell approached them. Seeing him temporarily separated from his men, the Indians seized the 31-year-old West Pointer. They killed him with clubs and arrows.

General Hitchcock reported Russell's death to the adjutant general in Washington, D.C. He added the disturbing news that California's trigger-happy volunteers had shot down a group of thirty Indians and kindled an "unextinguishable" desire for revenge on the part of the Indians. In the Army's view, warfare now existed on the upper Sacramento River.[35]

---

33 Townsend to Buchanan, Mar. 1, 1853, RG393.

34 Townsend to Wright, Feb. 8, 1853, RG393.

35 Hitchcock to Cooper, Mar. 31, 1853, RG393; PR, Ft. Reading, Mar. 1853, M267, R993; Bradford Ripley Alden, "The Oregon and California Letters of Bradford Ripley Alden," *CHQ*, vol. 27 (Sept. 1949), p. 203; *Shasta Courier*, Mar. 26 and Apr. 2, 1853.

Chapter 2
1853–1854

Scouts and Expeditions

*. . . in northern California and southern Oregon alone . . .
the lives of more than a hundred whites and several hundred
Indians have been sacrificed in collisions between the two
races. The force in that country is not now, and never has
been, sufficient.*

Annual Report of the Secretary of War (1853)

Lieutenant Russell's death near Fort Reading in March
1853 signaled warm weather and bad attitudes. Rain poured
down, exceeding seven inches by the end of the month.
Reports of Indians stealing property and settlers reacting
with gunfire and the hangman's rope filtered into the
Sacramento Valley. Packtrains battled unidentified attackers.
California legislators petitioned for a change of command
in the Pacific Division.[1]

Determined to restore peace quickly to the upper
Sacramento, Colonel Wright seemed unaware that Congress
had failed to ratify California Indian treaties. He first

---

[1] Lynda Lasswell Crist, *The Papers of Jefferson Davis* (Baton Rouge: Louisiana State
Univ. Press, 1985), vol. 5, p. 18; *Statistical Report on the Sickness and Mortality in
the Army of the United States* (Washington, D.C.: Gov. Printing Office, 1855), vol.
2, p. 589; San Francisco *Daily Alta California*, Mar. 30 and Apr. 19, 1853.

needed to get a supply train through to Fort Jones. Resupply of the post would assure the dragoons a base of operation for scouts and expeditions into the northern counties. Wright believed that vigorous leadership could push a packtrain through freshets and snowdrifts to Fort Jones. He turned to one of the officers in Company D, 4th Infantry—Lieutenant Francis H. Bates—to lead a mule column north.

Bates departed Fort Reading before mid March 1853, knowing rough trails awaited his train beyond Shasta. Ten days later he pulled his supply animals into Fort Jones. He also brought 1st Lieutenant Richard C. W. Radford, recently transferred to Company E, 1st Dragoons. Radford met Lieutenant Ogle and Surgeon Crane. Both had survived the winter well in their makeshift quarters.[2]

The main body of dragoons was slow in getting on the road from Fort Reading. Major Fitzgerald, his health somewhat improved, did not return to Fort Jones with his full squadron until April 22, a month behind Bates. Some eighty troopers strong, the dragoons had also added 2d Lieutenant Isaiah N. Moore of Company A to their rolls, thus bringing the total of officers at Fort Jones to six.

Rumors of new gold finds probably did more to scotch threats of open warfare on the Sacramento than the sight of eighty blue uniforms on horseback. Miners' interests were diverted from Indians to the search for yellow nuggets. Whatever the cause, affairs north of Fort Reading were characterized by a return to a slower tempo of cultural animosity and isolated killings.

[2] PR, Ft. Reading and Ft. Jones, Mar. and Apr. 1853, M617, R560,993.

Moving to regain lost prestige, the dragoons at Fort Jones set up a system of mounted escorts between Yreka and Shasta City. They patrolled the areas where packtrains met the most trouble. The display of federal military strength raised confidence among civilian travelers.

An infantry company of Regulars in Oregon was slated for transfer to Fort Jones one week after Fitzgerald returned. These infantrymen, which were to be added to Wright's command, would free Fitzgerald of many garrison duties. When the new troops arrived, the dragoons would be able to range much farther afield along the emigrant routes.[3]

Prior to the arrival of the new company, Colonel Wright inspected Fort Jones on May 24. The old Vermonter preferred to command from horseback instead of a headquarters hut. He personally reconnoitered as far north as Yreka and planned missions for his two cavalry and three infantry companies. Wright assigned Companies A and E, 1st Dragoons, the difficult task of protecting travelers on the California–Oregon Trail. Wright planned that when Company E, 4th Infantry arrived from Oregon, the foot soldiers would guard Fort Jones and build better facilities. According to Wright's plan, the two infantry companies at Fort Reading would act as a manpower reserve for Wright's Northern District of California.

Wright made one other change in his new command arrangements—a drastic change. He transferred Fitzgerald to Benicia. Perhaps sensing Fitzgerald's failing health, Wright had the dragoon officer accompany him south. Lieutenant Radford took command of Company A. Lieu-

---

[3] Townsend to Wright, Mar. 24, 1853, RG393; PR, Ft. Jones, Apr. 1853, M617, R560; Alden, "Letters of B. R. Alden," pp. 205–206.

tenant Ogle, a man who was as "quiet as an Indian," led Company E, 1st Dragoons.[4]

The Regular infantry from Oregon arrived on the last day of May 1853. Company E was under the command of Captain Bradford R. Alden, a West Point graduate in 1831 who had returned later as a member of the faculty. His company walked all the way to Fort Jones instead of taking a circuitous water route.

Alden, as senior line officer present, immediately assumed command of Fort Jones. Next in command was 1st Lieutenant Joseph B. Collins of the 4th Infantry, who took over demanding post logistics duties.[5]

Released from all garrison cares, the dragoon squadron filled the role of Regular Army fire brigade in northern California. Accompanied by Surgeon Crane, a strong party of horsemen under Lieutenants Radford and Castor rode out to guard emigrant wagon routes east of Fort Jones. By the end of July every able-bodied member of the 1st Dragoons stationed at Fort Jones served on field duty far away from that post. They performed well. The dragoons successfully prevented any attacks on emigrant trails between Yreka and the California border during the 1853 migration season.[6]

Captain Alden, rhapsodic over the natural beauty of the Scott River Valley, set to work improving Fort Jones. His men dug a well. Other soldiers laid floors in the rough log

---

4 Wright to Townsend, Mar. 10, 1854, RG393; PR, Forts Reading and Jones, May 1853, M617, R560,993; Alden, "Letters of B. R. Alden," pp. 212, 220–21. Fitzgerald died in 1860.

5 PR, Fort Jones, May and June 1853, M617, R560; Alden, "Letters of B. R. Alden," p. 207.

6 Wright to Townsend, March 10, 1854, RG 393; PR, Fort Jones, June and July 1853, M617, R560.

barracks. Building a post hospital and government store-house and operating a new post bakery, the garrison toiled through July. In accordance with standard War Department orders to establish gardens, they planted corn, tomatoes, and potatoes. Provisions from Fort Reading usually took four days to reach the post and were packed by trail at twenty cents a pound. Alden's efforts at self-sufficiency seemed prudent. He bragged about his wholesome daily rations. Commissary supplies included beef, rice, beans, bread, fresh milk, butter, and dried peaches.[7]

In July the calendar provided Alden a change of pace. Independence Day was celebrated even on the California frontier. As the most prominent federal official in the region, Alden accepted an invitation to deliver the Fourth of July oration at Yreka. Approximately fifteen hundred Americans assembled in the town. Alden spoke at length. Gold miners fired ragged rifle salutes to the United States. Enjoying his rustic life, Alden disclosed to his wife in New York: ". . . I am perfectly content."[8]

August shattered Alden's tranquility. Settlers and Indians tangled across the state boundary in Oregon. Oregonians, whatever the justness of their cause, insisted that they deserved Regular Army help. With his cavalry complement far afield, post commander Alden felt compelled to call on his infantry company for troops. In reality, the garrison lacked sufficient soldiers to meet the new emergency.

Able to muster but eleven riflemen for Oregon, Alden turned the post over to Lieutenant Collins. Collins would have to make do with the remaining eight men present for

---

[7] Alden, "Letters of B. R. Alden," pp. 211, 214, 216–17.

[8] *Ibid.*, pp. 213, 215, 218.

duty plus a few extra duty personnel and the sick. Collins watched Alden start the tiny expeditionary force north to the Rogue River Valley of Oregon.[9]

In California, settler apprehension about Indians around Fort Jones grew. Disquieting news and gloomy rumors reminded them that the Scott River Indians, a Shasta group, were linguistically related to Shasta Indians on the Rogue River. The Scott River group of a few hundred Indians had been peaceable, but they harbored genuine grievances. The Shasta were long-time residents of the pretty valley, considered it home, and had received false assurances that the area had been reserved for them. The Shasta watched settlers dam the Scott River in many places. Dams effectively destroyed Indian fishing and sustenance.

Either as a precaution to ensure public safety or to mollify the loudest settlers, Lieutenant Collins decided to act. He disarmed the Scott Valley Shasta Indians. Without disorder, Collins placed the Shasta rifles under his personal custody at Fort Jones.[10]

Successful in his enterprise to prevent angry gunfire in Scott Valley, Fort Jones's lieutenant acted on reports from Oregon. When he learned that Captain Alden had been wounded, Collins wrote to Mrs. Alden on the east coast and gave her the bad news. Captain Alden, invalided, returned to Fort Jones on September 22.

A new post surgeon, Francis Sorrel from Georgia, tended to Alden. Hardy Surgeon Crane and the entire dragoon squadron transferred to Oregon in Setember 1853. Fort Jones was now an all-infantry garrison, resulting in

9 PR, Ft. Jones, Aug. 1853, M617, R560; Alden, "Letters of B. R. Alden," pp. 207, 223.

10 Collins to Wright, Sept. 23, 1853, RG393; Heizer, *Indians*, p. 212.

loss of the capability to respond with speed to calls for help. Luckily, there were no further alarms.[11]

While peace prevailed along the Scott River in Siskiyou County, Colonel Wright's dissatisfaction over the lack of amity between settlers and Indians continued. He organized a fresh field force from the existing infantry at Fort Reading, because the services of his district's dragoon squadron had been lost to Oregon. Wright left the fort with his makeshift column on September 11, 1853. Lieutenant Payne of the 2d Infantry remained behind to temporarily command a small group of twenty-eight men at the Cow Creek post.

Wright scouted Shasta County without incident. Newly promoted to command of Company D, 4th Infantry, 1st Lieutenant Edmund Underwood joined Wright's expedition in the field. He and the men of the 4th entered their barracks at Fort Reading again on October 16.[12]

Underwood had transferred to Fort Reading from Fort Humboldt on the redwood coast, where Colonel Buchanan had suffered through an exasperating spring and summer. Attempts to open communication with Humboldt County Indians had turned uniformly futile.

Responding to stockmen's consternation over the destruction of their property, Fort Humboldt's commander sent Lieutenant Crook and a squad from the 4th Infantry. They identified and apprehended the lone Indian perpetrator of the misdeeds. Crook's squad took their prisoner back to the

---

[11] PR, Ft. Jones, Sept. 1853, M617, R560; Alden, "Letters of B. R. Alden," pp. 221, 351, 354.

[12] Bigler to Hitchcock, Sept. 20, 1853, RG393; PR, Ft. Reading, Sept. and Oct. 1853, M617, R993.

guardhouse at Fort Humboldt, safe from an irate Humboldt Bay community.

Evidently ungrateful for his safety, the prisoner fled during the night. Buchanan's wrath rose to a high pitch the next morning when he learned of the prisoner's escape. He termed the Indian's flight the "grossest negligence" and issued an official denouncement to his garrison: "This command was sent here to protect the citizens, and if prisoners cannot be held one single night by the guard, it may well be doubted that it can be relied upon for that purpose." Still furious, he requested a court-martial for the hapless private whose post was nearest the guardhouse from which the prisoner escaped.[13]

Trusting that military pride would prevent future occurrences similar to the guardhouse escape, Buchanan sent the first full field expedition from Fort Humboldt into the mountains. Led by Lieutenant Bonnycastle of Company B and accompanied by Lieutenant Crook and fourteen enlisted men, the party aimed for the south fork of the Trinity River in May 1853. They hoped to initiate communication with Indians who dwelt in the interior of Humboldt County.

Once contact was made, Buchanan expected his lieutenants to explain in no uncertain terms the danger to Indians of continuing petty annoyances to travelers between Humboldt Bay and the Trinity gold mines. Such acts by a few Indians would inevitably result in blind-swinging moves by volunteers to "chastize" all Indians, guilty and innocent.

Bonnycastle took an interpreter to facilitate talk with the Indians plus three mules to carry supplies. He fell short of

---

[13] Buchanan to Townsend, Apr. 2 and 15, 1853, RG393. Fort Humboldt's commander later withdrew charges against the private.

his Trinity River goal. Foiled by a rough route and hampered by deep gulches, he reached only the Mad River. Forced to turn around because they were low on rations, the initial attempt at communication with Indians seemed on the verge of failure. Bonnycastle tried to make contact with a few diffident Indians that he observed on the opposite bank of the Mad River before turning back. He thought he had secured their promise to come across and visit him, but he waited a day in vain. Bonnycastle's party gained the impression that the Indians were unusually apprehensive over reports of a Regular Army garrison on Humboldt Bay. Indian reserve confirmed to some extent earlier reports that somebody had circulated false stories about the Army. Allegedly, the Indians believed that the soldiers had come to Humboldt County with instructions to shoot them down wherever encountered.[14]

Encountering Indians and conversing with them continued to be a pressing necessity for troops at Fort Humboldt. In June further reports of Indian-inspired headaches to packers and travelers on gold-mine routes prompted Buchanan to launch another expedition into the hinterland. Resolutely, he turned to 1st Lieutenant Lewis C. Hunt, who had been born at a frontier Army post. Hunt arrived at Fort Humboldt in March and took command of Company F, 4th Infantry. He organized his security group and left on June 7 at the head of seventeen Regulars plus a hired civilian interpreter-guide.

Hunt met a failure more galling than Bonnycastle's. Two days after departing Fort Humboldt, Hunt ran into a party of nine civilians on horseback in the Eel River

---

[14] Buchanan to Townsend, May 24, 1853, RG393.

Valley. The civilians claimed that Indians had stolen four horses plus an equal number of mules and that they sought to recover the animals. The horsemen offered to accompany Hunt. Hunt knew that the theft described by the civilians was the type of minor incident that Buchanan wanted to stop. He naively accepted the local residents' offer.

Following an Indian trail up the Mad River Valley, they saw mule tracks but were unable to accurately trace them. In a small Indian rancheria, the combined military-civilian group met eight Indians of what was described as a Trinity tribe. Whatever their origin, Hunt found talk impossible because the interpreter knew no adequate dialect.

Moving on, Hunt's party came upon a second rancheria around sunset. All the inhabitants except a woman fled. The woman insisted through the interpreter, who knew her language, that her settlement held no stolen property. Hunt camped nearby for the night.

Next morning, the fresh tracks of mules dragging ropes — a sure sign of loose domesticated animals — caught Hunt's attention. He decided to pick up all Indian males in the area until the theft was resolved. Two Indians, one a youth, were soon taken prisoner. The soldiers hailed a third Indian who was close by.

While the soldiers tried to convince the third Indian to come into their group, all three Indians suddenly made a break to escape. One civilian raised his weapon and shot at an Indian. The youth, uninjured, froze motionless.

The fruitlessness of the search for the mules and the civilians' apparent eagerness to shoot Indians aroused Hunt to the possibility that the "theft" was a ruse. He got a report that the civilians had captured more Indians behind him.

Reversing his steps and wondering what next to expect, Hunt to his horror found two dead Indians. A woman and a child were prisoners of the civilians.

The trailside scene exceeded Hunt's ethical limits. He expressed his sorrow and gave the woman and child presents. Hunt asked the woman to tell her relatives and associates that soldiers intended to punish only "bad" Indians. With that, he released the pair.

Shed of his innocence about California Indian affairs, Hunt placed the youth first apprehended under his protection. Hunt returned to Fort Humboldt and reported his disastrous attempt at opening communication with mountain-dwelling Indians.[15]

At Fort Humboldt soldiers treated the young Indian with kindness, and named him Jim. The officers let Jim spend some time with the civilian interpreter employed by the garrison. In this manner they hoped that the hired linguist might acquire a thorough knowledge of Indian languages of the Eel River region.

Buchanan retained a determination to communicate with Indians. Despite misadventures, he still expected to improve feelings among Indians, soldiers, and settlers. Buchanan also showed his opinion of local volunteers. Whatever federal policy might be concerning cooperation between Regulars and volunteers, Fort Humboldt's commander would set his own policy. He was in northern California, not Washington. Buchanan prohibited future Fort Humboldt expeditions from allowing any armed volunteer to accompany them.

Buchanan renewed attempts to contact the native inhab-

---

[15] Buchanan to Townsend, June 27, 1853, RG393; PR, Ft. Humboldt, Mar. 1853, M617, R497.

itants of Humboldt County. Lieutenant Underwood led a
sergeant, a corporal, thirteen privates, and the post interpreter on the next expedition. The detained Jim and a
friendly Indian of the area, Tamarass, were also included
in Underwood's group.

They marched into the Mad River Valley. After five
days, Underwood arrived in the vicinity of Jim's capture.
He gave the boy preplanned presents, a message of assur-
ance to his family that blue-uniformed soldiers carried
only friendly intentions, and an invitation for Jim's chief to
visit Fort Humboldt.

Sending a greatly relieved Jim on his way, Underwood
next dispatched Tamarass to meet Indian leaders with
whom he was acquainted. Operating with Buchanan's
instructions to be friendly yet cautious, Underwood planned
to hold no formal conversations with anyone except chiefs.

Plans for conversations went unfulfilled. Tamarass spoke
with his own rancheria chief and returned with disconcerting
news. The Mad River Wiyut admitted killing a white
named Cooper in retaliation for unspecified wrongs. In
return, settlers had attacked them and cost the Indians
two lives.

The chief refused outright to come into Underwood's
camp. He believed that Underwood intended to kill all
Mad River Indians who fell into the soldiers' hands.
Settler retribution for Cooper served as an example to him
of the white man's justice. Tamarass's leader cited past
empty promises of provisions and blankets as further reason to avoid contact with the Army.

Underwood journeyed back to Fort Humboldt convinced that, despite many miscarriages, Buchanan's goals
had been met. Hunt's release of two Indians the previous

month appeared from Underwood's personal observations to have been a "medium of much good." The Indian band involved with Hunt's expedition had in fact moved farther upstream and away from busy gold-mine trails. Their voluntary relocation decreased chances of incidents. Underwood believed that Jim's return would also have the effect of keeping Jim's people away from white travelers. If unmolested by whites, Jim's band could subsist removed from miners' routes to the Trinity.[16]

Regardless of the unsuccessful attempts at contact, the Regular Army in the river valleys of northwestern California seemed to have a calming effect. By the end of July 1853, small parties of travelers moved easily and vital packtrains passed unmolested from Humboldt Bay to Weaver and the Trinity mines.

Civilians were not the only ones who were moving from one locale to another. Lieutenant Underwood's promotion and transfer to Fort Reading typified the constant personnel shifts that took place in soldier-short northern California. Likewise, Lieutenant Crook transferred from Fort Humboldt to Fort Jones and arrived at that northern post in October 1853.

The assigned strength of Fort Jones increased slightly with the arrival of a second rifle company, Company K, 2d Infantry. With only two officers and fourteen enlisted men, the addition of the company to the garrison proved insignificant.

Alden's wound had turned to partial paralysis and had forced him to leave Fort Jones and end his military career.

[16] Buchanan to Townsend, June 27 and July 28, 1853, RG393.

The 2d Infantry's captain, Brevet Major George W. Patten (later a poet of some note), became post commander in October. Patten had lost three fingers of his left hand when he had stormed the heights of Cerro Gordo in the Mexican War. However, Patten's tenure as commander turned out to be brief. The War Department broke up the 2d Infantry in California. Officers and noncommissioned officers were ordered to Pennsylvania, where the regiment was to be reformed and rejuvenated. The enlisted men were reassigned to existing regiments on the Pacific Coast.

After transferring seven privates to Company E, 4th Infantry, at Fort Jones, Patten and his crew left the position on November 21. Lieutenant Crook considered Patten "pompous, irritable, and flighty." The lieutenant felt no unhappiness at the departure of the stuttering poet. Farther south, at Fort Reading, fifteen privates and musicians shifted from the 2d Infantry to Company D, 4th Infantry.[17]

The War Department also notified northern California garrisons of orders to reorganize the Pacific Division. A new Department of the Pacific under the command of a major general headquartered in San Francisco was to administer them. Hitchcock was replaced by Brevet Major General John E. Wool.[18]

Reorganization hardly affected Colonel Wright's activities at Fort Reading, and civilian workers partially alleviated his troop shortage. Wright had to convince his superiors of the necessity for civilian helpers. In the face of War

[17] PR, Ft. Jones, Oct. and Nov. 1854; PR, Ft. Reading, Nov. 1854, M617, R560,993; Schmitt, *Crook*, pp. 14, 17. Major Patten is mentioned in Franklin Walker's *San Francisco's Literary Frontier*, but his name is misspelled as *Patton*.

[18] War Dept., Gen. Orders, No. 25, Oct. 31, 1853.

Department policy to economize, Wright vigorously defended his civilian-hire policy by pointing to the importance of Fort Reading as military district headquarters. The fort furnished supplies and arranged transportation for all Regular Army troops north of Sacramento in the interior of California—jobs that would not wait for a solution to the chronic troop shortage. Wright allowed his quartermaster officer to place thirty-three civilians on the government payroll to help with clerical work and the care of horses and mules. Thus, the civilian force was equal to over half the enlisted strength on post. In one month the civilian payroll totaled some $2,800.[19]

Captain Morris, the quartermaster, had reminded headquarters that the troop quarters at Fort Reading still lacked wall and ceiling linings and that he had asked for more stoves. In October 1853 he told the Department of the Pacific that stoves larger in size than ones in use the previous winter had not arrived. Morris declared that suitable stoves for every room were an "absolute requisite." Such habitation seemed luxurious compared to the log huts at Fort Jones where 1st Lieutenant John C. Bonnycastle followed Crook on assignment from Fort Humboldt.

Both Crook and Captain Alden had earlier remarked over the beauty of the Scott River Valley. Not so the infantry enlisted men. Despite improved conditions eighteen men deserted Fort Jones before winter set in.[20]

During the second winter at Fort Jones, supplies held

---

[19] Wright to Townsend, June 9, 1854, RG393; PR, Ft. Reading, Jan. 1854, M617, R993.

[20] Morris to Cross, Oct. 28, 1853, RG393; PR, Ft. Jones, June, July, Sept., and Nov. 1853, M617, R560; Schmitt, *Crook*, pp. 14, 15. During this same round of officer transfers, Lieutenant Collins moved from Fort Jones to Fort Humboldt.

steady through spring; the quartermaster could claim success. Military stores boasted pork, ham, bacon, flour, meal, hard bread, beans, rice, coffee, sugar, vinegar, salt, apples, and pickles. Throughout the winter of 1853–54, postal service also remained consistent; mail arrived at least once each month.[21]

Still another post commander, the fifth since the organization of Fort Jones, proved less steady than the logistics situation. Recently promoted to captain and ten years out of West Point, Henry Moses Judah came to Fort Jones at the end of 1853. Although he had been twice breveted for gallantry during the Mexican War, he gave Bonnycastle and Crook little cause to celebrate the advent of 1854. Captain Judah, in an Army of hard drinkers, drank to excess.[22]

Judah had to take to the saddle almost immediately. Prior to his arrival, Fort Jones's officers had suggested that the Shasta needed federal aid. Subsequently, the government acted. Alexander M. Rosborough of Yreka was appointed Indian agent.

Before the new Indian agent could act on Army advice or the views of civilized citizens could prevail, gunfire erupted on the upper reaches of the nearby Klamath River. Miners and Indians exchanged shots. Bearing a petition from residents of the mining camp of Cottonwood, a mufti-clad courier went to Fort Jones and called for military protection.

The courier spun a tale of a hundred Indians who lurked in a cave overlooking the Klamath. They had supposedly

---

[21] Bonnycastle to Wool, Mar. 18, 1854, RG393.

[22] PR, Ft. Jones, Dec. 1853, M617, R560; Schmitt, *Crook*, p. 19.

surrounded and killed some settlers who had tried to recover stolen stock. Judah, sober, reacted.

He marched two dozen Regulars out of Fort Jones over snow-covered ground on January 16, 1854. At the Klamath some twenty citizens tagged onto the column as a volunteer militia. Pushing ahead in heavy snow squalls and discomforted by below-freezing temperatures, the combined soldier-citizen force came upon stiff civilian corpses. At the top of a steep slope beneath high bluffs and above Judah, Indians barricaded a cave entrance with stones and logs. The courier's tale appeared to be true.

Desultory rifle fire killed a volunteer who attempted to peer into the cave from the bluff. At the foot of the slope leading up to the cave, Bonnycastle and Crook convinced their commander that a headlong rush by Regulars to the cave mouth would be foolhardy. Probably sick from a hangover, Judah quieted. He pulled back his troops and the volunteers and then sent Crook and Surgeon Sorrel to Fort Lane in Oregon for a howitzer.[23]

The commander of Fort Lane, Captain Andrew J. Smith, accompanied Crook back to the Klamath. He brought with him not only a howitzer with which to bombard the Indians but also an officer and fifteen men of the 1st Dragoons as reinforcements. Smith found that the Indian-held cave was too high for effective artillery fire. He also discovered that there was more to the story than Judah knew.

Smith learned that the Indians now cooped up in the cave sought only to defend themselves against further unprovoked attack. A party of gold miners had set upon them in

---

[23] Wright to Townsend, Jan. 21, 1854; and Smith to Wright, Jan. 31, 1854; and Judah to Wright, Jan. 31, 1854, RG393; Schmitt, *Crook*, pp. 17–20.

an organized attempt to abduct women and steal ponies. The Indians had hurriedly withdrawn into the cave. Seven of their number, unresisting, had been killed. After the initial assault, a second attack by miners had followed, at which time the Indians returned fire.

Smith took command of the situation and talked to the Indians. He accepted the Indians' promise to discuss matters in detail when warm weather came. Smith dismissed the entire expedition. Smith returned to Fort Lane, reproved by a Yreka newspaper for withdrawing the soldiers. Denied action against the Indians and Regular Army support, the volunteers shot an Indian pony, stole several others, and drifted away.

Completing their part in "the grand farce" on the Klamath, Company E, 4th Infantry, went back to Fort Jones. Seething over Judah's posturing and drunkenness in the field, Bonnycastle charged his superior with military misconduct. With little defense Judah offered to transfer himself if his officers kept quiet. He signed an order granting himself seven days of leave and departed.[24]

Harmony reigned over the garrison in Judah's absence. A third line officer, Brevet 2d Lieutenant John B. Hood (a West Point graduate and a year junior to Crook), joined the post and took over adjutant's chores. He termed California a "country of gold and extravagance." Hood and Crook hunted game together and supplied the officers' table with meat. They sent their surplus to Yreka's market to gain supplemental income. Sorrel as post surgeon kept the sick

---

[24] Smith to Wright, Jan. 31, 1854; and Wright to Townsend, Feb. 11, 1854, RG393; PR, Ft. Jones, Feb. 1854, M617, R560; Schmitt, *Crook*, p. 20. Carried on detached service, then on leave, Captain Judah officially transferred to Ft. Humboldt as a replacement for Captain U. S. Grant, who resigned.

rate low and, along with Hood and Bonnycastle, formed a Dixie-born trio in northern California.[25]

Bonnycastle acted as post commander while Judah was gone. He concentrated his attentions on Indian-settler problems. Explaining the situation to General Wool, Bonnycastle advised that Shasta Indian inhabitants of the valley of the Scott continued "remarkably peaceful." They once again owned rifles and kept their weapons in good condition. If protected from the outrages of ill-disposed whites, he said, the Shasta would cause no problem. Their greatest need was land, without which they would surely starve. Although an Army officer, not an Indian agent, Bonnycastle provided the Shasta with limited supplies of beef and potatoes furnished by Rosborough. With Crook as a witness to documents, Bonnycastle signed receipts for the food, terming it necessary and proper.[26]

Settlers near Fort Jones proved to be, in general, law abiding. According to Bonnycastle, the one continuing element of disturbance in the Shasta area was a "trifling little" newspaper in Yreka, which always called for Indian extermination.

From the Indians who had barricaded themselves in the Klamath River cave, word came to Bonnycastle in March 1854 that the chief of that tribelet, who was nicknamed Bill, was ready to meet. He wanted to discuss a safe location for his people, as previously agreed. Escorted by two Indians and an interpreter, Bonnycastle as lieutenant in

[25] PR, Ft. Jones, Mar. 1854, M617, R560; Alexander M. Rosborough, "Notes and Accounts as Special Indian Agent," Rosborough Papers, Bancroft Lib., Berkeley, Calif.; J. B. Hood, *Advance and Retreat*, (New Orleans: Hood Orphan Memorial Fund, 1880), p. 6; Harry L. Wells, *History of Siskiyou County*, (Oakland: D. J. Stewart & Co., 1881), pp. 134–35; Schmitt, *Crook*, p. 21.

[26] Bonnycastle to Wool, Mar. 17, 1854, RG393.

command met Agent Rosborough and citizen Elijah Steele. Together they journeyed along the Klamath and waited near the location of the winter battle. The chief entered Bonnycastle's camp with ten of his followers. Bill arranged his men around a fire. Everybody shook hands.

Bill explained that many of his compatriots were sick and unable to travel. Pointing out that food and game abounded in the vicinity, the Indian leader stated his preference for remaining where they were. Rosborough and Bonnycastle let the matter drop.

Not everybody agreed, however. Reaching the Klamath River ferry on the way back to Fort Jones, Bonnycastle saw several of Cottonwood's "lower class" assembled. Vengeful and incorrectly supposing that Bill would accompany the Army officer, the citizens planned to cause a disturbance at the stream crossing. Scornfully, Bonnycastle passed Cottonwood.[27]

Two months later, Bill lost his life, the result of a whole series of misunderstandings involving well-meaning citizens and Army officers. Taking advantage of the confusion, malicious whites and Oregon Indians had ambushed Bill and four associates. Bonnycastle, Lieutenant Hood, and Agent Rosborough defused a Shasta war of revenge.[28]

Meanwhile, nearly all the Shasta in the Scott Valley moved in and encamped near Fort Jones. Twice a week the Indian agent from Yreka issued them beef. The question of their land stayed unsolved. Bonnycastle expected a quiet summer. He requested a supply of presents for the Indians.

---

[27] Bonnycastle to Wright, Mar. 26, 1854, RG393; *Alta California*, Apr. 29, 1854.

[28] Bonnycastle to Wright, Apr. 18, 1854; and Bonnycastle to Wool, Apr. 27 and May 28, 1854, RG393; Alex J. Rosborough, "A. M. Rosborough, Special Indian Agent," *CHQ*, vol. 26 (Sept. 1947), p. 202.

Colonel Wright was determined that the vicinity around Fort Jones was not to be the only area of his command that should enjoy a peaceful summer. Along the McCloud River thirteen miners and thirty-seven Indians had died as they fought one another. Wright sought a policy that would preclude such violence in the future. He welcomed Indian visitors to Fort Reading in a cordial manner. Three groups, each of some forty Indians, called on Wright in the spring. Noting that the Indians had suffered much from want of food during the previous winter, the commander of Fort Reading gave them small quantities of Army provisions. With or without the concurrence of the Interior Department, commanders of the Army's three forts in northern California were feeding Indians.

Unlike Bonnycastle, Wright sensed that his visitors were dimly aware of proposals to assemble Indians on federal reservations. He informed the Department of the Pacific that with little encouragement these Indians would gather peacefully and move to a reservation. Knowing that reservation plans faced severe obstacles in California, Wright added, "I have made them no promises on the subject, as a failure in the execution would lessen their confidence in the government.[29]

Later, two Pit River Indian chiefs visited Wright, accompanied by a number of "warriors" and several respectable Californians who resided north of Fort Reading. They sought Wright's arbitration. The Pit dignitaries reported that some Indians had indeed stolen the citizens' stock. Armed stockmen had singled out and severely punished the Pit River Indians. They asked Wright to bring peace.

---

[29] Wright to Townsend, Apr. 9, 1854, RG393.

Wright saw frequent contact as the means of preventing more trouble. He issued the Pit callers safe-conduct passes to enable them to reach Fort Reading unhampered and report problems. Wright told the Indians to visit the post monthly. The chiefs promised to prevent their young men from causing further raids on animal herds. They and the stockmen seemed satisfied with the arbitration.[30]

Still displeased with overall conditions in his special military district, Wright pondered information from Bonnycastle at Fort Jones. The commander said that, off to the northeast, Pit River, McCloud River, and Modoc Indians kept settlers in fear—fear Bonnycastle believed was groundless. If some apprehension existed among settlers over northeast Indian groups, then that was where Wright would go. He reminded department headquarters in San Francisco that he was without cavalry.[31]

Instead of heeding Wright's hint for more cavalry, headquarters sent a cannoneer unit. Company D, 3d Artillery, appeared at Fort Reading on June 24, 1854. Without cannon, they were pressed into northern California service as infantry.

A shipwreck in the Atlantic had delayed the arrival of the 3d Artillery in California. Second Lieutenant James Van Voast headed Company D because its assigned commander, Captain Francis O. Wyse, was under investigation for refusing to board the ill-fated ship.[32]

With reinforcements, Wright saddled his command.

---

[30] Wright to Townsend, Apr. 22, 1854, RG393.

[31] Wright to Townsend, Mar. 10, 1854; and Bonnycastle to Wool, Mar. 17, 1854, RG393.

[32] PR, Ft. Reading, June 1854, M617, R993; War Dept., Gen. Orders, No. 8, June 5, 1854 as pertains to Francis O. Wyse.

Mounting the artillerymen on mules, he formed an expedition destined for the regions of the Pit and McCloud rivers. Wright planned to impress the inhabitants there with the benefits obtainable from peaceful Indian-settler relations. He conducted a mass meeting on the McCloud, a stream favored by the Indians because of abundant salmon. He warned that murder of settlers or theft of their belongings invariably brought troops seeking culprits. Accompanying Wright, the chief of the Cow Creek Indians and several others of that group helped assure Indian listeners that the Army officer's words carried weight.

Reassured that the massed Indians were peaceably inclined when left unmolested by miners and stockmen, Wright continued his horseback diplomacy. He distributed clothes and traditional goods among the Indians as tokens of friendship. In return, the Indians performed a spectacular dance in celebration.

Using converted artillerymen instead of cavalry, Wright's policy paid dividends. He successfully communicated with McCloud River Indians, probably a Wintu group, and some of the Pit River Indians. The appearance of his troops helped convince settlers that, if given a chance, order could exist in northern California.[33]

The peaceful progress of a railroad survey headed by Lieutenant Edward G. Beckwith through Wright's district was evidence of the increase in public safety. Beckwith departed from Salt Lake City and explored westward as part of the War Department's effort to survey four major transcontinental railroad routes. Passing from Honey Lake,

---

[33] Wright to Townsend, Aug. 15, 1854, RG393. Wright, perhaps a premodern environmentalist, complained to Department of Pacific Adjutant Townsend that salmon were less abundant since the coming of steamboats on the Sacramento River.

Beckwith dropped into the Sacramento Valley, where the temperature was 106 degrees Farenheit. He arrived at Fort Reading in July 1854 and found himself "courteously received" by Colonel Wright.

After his animals were shod at the Army post, Beckwith's small party continued to the Fall River, compiling terrain information about the route from Madeline Pass. He completed his work and returned to Fort Reading by the end of the month. From there Beckwith went to Washington, D.C., and prepared "a true picture of the country explored."[34]

Further evidence of Wright's success surfaced in September 1854. A deputation of principal chiefs from the McCloud and lower Pit visited Fort Reading. They told Wright how fortuitous the Cow Creek chief's presence had been at the previous meeting. Unknown to the soldiers, the Cow Creek headman had dampened a rumor started by some "evil disposed person" to the effect that Wright simply wanted to kill all the Indians on the McCloud.

The assembled chiefs then related the events that had ensued since the McCloud conference. Acting on Wright's advice, they had apprehended one of their number who had stolen a sack of flour from a citizen north of the Pit. The Indians returned the flour, executed the thief, and now sought Wright's nod of approval. He endorsed the Indians' actions.

Because there was no agent of the Indian Office in the area, Wright unofficially assumed an agent's duties.

[34] *Reports of Explorations and Surveys to Ascertain the Most Practicable and Economical Route for a Railroad from the Mississippi River to the Pacific Ocean* (Washington, D.C.: A.O.P. Nicholson, Printer, 1855), pp. 46–58; Frank N. Schubert, *Vanguard of Expansion* (Washington, D.C.: Gov. Printing Office, n.d.), pp. 96, 104.

The Department of the Pacific had supplied him with a box of red cloth to use at his discretion for Indian presents. Indian Superintendent Beale provided the cloth. Colonel Wright felt that Beale allocated an inordinate amount of congressional appropriations to southern California. Wright believed that Beale's neglect of his area forced the Army to improvise solutions to Indian problems in northern California.[35]

Buchanan at Fort Humboldt held a view of the Army's ability to solve Indian problems that was even less favorable than Wright's. In Buchanan's area, population expansion into Indian lands had added heat to the usual Indian problems. Estimating that ten thousand Indians now resided within the tactical limits of Fort Humboldt, Buchanan saw nothing but an endless spiral of violence.

For the edification of headquarters, Buchanan described the usual chronology of incidents that he experienced on the redwood coast. First hungry Indians stole a steer or a mule. Enraged, the owner killed the next Indian he saw. In retaliation the dead Indian's cohorts fell upon the first straggling white they spotted on a trail. Crying revenge for murder of a fellow citizen, settlers then turned out en masse and killed all the Indians they could locate. Nowhere in the cycle could the Regular Army inject itself. To this homily Buchanan added, "Then come very bitter feelings, and the Indians are declared to be in a state of open hostility."[36]

---

[35] Townsend to Wright, Nov. 14, 1853 and Sept. 26, 1854; and Wright to Townsend, Sept. 20, 1854, RG393; Heizer, *Indians*, p. 110.

[36] Buchanan to Townsend, Apr. 15, 1854, RG393. On the Army's lack of legal position, see Richard A. Preston's commentary in *The American Military on the Frontier* (Washington, D.C.: Gov. Printing Office, 1978), pp. 56–66.

Such "bitter feelings" boiled in October 1854, when Eel River Indians were accused of murdering a settler. Captain Judah, the notorious ex-commander of Fort Jones, had transferred to Fort Humboldt. He was the only officer on post besides Buchanan. Judah sped to the scene with twelve Regulars.

Judah found a hate-filled environment on the Eel. One settler was dead. Local citizens had seized an Indian man and a youth as hostages. Adult and youth were held in irons at a settler's house. The soldiers intervened immediately. Judah released the two Indians from their irons. When the Indian boy's worried father appeared, Judah explained the situation and released the young man to his care.

Acting as an intermediary, the father assisted Judah in finding the dead settler's real killers. He guided Judah to a Bear River rancheria near the coast, where Judah grabbed four tribal leaders. Judah assured them of his peaceful desires and then strongly voiced his determination to capture murderers.

The chiefs promised their assistance. Realizing that a squad of soldiers marching up the beach would tip his hand, Judah came up with a covert plan. He gave the four Bear Creek Indian residents rope and instructed them to find and tie up the killers.

After dark Judah got word that the chiefs had kept their promise. Filing up the rocky coast, the soldiers met their temporary allies and took two roped prisoners from them. A measure of calm returned to the Eel. After a week in the field, Judah restored his martial reputation. He returned triumphantly to Fort Humboldt with his captives.

Colonel Buchanan quickly notified the district attorney of Humboldt County, who was in Eureka, that the Army held the two law breakers. They were probably responsible for the death of one Mr. Wigmore. The duo seemed better guarded than in the previous occasion when Fort Humboldt held captives.

Walter Van Dyke, the county attorney, declined action. Adding to the legal standoff, a newspaper published near Fort Humboldt said that keeping two Indians prisoner until the next court session seemed too great an expense for county government. Instead of wasting money, the paper said that they should be promptly hung by a "Committee of Vigilance."

Perplexed, the Army saw no alternative but to discharge the Indians from the guardhouse. Proper civil authorities refused to receive them into custody. County Sheriff Peter Lothian offered a compromise. He stated his willingness to take charge of the two prisoners if the federal government would provide for their food and clothing. Acting as instructed by departmental headquarters and dissatisfied with the sheriff's reply, Buchanan freed the two Indians.[37]

Fort Humboldt's Indian prisoner problem educated General Wool in regard to the complexity of settler-Indian relations in California. In October he visited Fort Reading, the first visit to that post by a Department of the Pacific commander. Wright received him with full military honors.[38]

Wright had much to discuss with Wool. Colonel Wright had long complained about poor administrative support. Four months had elapsed since his troops were paid, an uncommon waiting period for soldiers who had to pay for laundry.

---

[37] Buchanan to Townsend, Oct. 11 and 19, 1854, Nov. 1 and 10, 1854, RG393; Bledsoe, *Indian Wars*, p. 94.

[38] PR, Ft. Reading, Oct. 1854, M617, R993.

At Fort Humboldt the situation seemed worse; no pay-master had visited the coastal post during the first year of the existence of the fort. Desperate to overcome this "decided inconvenience," Buchanan preemptorily sent one of his officers to San Francisco by steamer. His orders were to get government funds for the quartermaster and commissary subsistence. Buchanan also wanted a medical officer for the fort, to replace one who had died.

At Fort Reading the long-overdue pay finally arrived at the end of October. Delayed pay was but one sign of the military administration that bothered the semi-isolated Regular Army in northern California. Buchanan thought that without better inducements and greater pay he could expect no re-enlistments at his post. Spoiled food posed another problem. At Fort Humboldt the troops discovered that the pork received with government rations lost half the meaty mass when boiled. Four investigating officers at Fort Reading experienced a different, curious problem. There the pork, when unpacked from barrels, absolutely refused to cook, when boiled. They also found that the strange-tasting sugar issued with rations actually contained oats intermixed with other substances. Only Fort Jones escaped substandard meat, flour, beans, cornmeal, and coffee. In addition, the post gardens, which had been planted to supplement troop rations, proved an overall failure.[39]

Although less of a problem than pay for the troops, forage for animals was also a matter of concern. Forage

---

[39] Wright to Townsend, Oct. 5, 1852; and Buchanan to Townsend, Feb. 1, Apr. 1, and July 1, 1854, RG393; PR, Ft. Reading, Feb. and Dec. 1854, M617, R993; War Dept., Gen. Orders, No. 3, Feb. 9, 1854; Frazer, *Mansfield on Western Forts*, pp. 162, 164, 166. The War Department allowed 21 cents, 4.5 mills for daily rations in California at this time.

required financial expenditures from northern fort funds. The forts had to maintain large herds because other means for moving supplies were limited and the expense of civilian transportation was high. The herd at Fort Reading included 197 mules for packtrains and Army wagons. At Fort Jones fourteen mules hauled wood and water to the post and carried ammunition on field expeditions. Three horses at Fort Jones hastened Regulars in pursuit of deserters. The nine horses at Fort Reading served in the Army's own mail and express service.[40]

Problems of pay, food, and forage were overshadowed in 1854 at Fort Reading by official questions about the utility of the post. The questions were raised by the inspector general, Colonel Joseph K. F. Mansfield, who conducted a general survey of military conditions throughout the Department of the Pacific. Selected as the Army's principal inspector by Secretary of War Jefferson Davis, Colonel Mansfield visited Forts Humboldt, Jones, and Reading during the summer of 1854.

What concerned Mansfield about Fort Reading was the location and the amount of sickness. To Mansfield, who based his views on over twenty years' experience as a military engineer, Fort Reading seemed a poor position for defending populated areas against Indians. A more suitable spot to the northeast offered considerable advantage. It would place troops "between the wild Indians and the population." A northeastern site also assured better protection for the emigrant trail from the east. He also thought that Cow Creek was "a decidedly sickly locality" and

---

40 Wright to Townsend, June 9, 1854; and Crook to Bonnycastle, June 19, 1854, RG393.

objected to Fort Reading being situated where winter rains flooded the parade ground. He noted that Wright had been obliged to build a wooden bridge so that enlisted men could get to the kitchen in the rainy season. Mansfield concluded that the annual flooding caused the prevalence of fevers in the post garrison.

In contrast, Fort Jones seemed a good location for Indian control and Fort Humboldt seemed "well selected." Mansfield also pronounced himself satisfied with discipline at all three northern posts. The only exception was at Fort Reading, where he reported that a skirmish drill, put on for his benefit, seemed indifferent. Likewise, there had been no target practice or bayonet exercises to maintain soldierly talents.

Apprised of Mansfield's findings, General Wool agreed that Fort Reading seemed a likely prospect for closure. He, like Mansfield, favored a new Army post in the Pit River country. Before Wool or Wright could act, disorders broke out again near Fort Reading itself in November.[41]

Roaming parties of six to eight Indians, members of no particular tribe, stole and killed mules and oxen over a three-week period. Traversing Bear Creek and the eastern tributaries of Cow Creek, these acts caused citizens worry for their personal protection. Exaggerated reports to the contrary, however, no general attack against settlements or herds occurred in Shasta County.

Sending out Van Voast again with his mule-mounted artillerymen, Wright expressed regret over the incidents. To headquarters Wright reiterated the fact that no federal

[41] Wool to Lt. Col. Lorenzo Thomas, Oct. 23, 1854, RG393; PR, Forts Humboldt and Reading, July 1854, M617, R497,993; Frazer, *Mansfield on Western Forts*, pp. 87–88, 111–12, 119, 160–61, 163, 165, 184, 192.

Indian agent ever visited Fort Reading. In eight days of tough riding, Van Voast encountered no Indians, only mud. Warfare was not the Indians' object. Landless and neglected, the Indians were hungry.

Wright reported to San Francisco that the Indians were ". . . infinitely worse off than they were before the white settlements encroached upon their lands." Although Wright, Bonnycastle, and Buchanan's subordinates had proved effective as mediators with Indians, and Army officers had maintained cordial relations with Agent Rosborough, the Indians' straitened circumstances brought new pressures to the relationships. The decade to follow would mark a turbulent period in all matters relating to Indians in northern California.[42]

---

[42] Wright to Townsend, Dec. 10, 1854, RG393; Rawls, *Indians of California*, p. 200.

Chapter 3
1855–1856

Military Intervention

It is hard that the troops should be called upon to mediate between these contending parties, while they have also to restrain the Indians and try to protect them from destruction, yet such is mainly their duty in California.

Major General John Wool to Lieutenant Colonel Lorenzo Thomas, February 26, 1855

Gold miners poured into the Klamath River region northeast of Fort Humboldt. The newcomers disrupted the Indian inhabitants' annual salmon harvests and acorn-gathering parties. Karok Indians waited in vain for indemnities for damages inflicted on their food sources, a tribute Indian culture led them to expect. Instead, miners shot at Indians.

Encroachment on Indian lands continued in a crazy-quilt pattern along river valleys. During the winter months of 1855, despite mild weather and the proximity of the Regular Army, terror reigned on the Klamath. Stories circulated among the miners that Indians planned to combine forces and oust them. If true, such a political combination was a departure from the traditional lack of unity among California Indians. Culturally, the Karok and the Hoopa rejected authoritarianism. At Orleans Bar and also at the mouth of the Salmon River, idle whites, acting on dubious evidence, had decided that the nearby Karok plotted a general offensive against settlers and miners. Supposedly, the Indians' all-out attack would begin in the spring.[1]

Small mobs gathered early in January 1855 to preempt the reported Indian outbreak. They demanded that all Indians on the Klamath surrender their firearms and ammunition or face the consequences. One mob burned a number of Karok villages. Some Indians gave up their weapons to rampaging miners. Others defended themselves against unprovoked onslaughts. Two frightened Indian bands killed several of their attackers. Somebody also killed two miners.[2]

The Army was already frustrated as a result of futile attempts to keep steady contact with diverse Indian groups. Soldiers were also tired of their undefined status within California legal jurisdictions. With the outbreak of trouble in January 1855, Army patience ended. After two years of carrying muskets and pulling mules down dark forest trails to no avail, soldiers swiftly and forcefully intervened on the Klamath. At Fort Humboldt Buchanan moved on his own initiative, seeking no headquarters approval and disdaining any coordination with state officials. He pointed out that neither state nor county government maintained a single law officer on the river, and he justified military intervention under "no law but common humanity."

---

[1] Leigh H. Irvine, *History of Humboldt County, California* (Los Angeles: Historical Record Co., 1915), pp. 60–68; Rosborough, "Special Indian Agent," pp. 203–205; Heizer, *Indians*, pp. 175, 188.

[2] Wool to Thomas, Jan. 30, 1855, LR, M234, R34; *Humboldt Times*, Jan. 27, 1855.

After alerting the garrison on January 16 for quick action, Buchanan ordered Captain Henry M. Judah and twenty-six men to protect all persons in the neighborhood of the Klamath and Trinity rivers. Buchanan stripped the post of manpower, leaving himself only twenty soldiers for duty. He sent Assistant Army Surgeon Josiah Simpson with Judah to provide medical support for the men of the 4th Infantry. Judah marched out of Fort Humboldt as soon as there was enough light to see the trail.[3]

Walking into a delicate civil situation, Judah arrived on the Klamath and orchestrated a show of military determination. He openly placed the Regulars between Karok survivors and a small party of local miners who agitated for total Indian extermination. Judah's audacious stand backed earlier actions by other brave Klamath citizens who had shielded Karok Indians from further assault. Lacking strict legal authority, Judah remained in the vicinity under arms, flashing his captain's rank and exerting Regular Army prestige to calm unruly whites.

In addition to miners, Judah also dealt successfully with Humboldt County volunteers who assembled themselves when news spread of the disorders. Recognizing the prevalence of vigilante action on the frontier, he treated the volunteers with semi-military deference, yet left no question that he was the senior military man on the spot. Judah kept the armed volunteers in check.

Local volunteers and citizens warned the Regulars of still another element along the Klamath, the "white brother-in-laws," or "squaw men"—men who had taken Indians

---

[3] Wool to Thomas, Feb. 26, 1855, M234, R34; Ft. Humboldt, Gen. Orders, No. 1, Jan. 16, 1855, RG393; PR, Ft. Humboldt, Jan. 1855, M617, R497; *Humboldt Times,* Jan 20, 1855.

as common-law wives, lived apart from settlements of either culture, and generally abandoned most social mores. Many accused the squaw men of giving arms to certain Indian bands, but Judah discovered no evidence of arms trading.

Judah was able to confine the violence to the initial outburst between small groups of miners and a pair of Indian bands. He could do nothing to quiet the disagreement among the citizens. Some miners favored punishment of selected individual Indians. Others pushed for attacks on all the "red sons of bitches" who deserved "a damn good grubbing." The *Humboldt Times* expressed citizens' indebtedness to the Regulars "for the averting of a protracted war."

By February Judah had exhausted his rations. Unable to resupply his location because of bad weather, Judah and his force returned to Fort Humboldt on February 7. The Army's inability to supply Judah in the field caused, in the view of many civilians, an unstable situation that led to more bloodshed.[4]

Thomas J. Henley, newly appointed federal Indian superintendent for California in 1854, surmised that the Klamath "excitement" had passed for the time being. In San Francisco he studied reports from the scene of action. Henley discussed matters at Department of the Pacific level with General Wool. Henley agreed to send a special agent to the Klamath to represent the Indian Office on a full-time basis. Wool assured Henley that Buchanan would support the Klamath agent in every way possible. If

4 Wool to Thomas, Feb. 26, 1855, M234, R34; PR, Ft. Humboldt, Feb. 1855, M617, R497; *Humboldt Times*, Jan. 20, Feb. 3 and 10, 1855; Rosborough, "Special Indian Agent," p. 203.

necessary, Buchanan's garrison would be reinforced. Before proceeding to the Klamath, Henley's special agent would see Buchanan and get his estimate of Indian affairs around Humboldt Bay and vicinity.[5]

Wool found that he had a small command crisis on the redwood coast. After two years of thankless duty at Fort Humboldt, Buchanan was fed up with Californians. Buchanan realized, however, that on the frontier soldier and civilian needed to deal with one another. In a democratic society, military commanders had to get along with civilians. Buchanan put it bluntly: "It is very desirable that the officer in command of troops should be able to conciliate the people among whom he is serving and I find that with the opinions I entertain I cannot do so." Buchanan asked to be relieved of command.[6]

Wool agreed that Buchanan lacked clear authority to keep peace between Indians and whites. At the same time, he endorsed the initiative of Fort Humboldt and commended Buchanan for his moral influence on the "sober thinking" elements of the region. Pointing out to Buchanan that his difficulties were common to all post commanders in California, Wool told his subordinate that he would keep him at Fort Humboldt. He was confident that Buchanan would continue to perform his duties on a caliber equal to any Regular Army officer on the Pacific coast.

Part of Buchanan's frustration could be traced to the continual shortage of soldiers at Fort Humboldt. Help finally appeared in the form of three newly assigned

---

[5] Townsend to Buchanan, Feb. 22, 1855, RG393; Wool to Thomas, Feb. 26, 1855, M234, R34; Gerald Thompson, *Edward F. Beale & the American West* (Albuquerque: Univ. of New Mexico Press, 1983), p. 74.

[6] Townsend to Buchanan, Mar. 31, 1855, RG393.

lieutenants: Charles Rundell, Hezikiah Garber, and Alfred
Latimer, all West Point graduates. Also, a new captain
arrived to replace Judah—Captain De Lancey Floyd-
Jones, who had won honors during the Mexican War.

In addition, Buchanan received cheering personal news.
Buchanan was a brevet lieutenant colonel but only a captain
in Regular Army rank. The War Department promoted
him to a major in the Regular Army, twenty-five years after
his West Point graduation.

Reconciled to the prospect of further duty at Fort
Humboldt, Buchanan met Henley's special Indian agent,
Stephen G. Whipple. Buchanan ordered Captain Judah
and a thirty-man detachment of the 4th Infantry to accompany Whipple to the Klamath. Whipple and Judah set out
for the inland region in mid-March. They planned to
make permanent the peaceful measures instituted a month
earlier by Judah. Instead, the federal party found the
situation on the Klamath more reprehensible than ever.[7]

A white renegade had assassinated one of the most influ-
ential and understanding Indian leaders on the Klamath.
Anarchy ensued. More Indians had fled to remote mountain elevations in fear for their lives. A pair of unemployed
brothers named Woodward had organized two squads of
volunteers for "defense" against the Indians. The volunteers'
practice was to call Indian men from their dwellings, shake
hands as a symbol of friendship, and then kill them.
Mirroring their contempt for Indian life, the Woodward
squads carried off Indian women and violated them. One
account charged the Woodwards with twenty-six Indian
deaths and for taking twenty-three women prisoners. Indians

---

7 Ibid.; PR, Ft. Humboldt, Feb. and May 1855, M617, R497.

remaining on the Klamath begged protection from the lawless killers.

The law-abiding population had termed the volunteers "disgraceful" and had taken action without waiting for the federal government. They had armed themselves and guarded as many Indian villages as their numbers could cover. Some miners jeopardized their earnings to restrain malevolent whites and protect Indians who had yet to flee.

The Klamath's respectable population greeted Whipple and Judah with relief. A local newspaper, the *Humboldt Times*, took Buchanan to task for allowing Judah to withdraw in the first place, only to have the troops remain "idle" at Fort Humboldt. One observer at the Klamath thought that a Regular Army company and a United States marshal could settle most of the turmoil in three days.[8]

Judah tried. He possessed none of the legal authority of a U.S. marshal, but he commanded strength. Unlike Agent Whipple, Judah exuded confidence. He established a military camp near the junction of the Trinity River with the Klamath, some forty miles upstream from the Pacific coast. Next he sought talks with the Yurok and Karok groups in the area. Using the good offices of a pair of settlers who routinely kept contact with Indians, Judah sent word of his desire for a friendly meeting. Accompanied by the two settlers and six soldiers, Judah traveled twenty miles downstream by boat. Every Indian village on the Klamath seemed deserted. No meeting occurred.

Suspecting that large groups of Yurok might be at the mouth of the Klamath, Judah sent reassurances of his

---

[8] Wool to Thomas, Apr. 11, 1855, RG393; Henley to Manypenny, Apr. 9, 1855, M234, R34; *Humboldt Times*, Mar. 3, 1855; Bledsoe, *Indian Wars*, p. 205.

conciliatory desires, which were exemplified by the smallness of his party. He succeeded in his second attempt. Just
before dusk one evening, fifty Indians appeared near Judah,
armed with long knives and carrying bows and arrows.

Judah patiently listened to their complaints of despica-
ble acts by volunteers. He convinced the Yurok of his
friendly intentions. They promised to meet again near
Judah's military camp for a lengthier conference. Satisfied,
Judah hurried back upstream for a talk with the Hoopa,
who lived north of the scenes of violence.

On April 3, 1855, seventy representatives of the Indian
community assembled for a joint conference with Judah.
The Army officer stated his belief that a permanent Regular
presence was necessary to ensure peace between the native
groups, emigrant settlers, and transient miners. Turning
to the immediate problem at hand, Judah agreed to arm the
Indian groups represented at the meeting. Once furnished
with firearms, the Indian bands were to dispose of eight
Indians who had been adjudged as killers. As "Indian
allies" of the Army, these bands obtained small amounts of
government provisions and sent expeditions into the mountains to find the doomed men. Judah also told the county
volunteers to disband and go home.[9]

Soldiers understood that the Interior Department bore
responsibility for dealing with Indians, but local citizens
expected the Army to maintain peace. On the Klamath
River, Judah set government policy. He allied Indians
with the federal government for warlike or vigilante aims.
The Indian Office accepted Judah's action as a fait

---

[9] Ibid.; Humboldt Times, Mar. 31 and Apr. 21, 1855. The Army also warned
authorities that Woodwards' volunteers planned to seek government compensation
for "defending" the Klamath region.

accompli and permanently assigned Whipple to the area. Lacking any means or legal authority to establish a government Indian reservation on the Klamath, Whipple set up a "temporary rendezvous" there for Indians. In support of Whipple, Companies B and F of the 4th Infantry of Fort Humboldt maintained a field detachment at Judah's encampment. Judah transferred to again become a post commander at Fort Jones. His replacement, Captain Floyd-Jones, assumed command of the riverside camp.[10]

Floyd-Jones designated Judah's site as Camp Wool in honor of the department commander. Lieutenant Rundell, who had recently joined the camp, had matters more serious than names on his mind; he stayed busy keeping thirty enlisted men supplied and fed.

Assisted by a sergeant and three corporals, the officers moved about and actively endeavored to suppress difficulties between settlers and Indians. Calm returned to the area. According to one report, "miners are at work and every branch of business is going on prosperously."[11]

The lower Klamath remained quiet in the summer of 1855. Ninety-five additional enlisted men arrived at Fort Humboldt to fill depleted ranks in the 4th Infantry. Whipple termed the Regulars' efforts over a six-month period a "great service." Like Judah, he urged the establishment of a permanent Army post in the Klamath River area.

Army officers, however, complained about Whipple. They said he refused to pay their Indian "allies" the $150

---

[10] Henley to George W. Manypenny, Aug. 17, 1855, M234, R34; PR, Camp Strowbridge, Apr. 1855, M617, R1544.

[11] Stephen Whipple to Henley, Sept. 27, 1855, M234, R34; PR, Camp Wool, May 1855, M617, R1550; *Humboldt Times*, Apr. 7, 1855.

to $200 due them for the expedition into the mountains that Judah had arranged. Now that immediate danger had passed, the soldiers thought that Whipple seemed indisposed to coordinate his actions or exchange information with officers at Camp Wool. Harmony between federal agencies suffered.[12]

Lack of harmony with Whipple echoed through military channels to Washington. Secretary of War Jefferson Davis remarked to Whipple's and Henley's superiors that the history of steady outrages on the Klamath River required some action by the Secretary of Interior. Repetition of violence had to be prevented. Davis pointed out that the Army possessed no authority to prosecute or punish persons responsible for atrocities committed on Indians in California.[13]

Buchanan assured department headquarters that peace continued on the Klamath and all of its branches. He decided that his troops on field detachment would return to their home post before winter rains flooded trails. Despite the current peace, however, Buchanan and the Pacific Department staff still felt frustration over California Indian affairs. Obstreperous whites, bent on Indian destruction, routinely escaped punishment. Although the lawless element was but a minority, in the opinion of Army officers, California ethics "utterly arrests the course of civil law."[14]

Federal Indian Superintendent Henley expressed a few complaints too. Decrying his inability to be everywhere at

---

[12] Floyd-Jones to Townsend, July 3, 1855, RG393; Wool to Henley, Aug. 10, 1855, M234, R34.

[13] Jefferson Davis to Robert McClelland, Aug. 15, 1855, M234, R34.

[14] Wool to Thomas, Aug. 14, 1855; and Townsend to Judah, Aug. 30, 1855; and Jones to Buchanan, Oct. 18, 1855, RG393.

once and chagrined over Judah's withdrawal from the Klamath in January, Henley wrote to Indian Commissioner George W. Manypenny that "the people seem to look to me for the suppression of all Indian hostilities while the soldiers usually remain quietly at their posts.[15]

Henley deemed advisable a year-round military presence among his employees at the unofficial reservation on the Klamath. Henley offered Wool a deal. He would give the Army at cost a substantial dwelling at Cap El village for a barracks. In return, soldiers would protect Indian agents all winter long.

Unknown to Wool, politician Henley gave supervisors in Washington, D.C., a slightly different version. He told them that he had offered the Army free troop quarters on the Klamath and Henley questioned the Regulars' good faith. He wondered if Whipple's crew might "be left surrounded by several thousand Indians without any protection," while soldiers withdrew to "more comfortable quarters" for the winter at Fort Humboldt.[16]

Unaware of Henley's snide comments, Wool had already decided that Fort Humboldt should place outposts on the Klamath during the winter. He admitted that the superintendent occupied a difficult position in a state that lacked any legal "Indian territory." Headquarters penned orders to Buchanan.

Buchanan, uninformed of the higher-echelon letter-writing campaign, brought his thirty-man detachment back to Fort Humboldt on October 25. No mail arrived at

---

[15] Henley to Manypenny, Apr. 9, 1855, M234, R34.

[16] Wool to Henley, Aug. 10, 1855; and Henley to Wool, Oct. 16, 1855; and Henley to Manypenny, Oct. 20, 1855, M234, R34. In his letter to Wool, Henley omitted Agent Whipple's complaint that Buchanan had shifted troops about the Klamath without first coordinating the moves with the Indian Office.

Fort Humboldt for five weeks. Only then did Buchanan receive the orders to keep a detachment on the Klamath through the winter. Buchanan was angry at the thought of turning his men around. He retorted that if the Klamath Indian agent needed protection at Camp Wool, then "he ought to stay there and be protected." The soldiers at Camp Wool had claimed that Whipple was absent from his area some seventy-five percent of the time.

The mail brought another order that fed Buchanan's rising temper. Oregon was deep in Indian problems. Headquarters staff, reacting to fears that warfare in Oregon would flow down to California, ordered Buchanan to send a detachment from Fort Humboldt to Crescent City.

Hard weather hampered Buchanan's obedience to the displeasing instructions. Storms hit the coast, blew down the frame of a new barracks, and destroyed five hundred feet of lumber at Fort Humboldt. Blocked trails prevented immediate dispatch of a detachment back to the Klamath. Striving to comply with at least part of his orders, Buchanan hired a ship to send Captain Floyd-Jones and all of Company F, 4th Infantry, to Crescent City by water.[17]

The environs of Crescent City had witnessed violence twelve months earlier. Some of the "most triffling [sic] rabble" among local citizens had gone on an Indian-killing spree. They had been checked by law-abiding citizens who courageously acted without military or sheriff's help.

The ship contracted by Buchanan had been filled with enough provisions to sustain the troops for two months —insurance that the operation would not falter because of

---

[17] Buchanan to Townsend, Dec. 28, 1855, Jan. 28, 1856, and Feb. 2, 1856, RG393; PR, Camp Wool, Sept. 1855; and PR, Ft. Humboldt, Oct. 1855, M617, R497, R1550.

lack of food. Improved weather allowed Floyd-Jones to debark his fifty Regular Army soldiers on January 9, 1856. Rough seas drove the ship off before it could be unloaded completely, and Floyd-Jones looked on with some apprehension as the brig headed to sea again. Not until sixteen days later was the civilian ship able to put in near the Crescent City shore. Company F finished unloading supplies. The move from Fort Humboldt cost the government three-thousand dollars.

At Crescent City multiple missions awaited the Company. Guarding an accumulation of government supplies and escorting them overland to Fort Lane in Oregon Territory was a simple military task that required no detailed planning. Protecting Crescent City from an overflow of the violence on the Rogue River was an assignment that held nothing new to an experienced frontier field force. What complicated both these tasks was a third mission, that of protecting the seacoast-dwelling Tolowa Indians.

Captain Floyd-Jones judged that the Tolowa, known in Del Norte County as the Smith River Indians, were quiet and had no record of violence. Some California residents eyed the Tolowa suspiciously. In Crescent City the population feared a springtime attack by local Indians in concert with those of southern Oregon, and they made their fears known to the governor of California, John Neely Johnson.

The Army anticipated problems and worked to prevent violence before the governor could complain. Once more the Army intervened in local affairs by moving the Tolowa closer to Crescent City. Floyd-Jones placed them under military protection from attacks. The captain ensured that they would refrain from joining warfare in Oregon. Floyd-Jones continued the precedent set by other junior Army officers. He adopted a protective attitude for specific Indian groups, the province of the Interior Department.

Confident that they would not have to defend themselves against lawless whites, the Tolowa readily assembled under Army control. Because no federal Indian agent was available, Captain Floyd-Jones disbursed expense money to the displaced Tolowa. He ran up bills totaling nine-hundred dollars for their transportation and provisions. The captain also sent soldiers into the streets of Crescent City, where they walked guard.

After the arrival of the Army detachment, the wild stories of violence that had flown through Crescent City soon came to rest. Tales about houses in flames proved false, and citizens who had been reported killed were soon seen very much alive. Quietly completing his actions, Captain Floyd-Jones proclaimed his hope that Sacramento would send no state volunteers to further "protect" Crescent City.[18]

By the time Governor Johnson registered his concern over protecting Del Norte, the Army had already responded to the need. The Department of the Pacific quickly assured the governor that a "very efficient officer" already commanded a Regular force at Crescent City, where he could undoubtedly protect California from any attack.

General Wool reminded Johnson that the Army presented itself ever alert to "preserve and protect the inhabitants of the Frontiers of California from Indian Barbarity." He

---

[18] Floyd-Jones to Townsend, Jan. 30, 1856; and Buchanan to Townsend, Feb. 2, 1856, RG393; PR, Crescent City, Jan. 1856, M617, R266; Rosborough, "Special Indian Agent," p. 202; Crescent City *Herald*, Jan. 16, 1856.

then lectured the governor, writing that many Californians were determined to kill all Indians, indiscriminately. Such continual, irresponsible, and impolitic acts by armed citizens caused the deaths of many innocent and worthy people. Indeed, added Wool, could "the citizens be restrained from Private War I have no doubt peace and quiet would soon be restored. . . ."[19]

Certain of tranquility at the Smith River and less successful in restoring peace to southern Oregon, the Department of the Pacific moved Floyd-Jones and his men from California in March. The troop transfer left behind a small detachment to act as buffer between the Tolowa and fearful civilians.[20]

Buchanan had ordered Company B, 4th Infantry, back to the Klamath River in support of Indian Agent Whipple. Lieutenant Garber took temporary command of the Klamath-bound detachment until another officer became available.

Not until January 28, 1856, did troops start for the Klamath. A thirty-two man detachment commanded by Garber trudged over soggy trails to reach Whipple. They each carried two pairs of boots and three pairs of socks to cope with hard marching, rugged terrain, and wet weather. Garber placed his camp near the Indian village of Cap El, from which Interior Department agents operated instead of at the old site of Camp Wool.[21]

Garber detected no new signs of hostilities with Indians on the Klamath, but he was soon in a contest of wills with

[19] Wool to Johnson, Jan. 21, 1856, RG393.

[20] PR, Crescent City, Apr. 1856, M617, R266; Henley to Manypenny, May 30, 1856, M234, R35.

[21] Buchanan to Townsend, Dec. 28, 1855, Jan 28 and Feb. 2, 1856, RG393; PR, Camp Cap El, Feb. 1856, M617, R179.

Whipple. Possibly feeling triumphant over return of an Army detachment to his reservation despite Buchanan's feelings, Whipple informed Garber that he had shifted his own office downstream to a new location at Wak El. He let the lieutenant know that he would appreciate a squad of soldiers guarding him at his new location. Garber declined. Mindful of the fact that he had sole authority over the troops, Garber explained that his detachment was too small to split. He assured Whipple that the sturdy Regulars could move to any point on the reservation if danger became imminent.[22]

Lieutenant Rundell replaced Garber at the Cap El detachment on March 25. Garber departed the Klamath and shifted over the mountains to his own company at Crescent City. The seventeen-man force left behind by Floyd-Jones in Del Norte County seemed small for the task. Garber, tactful in his dealings with townspeople and Tolowa, maintained peace with some success.

Later in the spring, a verified case of arson caused a representative of Governor Johnson to sanction an operation by local volunteers in the Smith River Valley. The volunteers killed three Indians. Garber's Crescent City detachment remained aloof from the affair.

By the end of summer, Garber's detachment had dwindled to six privates and a bugler. Garber allowed the Tolowa to return to traditional fishing spots at locations removed from Crescent City. He stayed the autumn and spent the Christmas season at Crescent City. With no civilian present to accept responsibility for feeding the displaced Indians, Garber acted as temporary Indian agent

---

[22] Garber to Bates, Feb. 29, 1856, RG393.

for some four-hundred Tolowa. The Indian Office declined to accept responsibility for Indians away from the Klamath reservation. Garber ignored irritating remarks from Klamath reservation employees and continued to feed his charges.

Emboldened by twelve months of peace under the Army's aegis, certain Del Norte elements wondered if a propitious time had arrived for Indian extermination. The Tolowa reported to Garber that they had received serious, unattributable threats. An indignant Garber, seconded by General Wool, bluntly told Crescent City's population to expect no Army protection if they provoked Indians by lawless attacks.[23]

Garber's stance may have been firm, but he was not imprudent. With only a handful of men, he knew his chances of restoring order in the face of real trouble were small. Garber tried to head off violence by keeping the Tolowa away from settlements. He halted the citizens' practice of hiring Indians to do chores and denied them the use of Indian labor to dig potatoes at harvest.[24]

While Garber instituted his changes among the citizens, Lieutenant Rundell constructed a flagpole for his detachment at Cap El. On May 4, 1856, "amid the rattling of musketry and the enlivening sounds of the bugle," the soldiers ceremoniously hoisted the first American flag in the area.

---

[23] 1st Lt. Richard Arnold to Garber, May 7, 1856; and Maj. William W. Mackall to Garber, Dec. 16, 1856 and Jan. 15, 1857; and Mackall to Henley, Dec. 17, 1856, RG393; PR, Crescent City, Oct.-Dec. 1856, M617, R266; David W. Gilmore to Gov. J. Neeley Johnson, May 5, 1856, doc. no. F3753, 284, Indian War Papers, Calif. State Archives, Sacramento; Crescent City *Herald,* June 4, 1856.

[24] Garber to Mackall, Jan. 1 and 26, 1857, RG393.

Rundell, standing six feet six inches tall, continued correct but cool relations with Indian Office employees. Two sergeants and two corporals assisted him. The soldiers ran military patrols up and down the Klamath. Although the area had finally been declared as an official Indian reservation, the soldiers were wary as they patrolled the unsurveyed boundaries.

Hearing that whites had kidnapped the wife and two children of a principal Indian chief who resided in the Klamath locale, Rundell decided against armed pursuit. Kidnapping and selling Indians was not an uncommon occurrence in California and too strong a response seemed rash. Instead, Rundell tried legal measures. He asked the Indian leader, dubbed Coon Skin by settlers, to accompany him to a nearby civilian lawyer.

The wife stealers had obviously assumed their impunity from California courts since nonwhites were barred from testifying against whites in criminal cases. Under Rundell's guidance, however, Coon Skin swore a legal complaint against his family's kidnappers, and Rundell boldly signed it. Law enforcement authorities seldom paid attention to Indian witnesses, but now they had a document signed by a United States Army officer.

To Rundell's great satisfaction, he and Coon Skin observed a justice of the peace place a warrant for the kidnappers' arrest in a sheriff's hands. Word of the unprecedented action traveled fast. Prominent settlers' influence came to bear on the guilty whites. Social pressure proved sufficient. The embarrassed Indian snatchers released the victims. No court trial took place, but the kidnappers quietly paid all legal costs. Rundell felt satisfied that he had made a point and prevented bloodshed. He confided to other officers that the results were all that could be expected on an Indian's behalf from court action in a California county.[25]

While Rundell maneuvered local authorities in legal action, Buchanan transferred from Fort Humboldt. He was replaced by Major Gabriel J. Rains on June 11, 1856. Rundell stayed on the Klamath.

Convinced that the Indian Office knew little or cared little for Indians on the newly established Klamath reservation, Rundell hired an Indian interpreter. In this way he learned the concerns of the 3,500 Indians gathered in or near the reservation. Rundell had sensed a growing uneasiness. He reported to Fort Humboldt that the Indians felt Whipple had lied to them.

Rundell reported that the fishing rights of the reservation's inhabitants had not been preserved for them as promised. Instead of help in building shelter and providing food, they had been left to freeze and starve. Expecting protection from marauding whites, they had been

> . . . exposed to the brutal assault of drunken and lawless white men; their squaws are forced, and, if resented, the Indians are beated and often shot. So great is their dread, that upon the approach of whites the young squaws immediately run to the mountains to hide, and remain until the whites have left. A great many cases of ill-treatment might be mentioned, and they are so common here as scarcely to excite comment.

Rundell wondered about the limits of Klamath River Indian passivity.

The Indian Office pulled Whipple out. New agent

[25] Bates to Captain David R. Jones, May 24, 1856, RG393; PR, Camp Cap El, Mar. 1856, M617, R179; *Humboldt Times,* May 10, 1856.

James A. Patterson quickly voiced his dissatisfaction about Regular Army deployment. He wanted troops at both Cap El and Wak El so that, without fear for their lives, his employees could foster agriculture among reservation Indians.

The Army conceded to Patterson's complaint and ordered Rundell to split his detachment. A corporal and eight privates moved to Wak El. Camp Cap El and Wak El were healthful, rustic spots, but they could not keep the privates content. Possibly lured by dreams of riches in nearby gold diggings, ten men deserted from Rundell's detachment by the end of 1856.[26]

When the year 1856 ended, Army officers had compiled a twenty-four–month record of stepping into Indian Office matters on the redwood coast. Commanding detachments of Regular Army troops beyond the confines of Fort Humboldt, Judah, Bonnycastle, and Garber openly placed Indians under their protection. In each case they notified the civilian population of their intentions. Among the civilians, an orderly segment of the population cooperated with the Army in maintaining peace despite the violent acts of other citizens. On the Klamath, Rundell analyzed the shortcomings of the Indian agent. All actions were reported through military channels. No one in the War Department objected.

Rundell wintered again on the Klamath. The winter of 1856–57 blew so hard that miners and Indians were too

---

[26] Bates to Jones, May 24, 1856; and Rundell to Bates, June 1, 1856; and Patterson to Rains, July 18, 1856; and Orders No. 7, Camp Cap El, June 1, 1856, RG393; PR, Ft. Humboldt, June 1856; and Camp Cap El, Apr.-Dec. 1856, M617, R179, R497. The *Humboldt Times*, hearing of Buchanan's departure, characterized him as a "prudent and sensible officer . . . barring a little hauteur, too common in his profession."

busy surviving the elements to fight one another. Spring brought better weather and new gold discoveries just a half mile from Cap El. In an act almost foredoomed, a pair of gold miners tried to abuse some Indian women. Next they stabbed two Indians who came to the women's defense. But this time there was a change in the usual scenario. For the first time in Rundell's memory, the Indian Office acted promptly and effectively.

Indian Office agents shot one of the assailants. The second was arrested and taken to Crescent City, where he was bound over on five thousand dollars' bail. Rundell was surprised that no miner rose to the prisoner's defense.

Rundell stationed soldier-guards at the Indian settlement to ward off any further outrages. None occurred. He used his interpreter to calm the villagers. Reporting matters to Fort Humboldt, he told his military superiors that if the Indian Office backed the Klamath agent's act, it would, ". . . have more effect here than an army of soldiers."[27]

---

[27] Rundell to Bates, Feb. 16 and Mar. 4, 1857, RG393.

Chapter 4
1855–1856

Detachments and Exploring Parties

> *. . . exploration of the country between the valleys of the*
> *Sacramento and Columbia rivers [has] been successfully*
> *made . . . these surveys have been carried on, on a scale*
> *exceeding anything of the kind previously undertaken by any*
> *nation, and its results have been of a most beneficial character.*
>
> Annual Report of the Secretary of War (1855)

The experience of the Army in the three years of on-and-off strife around the Klamath contrasted with the tone of events east of the coastal range. Perhaps justifying Colonel Wright's criticism that the Department of the Interior had neglected Indians in northern California, Superintendent of Indian Affairs Thomas J. Henley established a federal Indian reservation in Tehama County shortly after he assumed his office in July 1854. Officials named the reservation Nome Lackee after the Nomlaki, the predominant Indian group in the area. The reservation lay at some distance from the supplies and protection of Fort Reading. The Nomlaki, who had suddenly been exposed to the terrors of gold-crazy Americans, welcomed protection from disturbers of their food supply and from brutal kidnappers of their women and children. [1]

Concerned about protecting more than eight hundred Indians assembled at Nome Lackee, and harboring thoughts of potential unrest by reservation inhabitants, Henley requested a Regular Army detachment for his Tehama County station. Before agreeing to Henley's request, General Wool detailed an experienced officer, Captain Erasmus D. Keyes, to reconnoiter Nome Lackee.

Keyes reported that the selected Indian reservation site was "perfectly adapted to the purpose for which it is intended." He picked a spot in the lower portion of the reservation for the incoming Army detachment to position itself. Keyes noted that Nome Lackee's total area seemed double the ten thousand acres allocated by Congress. He also observed that arable land on the reservation was limited. [2]

The Interior Department and the War Department were both committed to the concept of a reservation system. With no qualms over sending a detachment to a federal Indian reservation, Wool reacted rapidly to Keyes's report. A sergeant and nine privates from Company B, 3d Artillery, were ordered to accompany 2d Lieutenant James Deshler of that regiment on the protective mission. Department of the Pacific headquarters issued lengthy instructions for the remote Nome Lackee detachment.

Admonished to send only men of steady, reliable character, the 3d Artillery also received word to furnish the

---

[1] Wright to Townsend, Dec. 10, 1854, RG393; Henley to Manypenny, Sept. 25 and Oct. 19, 1854, M234, R33.

[2] J. Ross Browne to Manypenny, Dec. 1, 1854; and Henley to Manypenny, Dec. 8 and 28, 1854; and Keyes to Townsend, Dec. 12, 1854, M234, R34.

Nome Lackee detachment with a mountain howitzer. Headquarters added extra rifles and revolvers to the detachment's supplies for use by some two dozen reservation
employees. These weapons remained under Army control,
to be distributed if nonreservation Indians attacked Nome
Lackee. To guard against surprise attack, headquarters
prescribed that a military sentinel be on duty at all times.

Told to quarter his detachment near the houses of Indian
Office employees, headquarters expected Lieutenant Deshler
to use great caution in contact with Indians. His enlisted
men were to conduct themselves with the best deportment.
Whenever military duties allowed, Deshler could assist the
federal agent appointed for Nome Lackee. He was, however, to take great care to avoid interfering with the agent's
performance. Although within the territorial sphere of the
Northern District, Deshler would report directly to General Wool. Copies of the Nome Lackee detachment's communications would be sent to Colonel Wright at Fort
Reading as a source of information.[3]

Arriving with his detachment on January 4, 1855,
Alabama-born, West Point–educated Lieutenant Deshler
found Nome Lackee quiet and peaceful. Before the end of
January, an additional two hundred Indians from the
Trinity moved without incident to the reservation.

Such incidents that did occur were handled by Interior
Department appointees. One problem involved Indian
labor. Under state law citizens of California, by appearing
before a justice of the peace, could place Indian youths
under apprenticeship. The law, passed in 1850, made
Indian males under the age of 18 and females under 15

3 Dept. of the Pacific, Special Order No. 114, Dec. 26, 1854, M234, R34.

eligible for what, in effect, became free labor. The fact that so many Indians went to Nome Lackee removed many apprentices from the labor pool, and some Californians objected to the reservation for that reason. Certain local whites appeared at Nome Lackee demanding return of their Indian "property."[4]

While reservation affairs presented no problem to Regular Army soldiers at Nome Lackee, their own situation caused embarrassment. Through some oversight, the Department of Pacific quartermaster had not sent tents to the detachment. Nome Lackee was deep in winter weather, so Indian Office Agent Henry L. Ford lodged the soldiers in one of the reservation sheds. Deshler told General Wool of his predicament. He also advised headquarters that a lumber shortage existed in the vicinity, which complicated the possibility of building soldier shelter.

Displeased with a display of military inefficiency at an Indian reservation, Wool ordered Colonel Wright over from Fort Reading to set things straight at Nome Lackee. Wright conferred with Deshler. He directed Deshler to always keep on hand one month's provisions as a precaution. Fort Reading's commander also wanted the detachment to build a storeroom to house the mountain howitzer and other Army property that needed protection from the elements. Additionally, Wright called for two inexpensive frame buildings, one for the officer in charge of the detachment and the other for the enlisted men. From his own

4 Deshler to Wool, Jan. 9, 1855, RG393; PR, Nome Lackee Detachment, Jan. 1855, M617, R867; David L. Hilsop, *The Nome Lackee Indian Reservation, 1854–1870* (Chico, Calif.: Assoc. for Northern California Records and Research, 1978), p. 25; Robert F. Heizer and Alan J. Almquist, *The Other Californians* (Berkeley: Univ. of California Press, 1977), pp. 54–56, 212–15; Rawls, *Indians of California*, p. 164.

command, Wright would send Deshler (to whom he referred condescendingly as "the young officer") an old hand, Lieutenant Underwood, who could render assistance in organizing the Nome Lackee detachment. In Wright's opinion the detachment was too small for military emergencies at Nome Lackee. Using command judgment and initiative, he sent a corporal and six privates from Fort Reading to supplement manpower at the miniscule detachment. A laundress accompanied them as an official camp follower. The reinforcing squad arrived in May. Now seventeen enlisted men composed Deshler's force at Nome Lackee.[5]

Deshler, transferred from artillery to a new infantry regiment, left Nome Lackee in June despite Henley's request to Wool that he be detained regardless of Army reorganization. First Lieutenant John Edwards of Company B, 3d Artillery, replaced Deshler. Edwards brought with him a few more men from his company at the Presidio of San Francisco.

Captain Erasmus Keyes revisited Nome Lackee in July and reported to Wool that all seemed in order. He noted approvingly that Henley's management entertained no "fantastic hope" of "civilizing" or Christianizing Indians. Military routine occupied Edwards's summer. At Nome Lackee the detachment of twenty-two soldiers spent without incident the winter of 1855–56.[6]

Wool, Wright, Keyes, and Edwards assumed that Henley was pleased with Army support. Henley's opinion was

---

[5] Deshler to Cross, Jan. 19, 1855; and Deshler to Wool, Jan. 9, 1855; and Wright to Townsend, Feb. 8, 1855; and Deshler to Townsend, May 11, 1855, RG393; PR, Nome Lackee Detachment, May 1855, M617, R867.

[6] Keyes to Townsend, Aug. 15, 1855, M234, R34; PR, Nome Lackee Detachment, June 1855, M617, R867.

different. He was silently dissatisfied with Army officers in southern California. Henley also resented Wool's refusal to keep Deshler at Nome Lackee. Calling Deshler a cooperative and efficient officer, he cited the lieutenant's transfer as an example of the Army's refusal to help the California superintendent's office. Henley admitted to his supervisor in Washington, D.C., that he had bared no such feelings to General Wool or his subordinates. Still, he unhesitatingly told him that ". . . a large proportion" of Army officers in California opposed the reservation system.[7]

No Indian reservation existed near Yreka, where trouble between settlers and Indians descended over the summer landscape. Rejuvenated and again in command of Fort Jones on June 18, 1855, Captain Henry Moses Judah rose to the occasion. Receiving reports of unprovoked Indian attacks and petitioned by Scott Bar citizens to come and chase Indian murderers, Judah mustered what force he could from the single unit still assigned to the fort, Company E, 4th Infantry. He marched out of Fort Jones on July 29 with two squads, taking the unusual step of bringing along thirty government rifles with which to arm volunteers. In an even more unusual action, Judah, the only infantry officer on post at the time, placed Surgeon Sorrel, the medical officer, in temporary command of Fort Jones.

Judah verified the deaths of ten miners and was dismayed by the intense, vengeful feelings of local whites for all Indians. He hastened to the summit of Siskiyou County, a wooded, rocky, mountainous labyrinth where five volunteer companies had already gone. The volunteers planned to

---

[7] Henley to Manypenny, May 31, 1855, M234, R34.

attack Rogue River Indians over the state line in Oregon Territory. Judah, whose force was vastly outnumbered by the volunteers, attempted to dissuade them from such harmful action. He pointed out the disastrous retaliation they could expect from Oregon. Unsuccessful in his talks with the Californians, Judah marched to Fort Lane and warned its commander of the coming explosion.[8]

While Judah led soldiers over mountain trails, Dr. Sorrel commanded Fort Jones with extraordinary skill. Certain settlers in the county executed an Indian on suspicion of complicity associated with the miners' troubles near the upper Klamath. Fearing Indian retaliation, citizens in the valley of the Scott formed armed bands to exterminate nearby, albeit unoffending, local Indians.

Sorrel believed it his duty as post commander to prevent hostilities and protect peaceful Indians. He found a large body of Shasta Indians who had fled in justifiable fear. On the way he obtained promises of cooperation from settlers who shared his view. Identified by both Indians and whites as an Army officer, Sorrel proposed moving the Shasta to Fort Jones and protecting them with his troops.

Under the Regular Army's wing, the entire Indian group took refuge at Fort Jones on August 2. Several respectable citizens from Scott Bar brought nineteen additional Indian women and children to the fort for protection. Digging into Army rations, Sorrel fed a hundred Indians with beef and flour.

From Fort Lane, Judah started back to Fort Jones. At the Klamath ferry, the operator told of Indians sniping at him. While accepting the ferry proprietor's statement as

---

[8] Judah to Townsend, July 28 and Aug. 13, 1855, RG393; PR, Ft. Jones, July-Sept. 1855, M617, R560; Wells, *Siskiyou County*, pp. 138–41.

true, Judah feared for innocent Indians, a number of whom he observed in the vicinity. He gathered another Shasta group and escorted them to his growing Fort Jones family.[9]

Judah recommended that the Indian Office quickly send a representative to Fort Jones. He reconnoitered a small valley parallel to the Scott River as a potential federal reserve for the increasing body of Indians at the Army post. Meanwhile, the Interior Department abolished Rosborough's office of Indian agent. Claiming that he had been acting as special Indian agent to fill the void, Judah asked headquarters to pressure Henley into relieving him of such unmilitary duties.

Judah was convinced that northern California gold miners wanted nothing less than to shoot down any male Indian passerby. By the end of August he felt compelled to strengthen the guard force at his post. He gained cooperation from a number of persons who promised to warn him if any mobs formed to attack Indians at the fort. Judah openly declared his intention to meet force with force. Even the Yreka newspaper commended Judah for his "energy, perseverance and tact."

Efforts by infantry officer Judah and medical officer Sorrel to create an atmosphere of justice and order in Siskiyou County met with limited success. Informed that four rifle-carrying men had killed an Indian youth, Judah decided to demonstrate the legal process. After collecting facts, he steeled himself and appeared before a state judge. Presenting himself as an Army officer, he made an affidavit accusing one of the Indian's attackers by name. Judah

---

[9] Sorrel to Townsend, Aug. 2, 1855; and Wool to Henley, Aug. 10, 1855; and Judah to Townsend, Aug. 13, 1855, RG393.

asked the law officer to transmit his sworn statement to a federal judge.

The state judge complied and Judah waited. A week later military headquarters advised him that a federal judge in San Francisco had ruled that he lacked jurisdiction in Judah's case. Wool's adjutant, Major E. D. Townsend, told Judah frankly that Indian cases held little hope for fairness in the legal system.[10]

Any misgivings Judah may have harbored concerning his actions, including that of turning over command of a fort to an Army doctor, evaporated with reassurances from General Wool and praise from Superintendent Henley. Pleased with affairs at Nome Lackee, despite a grasshopper attack on the vegetables, Henley decided to expand the reservation system. He directed Nome Lackee Agent Ford to occupy an area on the Mendocino coast between the Noyo and Hale rivers until he could get presidential approval for the site. Henley judged the area as offering ample potential for food production.[11]

Wool informed Henley that food was a problem for the Army and that Judah's garrison at Fort Jones now fed 150 Indians, mostly women and children. He asked if the Indian survivors might be moved to peaceful Nome Lackee and supervised by the Indian Office. In the Army view " . . . something ought to be done for these miserable creatures, who it appears were not in the wrong, and whom the white inhabitants are determined to exterminate."[12]

---

[10] Judah to Townsend, Aug. 23 and 28, 1855; and Judah to Judge Ogden Hoffman, Aug. 23, 1855; and Townsend to Judah, Aug. 22 and 30, 1855, RG393; Crescent City *Herald*, Aug. 22, 1855.

[11] Townsend to Judah, Aug. 10, 1855; and Henley to Manypenny, Aug. 17, 1855; and Henley to Wool, Sept. 19, 1855; and Henley to Ford, Nov. 3, 1855, M234, R34.

[12] Wool to Henley, Sept. 15, 1855, RG393.

Henley offered no solution unless somebody transferred the Indians from Fort Jones to Nome Lackee. Army policy steadfastly avoided the use of soldiers as escorts of Indians to reservations. New Interior Department orders prohibited Henley from employing any special agents to induce Indians to move.

Pleading that "Indians respect the Military," Henley again sought military escort to remove Indians from gold-mining districts to reservations. Soldiers admitted that such removals were often complicated by whites who had Indian mistresses. Sometimes quick on the trigger, these men objected to removal of their companions to reservation life. Realizing that armed squaw men placed Henley in a difficult position, the Army position softened.

Seeking to facilitate voluntary removal of the Shasta at Fort Jones, the Department of the Pacific bore the expense of sending Lieutenant Bonnycastle back to the Siskiyou post on temporary duty. Bonnycastle's advice to the Indians fell on deaf ears. The Shasta showed no desire to leave their traditional tribal home for Nome Lackee. Bonnycastle's failure fueled acrimony between the Army and the superintendent. Wool pointedly reminded Henley that removing Indians to reservations remained the exclusive duty of the Indian Bureau. [13]

In contrast to the turmoil in Humboldt and Siskiyou counties, Fort Reading reposed in normal military routine. Captain and Brevet Major Francis O. Wyse, restored to duty, replaced Lieutenant Van Voast as commander of Company D, 3d Artillery, at Fort Reading in January 1855.

---

[13] Henley to Manypenny, Aug. 17, 1855; and Henley to Wool, Sept. 19, 1855, M234, R34; Henley to Wool, Aug. 14, 1855; and Wool to Henley, Jan. 26, 1856, RG393; Hilsop, *Nome Lackee*, p. 24.

In the Golden State, Wool, feeling that he had a firm grip on events in the upper counties, dissolved the Northern Military District of California. Congress enlarged the Army and elevated post commander Wright to full colonel and placed him in command of a new infantry regiment assigned to duties outside California. Five other officers, promoted and transferred in their new grades, departed from the northern post. Major Wyse took command of Fort Reading. The Department of the Pacific boosted Wyse's complement at Fort Reading by assigning sixty-three recruits to Company D, 4th Infantry.

Constrained from drilling the garrison by a shortage of musicians and concerned over the health of his men, Wyse sent fresh requests to headquarters. He asked for drummers and fifers, and supported by the surgeon, he sought one extra daily ration of coffee and sugar for his troops because he thought it would help prevent fevers. Instead of meeting his requests, the Department of the Pacific ordered Wyse to support an army-managed exploring party.[14]

Fort Reading had been chosen as the site to launch explorations for railroad lines. As part of the War Department's wide-ranging survey to find feasible routes for a transcontinental railroad, the exploring detachment at Fort Reading would have two goals. Under Lieutenant Williamson, who had been one of Colonel Wright's staff when he took command of Fort Reading, the military explorers sought a crossing over the Sierra Nevada. They also planned to determine potential railroad routes between California and Oregon.

Assisting Topographical Engineer Williamson were

---

[14] Hammond to Wyse, June 1, 1855, RG393; PR, Ft. Reading, Jan., Mar., May, and July 1855, M617, R993.

Lieutenant Henry L. Abbot and several civilian aides. Abbot belonged to the same corps of military engineers as Williamson. The civilians included a geologist-botanist, a physician-naturalist, a civil engineer, a recorder, and a trained draftsman.

Accompanied by an eighteen-man crew and a packtrain, Williamson's party seemed a tempting target for marauders, particularly since they would be forced to travel the Pit River country. Williamson himself had witnessed the death of Topographical Engineer William H. Warner from an Indian attack during an 1849 expedition through the same region. The Army was determined to prevent another incident like that of Captain Warner. A strong military escort for Williamson assembled at Fort Reading in July 1855.

Commanded by 1st Lieutenant Horatio G. Gibson, the one-hundred-man escort included soldiers from Gibson's own 3d Artillery, Lieutenant Crook and men from the 4th Infantry at Fort Jones, and dragoons under Lieutenant Hood. Major Wyse extended the hospitality of the post to the engineers. When they started north at the end of the month, he sent Fort Reading's civilian supply clerk and an experienced packer to help.

The success of the exploring project seemed ensured. With scores of soldiers, security presented no worry. Experienced field officers, accompanied by engineers of proven skill, headed the reconnaissance. Enthusiasm spread. Unfortunately, the detachment got off to a shaky start. Gibson fell sick. Rather than delay, Gibson sent Crook ahead.

Crook left with the packtrain and the infantry element

on July 26. The detachment soon learned that the number of pack animals supplied by Fort Reading was insufficient. Overloaded mules carried as much as three hundred pounds of supplies and equipment. The heavily burdened pack animals would offer no temporary transportation for injured or ill soldiers. A shortage of pack animals caused delay.

Lieutenant Abbot compounded the detachment's woes. He started out two days behind Crook and promptly got lost. After spending a night without blankets or cooked food, he led his group into Crook's bivouac the next day. Gibson eventually rejoined the party. Journeying through Nobles Pass, the detachment killed a deer. Abbot, fresh from West Point, dined for the first time on venison. They crossed Hat Creek Valley, luxuriant with grass, on July 31. The next day they suffered a fresh blow to their survey efforts when a cart overturned, rendering the chronometer useless.

Continuing, the detachment traversed valleys and lava-filled table lands. Reconnoitering routes to the Pit River, they checked mountain passes and drew military maps. From time to time detached patrols split off from the main body to check possible railroad routes.

Strangers appeared from the south on August 4, but their entry into camp gave cause for festivities instead of defensive action. Officers recognized an old acquaintance, 2d Lieutenant Philip H. Sheridan, among the visitors. Eager to join the railroad exploring party, Sheridan had overcome objections at Fort Reading and had ridden hard to catch up. He was to replace Hood, who received orders to join a cavalry regiment.

On his way north, Sheridan thought that he had spotted

dangerous Indians trailing Williamson's group. In fact, he found unclothed and unfed Pit River Indians. Instead of attacking Sheridan, an easy target, the Indians showed him the best place to cross a stream and followed him toward the explorers' camp. Williamson fed the hungry Indians while the enlisted men introduced them to the joys of plug tobacco. Hood turned over the dragoons to Sheridan and departed California.

Regardless of the heavy security escort for the explorers, local Indians managed to steal government mules on two different nights. After loss of the second mule, the less-than-vigilant soldiers traced the animal to an Indian settlement and recovered it.

Overall, Indian troubles scarcely plagued the travelers. Quite the contrary. Indians expedited the detachment's progress by offering useful information about routes and travel conditions. When the exploring detachment approached the Klamath, Indians guided them to a fording site and then, to keep soldiers' packs dry, provided boats to convey the baggage across the stream. In bivouac, to Lieutenant Abbot's surprise, Indians kindled a campfire by merely rubbing two pieces of wood together.

Although railroad geography remained the prime reason for the terrain march, science gained, too. Williamson's party collected some fifty mineral specimens and seventy plants in northern California. In addition, they named a species of tree after Lieutenant Williamson, *abies Williamsonnii*.

Beyond the Pit River, soft soil made for slow going. The exploring detachment divided at the Cascade Mountains. Williamson and Abbot each took a separate party on

The Spruce tree named *abies Williamsonii*
From the Pacific Railroad Surveys publications

what appeared to be feasible north-south routes for a railroad. Inadvertently, by proving the practicality of a railroad line above Sacramento, the two engineers assured San Francisco's claim to the transcontinental railroad's terminus. In two months of travel from Fort Reading, Williamson and Abbot successfully explored, gathered considerable data on northern California, and reached Oregon without incident.

In Oregon events quickly broke up the detachment. Gibson heard of troubles leaping up the Rogue River Valley and rushed his troops to Fort Lane. Williamson, in poor health, set out for San Francisco by coastal steamer. The remnants of the depleted detachment started south to Fort Reading under Abbot and Crook.

Captain Judah of Fort Jones was also heading to Fort Lane in response to the emergency there. He spotted Abbot's group and, exasperated over the lengthy absences of all his lieutenants, ordered Crook to stay at Fort Jones. Crook's original instructions were to return to Fort Reading to settle the detachment's supply accounts. Judah's order deprived the exploring detachment of the last experienced line officer. After a cold, snowy night at Fort Jones, Abbot continued alone to Fort Reading, where he arrived on November 15.[15]

Fort Reading furnished more support to explorers in October 1855. The surveyor general requested protection

---

[15] Gibson to Townsend, Nov. 24, 1855, RG393; *Reports on Explorations*, vol. 6, p. 56, 59–63, 110–11; Schubert, *Vanguard*, p. 109; Henry L. Abbot, "Reminiscences of the Oregon War of 1855," *Journal of the Military Service Institution of the United States*, vol. 45 (Nov. 1909), pp. 436–37; Philip H. Sheridan, *Personal Memoirs of P. H. Sheridan* (New York: Charles L. Webster, 1888), pp. 37–46; Schmitt, *Crook*, pp. 26–30. California mountain peaks were later named in honor of Lieutenants Williamson and Abbot.

for C. C. Tracy while he charted a meridian line to the northern boundary of California. After joining Company D, 3d Artillery in August, 2d Lieutenant Dunbar R. Ransom commanded the survey party's escort. They traversed the California countryside from October 6 to November 2, 1855, and facilitated the completion of the survey.[16]

Both the railroad detachment and the meridian survey party sought troop protection because of stories about the Pit River Indians who lived northeast of Fort Reading. These tales had caused Inspector General J. K. F. Mansfield to recommend that a military post be placed in the area. When Superintendent Henley visited Shasta County, he discussed with Major Wyse the potential for an Army-protected Pit River Indian reservation. From a military viewpoint, Wyse thought he should move his entire command to the Pit River Valley. He termed Fort Reading an unhealthy post, worse than Florida. Protecting neither settler nor Indian, in his opinion, Wyse bluntly told his superiors: "This post is of no earthly use here. . . ."[17]

While Wyse and Henley discussed the Pit River country, Fort Jones witnessed still another breakdown of Indian-settler relations. Accusing Indians of two murders, Cottonwood residents held a public meeting. The meeting resulted in a petition signed by 129 persons asking for aid, arms, and ammunition to pursue the Indians.

---

[16] J. C. Hays to Wool, Aug. 6, 1855; and Townsend to Wyse and Judah, Aug. 10, 1855, RG393; PR, Ft. Reading, Oct.-Nov. 1855, M617, R993.

[17] Wyse to Townsend, Sept. 3, 1855; and Judah to Townsend, Sept. 27 and Oct. 10, 1855, RG393; Henley to Wool, Sept. 19, 1855, M234, R34; Frazer, *Mansfield*, p. 111; PR, Ft. Jones, Sept. and Oct. 1855, M617, R560. One elderly Indian woman returned to Fort Jones with the scouting expedition.

Seeking to prevent Indians from committing hostile acts in response to rampaging whites, Judah planned a repeat of his earlier successful tactics. At the end of September, he formed a twenty-man scouting detachment from his garrison and again placed Surgeon Sorrel in command. Sorrel held the line at Fort Jones for the second time in a year, which was surely a command record of some sort for an Army medical officer.

Scouting laboriously without success for ten days in the Siskiyou Mountains, Judah decided to abandon his search for hiding Indians. Returning to Fort Jones on October 8, his concern for local harmony magnified with news that volunteers had attacked Indian reservations near Fort Lane in Oregon.

Judah worried about Shasta Indians protected by Fort Jones. Having earlier advised them to scout nearby mountains for traditional foods before winter set in, Judah determined to bring the Shasta back to camp and under the fort's guns. Word that Indians had attacked settlers near Happy Camp on the Klamath speeded his resolve to take to the field and maintain peace.

Left in command again, Dr. Sorrel recognized trouble when Shasta began gathering at Fort Jones. He saw among the tribesmen an individual many months absent from the Siskiyou area. The Indian appeared at Fort Jones riding a colt that bore the brand of a well-known citizen in the Rogue River Valley of Oregon. Such a sight evinced two distinct possibilities: Shasta Indians, seeing a successful thief, might be tempted to organize a horse-stealing foray across the state border, or trigger-happy Californians might attack the Indian camp adjacent to Fort Jones.

Sorrel played his temporary role as an Army line officer well. Leaving post headquarters, he arrested the man, walked him into the Fort Jones guardhouse, and locked him up. Apprehensive over any difficulties, Sorrel placed his prisoner in chains.[18]

Events at Fort Jones remained peaceful. Through most of October and again in November, Judah led detachments into the Siskiyou Mountains and over the Oregon border. Acting in conjunction with the commander of Fort Lane, he chased Indians accused of murder and gained a sprained ankle for his exertions. Crook, arriving at Fort Jones from the exploring party by Judah's order, became temporary post commander until Judah's return.

Judah resumed full command of Fort Jones on December 10. Although his military conduct gained approbation from General Wool and his peace-keeping efforts were generally well received, his enlisted men thought otherwise. Marching over mountains did not inspire all the Fort Jones soldiers. Fourteen had deserted by the end of the year. Five more deserted before spring.[19]

Judah, instead of facing the problem of deserters, embroiled himself in the problems of the commissioner of Indian affairs. Displeased over the lack of an Indian agent in Siskiyou County, Judah chided Superintendent Henley for his ignorance of the situation, a charge Henley denied. Judah reported that citizens in the Valley of the Scott were performing Indian Office duties for the hungry, shelterless Shasta, with no compensation from San Francisco. As the Shasta "agent," Judah threatened to seek charity from

[18] Ibid.; Sorrel to unknown, Oct. 20, 1855, RG393.

[19] Judah to Townsend, Oct. 29 and Dec. 13, 1855, RG393; PR, Ft. Jones, Sept.-Dec. 1855, M234, R35.

Washington, D.C. Meantime, the commander of Fort Jones said he would feed the Indians.

Henley countered that Judah's superiors had prevented him from moving the Shasta to a suitable reservation. Wool's policy of allowing soldiers to participate in none but voluntary removal of Indians from untenable positions continued to bridle the superintendent. Henley said that the Shasta would never consent to move. He pointed out that the Army fed the Indians gratuitously and kept them in idleness. There matters rested until spring.[20]

Things also remained quiet at Fort Reading. In late October 1855 Brevet 2d Lieutenant William B. Hazen had reported for duty at Fort Reading with Company D, 4th Infantry only to discover that despite the season, the Department of the Pacific wanted the infantry company to move. Responding to orders, the infantrymen marched for Oregon Territory on November 13, leaving Wyse and Ransom with just the thirty-one men of the 3d Artillery.

Ransom acted as post commissary and quartermaster officer. He rounded out his logistics staff with civilian herdsmen, a quartermaster clerk, a foragemaster, and a blacksmith, whose salaries totaled $380 per month. With the medical officer transferred and winter approaching, San Francisco authorized Major Wyse to employ a civilian physician at seventy-five dollars per month. In March 1856 Fort Reading received forty-five recruits to reinforce the garrison's field strength.[21]

Regardless of the new recruits' state of training, headquarters directed Wyse's command to Oregon. Difficulties

---

[20] Judah to Henley, Nov. 1 and Dec. 13, 1855; and Henley to Manypenny, Dec. 29, 1855, M234, R35.

[21] PR, Ft. Reading, Oct.-Dec. 1855 and Mar. 1856, M617, R993.

abounded in the Rogue River Valley. Fort Jones had already sent a strong detachment there under Lieutenant Crook. Establishing a small guard force under a sergeant to secure Fort Reading, Wyse prepared Company D, 3d Artillery, for field duty as infantry and marched north.

After covering seventy miles, Wyse halted upstream on the Sacramento River. At this point headquarters had second thoughts. Rogue River troubles could produce a reaction among Shasta and Modoc in California. From Fort Jones, Judah ominously reported seeing Modoc in the vicinity. Shasta Indians reaffirmed their desire for U.S. Army protection. Orders changed and directed Wyse to go permanently to Fort Jones.[22]

The Army evacuated Fort Reading in April 1856. The fort had provided ombudsman service to the Sacramento Valley Indians, succored early emigrant trains, and sheltered and supplied numerous military expeditions. By 1856 an alarming sick rate and a steadily deteriorating tactical location had made Fort Reading less useful than other northern California posts.[23]

To comply with the new orders, Wyse moved in heavy rainstorms and crossed swollen streams to make Fort Jones, where he arrived on April 6, 1856. Wyse, much senior to Judah, automatically became post commander. Judah, basking in headquarters favor for the "untiring energy" he had displayed in settling Indian problems, had no plans for

[22] Judah to Townsend, Mar. 21, 1856; and Wyse to Wool, Mar. 27, 1856, RG393; PR, Ft. Jones, Feb. 1856; and PR, Ft. Reading, Mar. 1856, M617, R560, R993.

[23] Wyse to Jones, Apr. 6, 1856; and J. B. Vinton to Cross, May 4, 1856, RG393; PR, Ft. Reading, Mar. 1856, M617, R993. The Army returned to Fort Reading briefly in May 1857 when Company A, 1st Dragoons halted there on the way north to establish Fort Crook.

taking second seat. Armed with a surgeon's certificate stating he needed convalescence, Judah waved goodbye and left Fort Jones on official leave.

Wyse found the situation around Fort Jones and Yreka quiet, but he stayed on the alert for Modoc. The new commander organized a reaction force from Company D, 3d Artillery, and Company E, 4th Infantry. He equipped thirty Army mules with saddles and bridles and grazed them near the barracks. Inside the barracks an equal number of men maintained their equipment and readiness to take to the trail on the shortest notice. With Crook away in Oregon and Judah on official vacation, Fort Jones witnessed another unusual command assignment: no infantry officers were present for duty, so Lieutenant Ransom, an artilleryman in good standing, took command of Company E, 4th Infantry.[24]

Seeking better living conditions in the crude log cabins that distinguished Fort Jones, Wyse hired a plasterer at eight dollars per day. For the post commissary the services of a civilian employee were obtained at seventy-five dollars per month. Suffering from chills and a fever, Wyse attended to post administration as best he could, and he sent Ransom scouting.

Ransom rode through rain and snow to the upper Klamath, where Indians reportedly had stolen cattle. In seven days he discovered only that his men rode mules poorly and packed them worse. Things worked better for Ransom on a second field trip from Fort Jones. He commanded a twenty-man detachment escorting a supply

[24] Wyse to Jones, Apr. 1, 6 and 30, 1856, RG393; PR, Ft. Jones, Apr. 1856, M617, R560.

train to Oregon with "nothing of interest to break the monotony of the march."

Next Ransom received responsibility for the security of the trail between Yreka and Crescent City. Ransom left Fort Jones on May 19 with a strong detachment. He was determined to keep public thoroughfares free from lawless interference. In this he succeeded. Wyse reported to headquarters that "the Crescent City trail is open—Clear of Indians." Ransom remained away from the post until July 14. At the end of July, Crook also returned with his men.[25]

Some people around Yreka apparently were dissatisfied with Wyse's efforts, enough so that Governor Johnson complained to Wool. Saying that his northern frontier was menaced with Indian warfare, Johnson threatened to call out his volunteers unless sufficient Regulars appeared on the scene.

Twenty-two Siskiyou County citizens disputed the governor's claim about the Indian menace. They also signed a petition requesting a linguistically qualified Indian agent. Appealing to the Secretary of Interior, they asked for a reservation to house and feed Northern California Indians who, because of settlement, had been deprived of most of their native means of subsistence. Scrutiny of the signatures showed among them, "F. O. Wyse," the commander of Fort Jones.

The comparative numerical superiority of Wyse's company caught the Department of the Pacific's attention. Needing greater numbers farther north, Wyse and his troops departed California under new orders in August.

---

[25] Wyse to Jones, Apr. 30, May 19 and June 7, 1856; and Ransom to Wyse, May 17, 1856; and Wool to Wyse, May 6, 1856.

Moving small, understrength Regular Army companies like checkers on a board, headquarters jumped Company D, 3d Artillery, to Washington Territory, where Indian-settler problems demanded more attention. Seeking troops to fill the gap in California, the department withdrew Company D, 4th Infantry, from Oregon to Fort Jones. Judah returned to Fort Jones for duty and commanded the two-company post by default after Wyse's departure.[26]

From Fort Jones Judah scornfully reported that Governor Johnson had made good his threat and had turned loose a state-financed expedition to the Klamath Lakes. Returning scorn, a member of the volunteers' staff described the Regular Army garrison at Fort Jones as totally inadequate for handling problems among settlers, miners, and Indians.

Judah resolved to take no action in support of the state volunteers. He judged that volunteer action was totally uncalled for. When and if the state volunteers ceased their warlike acts, Judah would offer his services as well as those of former Indian Agent Rosborough to negotiate peace.[27]

Not everybody in northern California sought Indian death as the best means of terminating local misunderstandings. Addressing the commander of the Department of the Pacific, one Siskiyou County group suggested the propriety of building a fort in the Pit River area, an idea that Henley had mentioned to Wool a year earlier. Surprisingly, Wool now assured his northern California correspondents that he had just such a thing in mind when troops became available.[28]

[26] Wool to Johnson, June 17, 1856; RG393. Henley to Manypenny, Aug. 7, 1856, M234, R35; PR, Ft. Jones, May, July, Aug. and Sept. 1856, M617, R560.
[27] Judah to unknown, Aug. 7, 1856, RG393; Goodall to Henley, Aug. 30, 1856, M234, R35; Wells, *Siskiyou County*, pp. 141–44; Murray, *Modocs*, p. 32.
[28] Mackall to W. A. Robertson et al., Aug. 11, 1856, RG393.

Before a Pit River post could be established, the Indians of that region, possibly reacting to the latest Indian "hunt," hit travelers between Yreka and Red Bluff. Sensitive to threats on public transportation, Judah formed a strong, mobile detachment to take the field. He turned post administration over to Crook and crossed over to Shasta Valley.

Reaching Lockhart's Ferry on the Pit with his detachment on September 1, a march of 110 miles in five days, Judah found nearly all Indian bands east of the Oregon wagon road seething with new hostility toward settlers. Unsuccessful in communicating with the one remaining friendly chief in the region and unsure of the cause of the trouble, the soldiers learned details of the Indian attack. Indians had ambushed a California Stage Company conveyance, killing two men. Near the ferry, other attackers attempted to set fire to a residence.

Perplexed, Judah headed for Hat Creek, reportedly the center of new bitterness and the source of the stagecoach attack. Marching over rocky ground in extreme weather, which included the formation of ice at night, the Army quickly lost hope. Indians had burned dry grass, obliterating all tracks for the Regulars to follow.

Reversing his column, Judah got back to the ferry crossing after three days of hiking. He succeeded with new attempts to meet an Indian ally. The next day Judah marched back into the hills and identified the band involved in the wagon attack. Judah surprised the Indians and ignored the ineffective volley of arrows they sent out in defense. Judah's detachment killed six men, the first time in years that a Fort Jones detachment had mortally shot a California Indian. Hoping that his drastic, uncharacteristic action had dampened further plans for plunder on public

roads and running short on rations, Judah returned to
Fort Jones.[29]

A new post doctor, Assistant Surgeon Charles C. Keeney,
and a pair of infantry officers, 1st Lieutenant Hiram Dryer
and 2d Lieutenant James K. McCall, had arrived. McCall
soon learned the place of junior officers in Judah's garrison. He spent a month escorting a hundred surplus
government mules from Fort Jones to Fort Vancouver
near Portland.[30]

General Wool emphatically wanted to lessen military
involvement with California Indian reservations. When
Superintendent Henley advised Wool that the President
had recently authorized a new Indian reservation in
Mendocino County, the Army rejected outright the thought
of stationing troops there unless certain conditions were met.
The new Indian reservation was to be on the Mendocino
County coast, one hundred miles south of Fort Humboldt
but inaccessible from the fort. The Army wanted proof of a
White House decision establishing the reservation. If the
claim was valid, the Army wanted a government land
survey of the area. Furthermore, the Department of the
Pacific was convinced that Nome Lackee lacked legal
authentication, and the Army intended to relieve the military detachment at the reservation of all duties. Demon-
strating the Army's hardening attitude, the dismounted
artillerymen pulled back from Nome Lackee to their home
garrisons in August 1856.

Army officers carried on their exchanges with Henley

[29] Judah to Mackall, Aug. 28 and Sept. 9, 1856, RG393; PR, Ft. Jones, Aug.
1856, M617, R560.

[30] Mackall to Judah, Oct. 17, 1856, RG393; PR, Ft. Jones, Sept.-Dec. 1856,
M617, R560.

from good ground. Post and detachment commanders gave considered observations on the conduct of Indian affairs and kept the Department of the Pacific well-informed. In the spring of 1856, General Wool went so far as to employ a "confidential" civilian observer to check on what subsistence, if any, was being supplied to Indians on the Klamath reservation. A local citizen strengthened the Army's case and distaste when he wrote to President Franklin Pierce and described Agent Patterson of the Klamath as an incompetent drunkard. Federal appointees on California Indian reservations, in the words of a modern historian, had amassed a "record of fraud and corruption remarkable even for the Indian Bureau."[31]

The Army noted that the boundaries of Patterson's jurisdiction had not been officially surveyed. On this technicality or from an accumulation of reports, the Army withdrew from the Klamath Indian reservation. The detachment at Cap El returned to Humboldt Bay on April 13, 1857. Unrelenting in the drive to distance itself from Californian Indian reservations, the Department of the Pacific turned to Crescent City, where no pretense of a federal reserve existed. Garber's detachment sailed for Fort Humboldt in October 1856. Garber himself remained at Crescent City until February 1857, trying to arrange for the Indian Office to feed the Tolowa.[32]

Stunned by the arbitrary action of the Department of the

---

[31] Arnold to Garber, May 7, 1856; and Henley to Wool, Aug. 7, 1856; and Mackall to Henley, Aug. 8, 1856; and Henley to Wool, Aug. 13, 1856, RG393; Alexander Hamilton to Franklin Pierce, Sept. 27, 1856, M234, R35; Robert M. Utley, *The Indian Frontier of the American West* (Albuquerque: Univ. of New Mexico Press, 1985), p. 52.

[32] Mackall to Garber, Oct. 20, 1856 and Feb. 19, 1857, RG393; PR, Ft. Humboldt, Apr. 1857, M617, R993.

Pacific, Henley expressed, to his superiors in the nation's capital, fears for the safety of reservation employees and government property. Writing to the commissioner of Indian affairs, Henley stated that "General Wool will not, if it is left to his discretion, furnish any protection or assistance whatever to the Reservation." Meanwhile, Henley instructed his reservation employees to prepare for their own defense against insurrection.

Describing local commanders' actions in California as ill-advised and poorly timed, Interior Department officials sought help from the War Department. Secretary of War Jefferson Davis interceded and tried to conciliate disputes between military commanders and Henley. Davis hesitated to give Wool a direct order to establish military detachments wherever Indian reservations might be organized. Instead, Davis announced his desire that Wool afford military protection to Indian reservations if men and funds were available.[33]

After less than a year of respite from duty on the reservations, Northern California Regulars again prepared for life among federal Indian agents. The Army took its time and waited for good weather. General guidelines for the use of troops remained unchanged. Soldiers would not compel Indians to move to reservations against their will; they might protect them en route when voluntarily moved. Troops would administer no punishments to Indians on reservations, and they would protect reservations "against

---

[33] Wool to Thomas, Aug. 19, 1856; and Cooper to Wool, Dec. 4, 1856, RG393; Henley to Manypenny, Oct. 4, 1856; and Davis to McClelland, Nov. 19, 1856; and McClelland to Manypenny, Nov. 11 and 24, 1856, M234, R35. The first draft of the War Department's letter told Wool: "You will extend military protection . . ." but "will" was subsequently lined out.

aggressions of evil-disposed whites." The Army would also quell outbreaks that might result in injury or destruction among reservation Indians. Post and detachment commanders were expected to continue to use their personal judgment in dealing with Indian Office employees. Specifically, detachment commanders at California Indian reservations would render semimonthly reports straight to the commanding general of the Department of the Pacific.

Forced to send troops back to northern California Indian reservations in 1857, the Army intended to be vigilant. Attending to military duties, soldiers also would closely watch the activities of the Indian Office.[34]

---

[34] Cooper to John B. Floyd, Apr. 14, 1857; and Floyd to Jacob Thompson, May 23, 1857, M234, R35; Jones to Deshler, May 26, 1857, RG393.

Fort Bragg Garrison in Frock Coats, Mendocino Reservation

From an 1858 painting by Alexander Edouart

Chapter 5
1857

Onto the Indian Reservations—Again

Our regiments, horse and foot—including artillery (serving, mostly as infantry)—are . . . anything but a peace *establishment.*

Annual Report of the Secretary of War (1857)

As the Army took its time moving soldiers back to California Indian reservations in 1857, Superintendent Henley and U.S. Treasury Special Agent J. Ross Browne, fidgeted. They thought that Regulars should act promptly to protect Indian Office employees, deploy as reservation policemen, and assist in moving tribes to reservations. Browne described the Regular Army in California as useless and averse to assisting either federal or state authorities.

Officers in the War Department defended the Department of the Pacific against charges of laxity. They advised the new Secretary of War, John B. Floyd, that troops had been deployed when proper or practical. Floyd decided that no interference from his office was necessary despite civilian complaints. Commanders in California could run

their own affairs as long as they conformed to General
Orders. By the time Floyd completed his review of the
situation, Regulars had begun moving to northern California Indian reservations again.[1]

After spending a winter at the Presidio of San Francisco,
men from Company B, 3d Artillery, re-established themselves at the Nome Lackee Indian reservation in June
1857. The soldiers were to protect reservation employees
and, when possible, to prevent difficulties between Indians
and Tehama County voters. Commanding the twenty-man
detachment, 1st Lieutenant Michael R. Morgan told
department adjutant William W. Mackall that, to perform effectively, he needed a horse.

Morgan reported faithfully and routinely to the Department of the Pacific. He gave a new Indian agent, Vincent
E. Geiger, good marks for earnestness, but Morgan admitted that the Indians were discontented with the new culture
of confined reservation life. The detachment found duty at
the reservation boring: "As usual, some Indians have run
away from the Reservation and some have been caught
and brought back."[2]

When part of the 3d Artillery made its way back to
Nome Lackee, another detachment under 1st Lieutenant
Horatio G. Gibson from the same regiment moved north
to the lonely Mendocino coast. Leading one sergeant,
one corporal, and eighteen privates to provide military
security for the newly established Mendocino Indian reservation, Gibson arrived at the Noyo River the evening of

---

[1] Browne to James Guthrie, Mar. 3, 1857; and Cooper to Floyd, Apr. 14, 1857;
and Floyd to Thompson, May 23, 1857, M234, R35.

[2] Morgan to Mackall, June 15 and Oct. 1, 1857, RG393; PR, Nome Lackee,
June 1857, M617, R867; Hilsop, *Nome Lackee*, pp. 38–44.

June 8. He named the post Camp Bragg in honor of Braxton Bragg, his artillery company commander in the Mexican War.

Gibson was satisfied with the reputation of reservation agent H. L. Ford, but he felt otherwise about Ford's eighteen subordinates. He heard that they were "mostly worthless, drunken characters," and Gibson resolved to keep his soldiers removed from such influences. Gibson sited the military post a mile from the reservation headquarters, where he waited three days for his baggage to appear.[3]

Camp Bragg's garrison, Detachment M, 3d Artillery, set to work building quarters. Constructing an Army post required all hands, with no time for marching about a parade ground or keeping surveillance over the four thousand Indians supposedly on the reservation. The soldiers borrowed tools from Agent Ford, hewed timber for buildings, and by September had erected three structures. In September 1857, with approval of Gibson's immediate superior in the 3d Artillery, Captain Keyes, the garrison started calling the post a fort instead of a camp.

Troops found Fort Bragg mail service wanting; the new post was even more isolated than Fort Humboldt. Fort Bragg also lacked medical services, so the Army paid seventy-five dollars a month for visits by a civilian physician. After a soldier died from disease, Gibson fired the doctor and asked for an Army surgeon. He also requested a howitzer for his all-artillery garrison.[4]

---

3 Gibson to Mackall, June 8 and 18, 1857, RG393; PR, Ft. Bragg, June 1857, M617, R138; Fred B. Rogers, "Bear Flag Lieutenant," *CHQ*, vol. 30 (June 1951), pp. 164–65; Lyman L. Palmer, *History of Mendocino County* (San Francisco: Alley, Bowen & Co., 1880), pp. 169–70.

Gibson warned headquarters that the Indian Office apparently lacked the ability to feed its charges on the Mendocino reservation. He accompanied Ford to investigate reports that Indians had killed stock some forty miles away in Long Valley. Indians often cut stock from herds to satisfy hunger. In Long Valley, a portion of Mendocino County noted for good grazing, Gibson discovered that, in addition to three cattle, Indians had also killed two horses. More startling still, they found that Indians had burned off range grass to prevent animals from using the valley for further grazing.

Acting in concert, Indian agent and Army officer successfully dissuaded a pair of settlers from organizing a retaliation party against Indians. Other than preventing this Indian-killing expedition, the Fort Bragg garrison attempted no operational missions throughout the summer and autumn of 1857. Gibson made no secret of his housing predicament. He reported that all military training had been "unavoidably suspended since June 11, the troops being employed in the construction of [the] post." Gibson's experience at Fort Bragg paralleled those of commanders at Fort Reading and Fort Humboldt. Building a small Army post by using soldier labor and with limited tools saved money. It also took an inordinate amount of time and detracted from the main tactical mission. Northern California rains made absolutely necessary some structures to shelter food, weapons, and powder. Latrines had to be dug for simple sanitation. In November, Gibson hired a

---

4 Gibson to Mackall, June 18 and Sept. 15, 1857, RG393; PR, Ft. Bragg, July, Sept., Oct. 1857 and Jan. 1858, M617, R138; Browne to Guthrie, Mar. 3, 1857; Statement of Indians on Mendocino Reservation, Mar. 31, 1857, M234, R35.

civilian mason at five dollars a day to help soldiers complete their quarters.[5]

Exasperated over slow construction, Gibson worried even more over a food scarcity at the reservation. Increasing numbers of undernourished Indians slipped away, and Gibson's concern for security in the area grew. As if to bear out Gibson's doubts, a traveler was murdered north of the reservation, the third such occurrence since the arrival of the 3d Artillery.

Gibson's suspicions grew with his concern. The Indian Office had allocated seventeen-thousand dollars for a three-month period at the Mendocino reserve. The number of inhabitants at the reservation had dropped to just two hundred. Why was food in short supply? Early in May 1858 Gibson notified his military superiors that government-supplied food for Indians had disappeared altogether.[6]

Before Gibson could confirm further misgivings about management by the Indian Office, open hostilities in Washington Territory caused the department to relocate his unit. Detachment M, 3d Artillery, left Fort Bragg on June 7, 1858, leaving behind Sergeant William G. Lee to protect military property. Lee proved unable to defend the buildings against a plague of mice, which overran them.[7]

Hostilities were not confined to Washington Territory. Lacking Indian contacts from the Pit River after the

---

[5] Gibson to Mackall, Sept. 15 and Oct. 1, 1857, RG393; PR, Ft. Bragg, Nov. 1857 and June 1858, M617, R138; R. R. Olmsted, ed., *Scenes of Wonder & Curiosity from Hutchings' California Magazine* (Berkeley: Howell-North, 1962), p. 254.

[6] Gibson to Mackall, Jan. 6 and 24, Apr. 9, and May 5, 1858, RG393.

[7] Gibson to Mackall, June 15, 1858; and Lee to Mackall, July 29 and Sept. 23, 1858, RG393; Gibson, taken ill, had to delay his own departure from Fort Bragg until June 15.

closure of Fort Reading, the Army received startling news in February 1857. According to Captain Judah at Fort Jones, Lockhart's Ferry on the Pit had been destroyed, five settlers killed, and all stock slaughtered. In Judah's opinion, deep snow and high mountains precluded any immediate reaction from the valley of the Scott. Instead, he journeyed to Benicia and gave his personal analysis to the department commander.

The Department of the Pacific agreed to Judah's delay so he could form an expedition in dry weather. He would then keep a detachment in the Pit River area for the protection of travelers and residents. By the time Judah arrived, Yreka volunteers had already visited the Pit. According to diarist Joaquin Miller, they had killed fifty-four Indians, lynched two, and had taken sixteen children back to town.

The Army tried to separate itself from the acts of California volunteer groups just as it had tried to distance itself from agents of the Indian Office. The Army set ground rules: only the department commander could authorize recognition of volunteers' legitimacy. In any extraordinary case where recognition of volunteers' status seemed necessary, Californians would first be mustered into federal government service.[8]

Unlike the corral at Nome Lackee, where Lieutenant Morgan had not a single government mount, the corral at Fort Jones contained a plentiful supply of animals. Judah had enough mounts to put Companies D and E, 4th Infantry, on mules to travel to the Pit River. Spurred by

---

[8] Judah to Mackall, Feb. 8 and May 17, 1857; and Mackall to Judah, Feb. 17, Mar. 31, and Apr. 24, 1857, RG393; Schmitt, *Crook*, pp. 34–35; Joaquin Miller, *His California Diary* (Seattle: Dogwood Press, 1936), p. 73.

news that the whole garrison had orders to turn out against the Indians, eight soldiers deserted. The remainder found snow impeding their progress, despite the lateness of the season. On May 22 they finally crossed the river, where one mule fell off the ferry and was lost.

Marching through tule and timber with sixty-five Regulars, Judah verified that settlers had been killed and stock taken. Unable to contact Indian leaders or find missing stock, Judah returned to Fort Jones on May 30. He left Lieutenant Crook at Lockhart's Ferry with twenty-five men.

Meanwhile, Crook had been instructed to provide security for the Shasta–Yreka wagon road and the ferry crossing and to scout between Bear River and Hat Creek Station. Crook relished the chance to use his own judgment. Leading a three-man patrol southeast of the ferry, Crook chanced upon a group of Indians. Discretion overcame valor, and he beat a path back to the ferry for more soldiers. Returning with his enlarged force, Crook pursued the aroused band, escaped a shower of arrows, and killed one Indian.

Crook returned to camp, certain that no information could be gained in the vicinity of his skirmish. Notified that Indians had stolen three horses from settlers, Crook took a five-man patrol north along the river in the opposite direction. On the riverbank he spotted an Indian encampment. Arrows rained, and one struck Crook's thigh. Wounded and believing the arrow poisoned, Crook, aided by his men, withdrew to his camp in agony.

Crook asked help from Fort Jones in extracting the arrowhead. Fort Jones exploded with activity after learning of Crook's crisis. Lieutenant Dryer, Assistant Surgeon Keeney, and twenty-five men marched from the post before sundown. Mounted on mules, they rode until two in the morning, covering forty miles. Resuming their march when the sun was high, Dryer, Keeney, and men of the 4th Infantry reached Crook on the afternoon of June 16. They had traveled 110 miles by mule in sixty-nine hours.

Deciding it best to leave the arrowhead embedded, Keeney went back to Fort Jones. Crook, his health dramatically improved, and Dryer resumed patrols along the troubled Pit. A fresh encounter resulted in another Indian death. Complying with orders from Judah, Dryer returned to Fort Jones at the end of June. Crook remained east of the Trinity Mountains, where muskets and arrows fueled open warfare.[9]

The area of concern included 150 miles of fish-bearing streams and three waterfowl-covered marshes that fed the Pit and Hat Creek Indian groups. (The Indians called themselves the Achumawi and the Atsugewi, respectively.) Some sixty rancherias lined the Pit River, Burney Creek, and Hat Creek. At the falls of the Pit, the Achumawi monopolized salmon fishing. Both groups had earned a reputation for harassing travelers between the Sacramento Valley and Oregon. A Pit River reservation might be feasible; Superintendent Henley decided to send an agent to the area.

The Army reacted more rapidly than Henley. New to his command of the Department of the Pacific, in May 1857 Brigadier General N. S. Clarke ordered Company A of the 1st Dragoons to garrison the Pit. For the first

---

[9] Crook to Mackall, May 31, 1857; Judah to Crook, May 27, 1857; and Crook to Judah, undated, RG393; PR, Ft. Jones, May 1857. In his autobiography Crook states that Judah and many of his soldiers were drunk at the start of the expedition; Judah to Mackall, June 14 and July 7, 1857; and Dryer to Judah, July 6, 1857, RG393; Schmitt, *Crook*, pp. 36–43.

time in four years, Regular Army cavalry would be seen
in northern California.

Commanded by Yankee-born, West Point–educated
Captain John William Tudor Gardiner, Company A rested
briefly at old Fort Reading on the way north. Gardiner's
instructions were to establish a fort where he could protect
travelers as well as the crossings of the Pit River. He was
expected to impress and control the Indian groups.
Gardiner, who had served seventeen continuous years in
the 1st Dragoons, gathered information and pushed supplies to ensure that he was well-stocked before winter.[10]

Original plans placed the fort at the Pit River ferry
crossing. Gardiner decided, however, that a position on
the Fall River, some seven miles away from the crossing,
offered a better location. He occupied his position on July
1, 1857. East of the redwoods and at over 3,300 feet
elevation, the fort included dragoon 2d Lieutenant William
P. Sanders, Assistant Surgeon Calvin Hollenbush, and
forty-seven horse soldiers. On July 12 Crook and Company
D, 4th Infantry, were operating in the nearby hills, and so
came under Gardiner's temporary supervision.

Gardiner took the unusual step of naming the new post
Fort Crook "as Lt. Crook 4th Infantry has been very active
in scouting through the country and has been wounded in
one of his encounters with hostile Indians." Lieutenant
Sanders assisted Gardiner, who sometimes found movement difficult because of rheumatism. While the dragoons
busied themselves building the new fort, Crook and his

---

[10] Mackall to Gardiner, May 11, 1857, RG393; Henley to Denver, Nov. 23,
1857, M234, R35; PR, Ft. Reading, May 1857, M617, R993; Heizer, *Indians*,
pp. 225–30, 236, 238, 242–43.

infantry supplemented the cavalrymen's government rations by hunting game.

Unimpressed with the slow progress and crude results of infantry construction, Gardiner hired civilian carpenters, masons, and laborers to speed the building of Fort Crook. Seven to fourteen civilian craftsmen worked on quarters, kitchen, and corrals throughout the summer and autumn. They were assisted by some thirty cavalrymen.

Exemplary in his industry to get the command sheltered before winter, Gardiner also set to his security mission with vigor. Scouting was a cavalry specialty. Three days after arrival at Fort Crook, Company A, 1st Dragoons, sent out a reconnaissance detachment. Led by Lieutenant Sanders, the eighteen-man party surveyed terrain for two days, encountering no Indians.[11]

Lieutenant Crook also foraged for trouble in July. He found it among some bluffs north of the post. He spotted several hundred Indians, their hostility indicated by settler plunder strewn about the camp. Crook attacked just after daybreak. His troops engaged a determined foe in close combat, killed a number, and held the field. When the Indians retreated to foothills in the south, the soldiers destroyed food that the group had been gathering for the winter.

In August Crook led a combined party of Company D, 4th Infantry, and Company A, 1st Dragoons beyond the fort. Once again he encountered Indians ready to do battle. One of Crook's foot soldiers was wounded in the engagement and two Indians died. Alarmed over Gardiner's

---

[11] Gardiner to Mackall, July 1 and Aug. 5, 1857, RG393; PR, Ft. Crook, July–Dec. 1857, M617, R217; Schmitt, *Crook*, pp. 45–54.

Union Brigadier General William P. Sanders
Served with Fort Crook's initial garrison in 1858
Courtesy of U. S. Army Military History Institute

forcefulness in meeting his requirements and worried about what effect the actions of Gardiner's lieutenants would have on Henley's agent, the Department of the Pacific ordered Fort Crook to cease action against Indians.[12]

Despite frontier conditions, Gardiner remained an active Episcopalian. Slightly chagrined by his own headquarter's implied criticism, Gardiner defended his actions. Referring to local Indians, he wrote: "they were undoubtedly shamefully treated last year by some of the whites," but he had nevertheless been ordered to impress Pit River Indians with the government's authority. Gardiner felt that he had done just that, striking each band known to have been involved in killings and talking with them later. He assured the department commander that his combative actions against the Indians were conducted not "a moment longer than I consider absolutely necessary."

Captain Gardiner reported Indian Agent Edward A. Stevenson's arrival at Fort Crook in August. The Indian agent found Gardiner "a perfect gentleman, and willing to render any assistance in his power." Stevenson planned to check the vicinity for a potential Indian reservation, but he decided to journey first to Yreka and Fort Jones.

Stevenson returned to Fort Crook on August 16. Accompanied by Lieutenant Crook, he moved northeast, seeking peaceable Indian contacts. They came across twelve boatloads of wary Indians who wanted to test Stevenson and Crook's sincerity. The Indians suggested that one of their number, a woman, be taken to Fort Crook. She would

[12] Gardiner to Mackall, Aug. 5 and 11, 1857, RG393; Henley to Denver, Nov. 23, 1857, M234, R35; PR, Ft. Crook, Aug. 1857, M617, R217; Rosena A. Giles, *Shasta County*, 1949, p. 39; William I. Kip, *The Early Days of My Episcopate* (New York: Thomas Whittaker, 1892), p. 203.

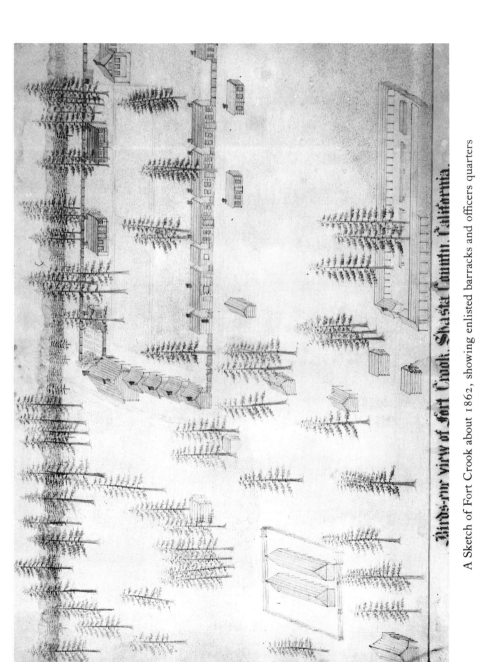

A Sketch of Fort Crook about 1862, showing enlisted barracks and officers quarters

Courtesy of Fort Crook Historical Society

return from the Army post the next morning to report her observations if the soldiers did not harm her. Complying, Stevenson and Crook escorted the woman to the post.

Meeting with Captain Gardiner and socializing with Army families at Fort Crook, the Indian delegate was convinced that no plot existed to ambush her cohorts. She and Stevenson went back to her group the next day. Gradually, as many as 150 Indians gathered to see the woman and Stevenson, but only eight or ten showed sufficient confidence to visit Fort Crook. For two days they observed soldier activities at the post. Suddenly one night at 11:00, the Indian guests jumped up and ran off, leaving a 2-month-old child to the care of the confused garrison. After their nerves settled from some terrifying idea that the Army was about to kill them, they returned to the fort.

Pleased with the success of the Stevenson–Crook effort, Gardiner sent his civilian interpreter and eight soldiers with Stevenson when the agent decided to communicate with the Modoc. Stevenson met with some fifty Modoc and assured them of the government's good intentions. The party returned to Fort Crook, where they found Gardiner feeding fifty-two Indians from the Pit group. Taking their voluntary acceptance of Fort Crook's protection as a good sign, Stevenson recommended an Indian reservation for the Pit River region.

Whether Stevenson's talks or Gardiner's scouting parties produced the effect, peace reigned in Shasta County at the end of summer. By contrast, settler-Indian relations in Humboldt County bubbled from minor irritants. Fort Humboldt, its strength drained because twenty-three men had failed to re-enlist and five more had deserted, still managed to field a roving, twenty-five–man detachment under Lieutenant Rundell. His packtrain tour of the countryside made an ostentatious display of military power, and Rundell hoped it would produce a salutary effect. He scoured the Trinity and Klamath riverbanks in July and August 1857, but the infantry lieutenant reported little of substance—stolen blankets from one group of locals, a cow killed by an arrow, and a less-than-distinguished traveler from Eureka complaining that Indians had fired at him.

Rundell characterized the Indian population as generally friendly, "though the whites are continually inflicting upon them the grossest outrages." He worried about the thousand Indians at Hoopa Valley. They were peaceable but no cowards, and they owned firearms. Completing his reconnaissance, Rundell forecast no serious trouble from the juncture of the Trinity to the mouth of the Klamath.[13]

Indian Office officials disagreed with Rundell's estimate. They continued to pester his superiors for a permanent troop detachment on the Klamath to replace the military presence removed earlier. In September Del Norte County citizens petitioned General Clarke for an Army post on the Klamath reservation. Casting about for spare troops, the attention of headquarters was drawn to Lieutenant Crook's company because of Judah's pronounced fury over Gardiner supervising a Fort Jones unit. The Department of the Pacific noted that Judah had survived for several months at Fort Jones without Crook's company of infantry. Aware that a significant number of recruits were destined for Judah's command, presuming also that Fort Crook's operations would lighten the burden of Fort Jones, the

---

[13] Rains to Mackall, July 14, 1857, and Rundell to Rains, Aug. 2, 1857, RG393; PR, Ft. Humboldt, Jan.-July 1857, M617, R993; *Humboldt Times*, Feb. 28, 1857.

department ordered Lieutenant Crook to march promptly for the Klamath.[14]

Crook's fifty men hiked over the mountains to Fort Jones, then dropped to the coast at Crescent City. Moving up the Klamath River, they arrived at the reservation on October 13. Crook found no spot suitable for an Army post. Told to position his troops where they could support and protect the Indian agent and cautioned to keep strict discipline among his men while in such proximity to reservation Indians, Crook moved across the river the next day to a more favorable spot backed by redwoods. Discerning that local Indians called the grounds of his proposed fort "Ter-waw," which Crook translated as "beautiful place," he proposed that his post adopt the Indian name. Fort Ter-waw it became, supervised by one infantry officer and seven noncommissioned officers.

Crook's company had watched the 1st Dragoons construct a comparatively elaborate post a few months earlier; they learned that they were to limit their own building efforts to economical shelter sufficient for health and comfort. Using tools borrowed from the Indian agent, Regular soldiers worked to make the Klamath post habitable. Meanwhile, reservation Indians hauled military stores to Fort Ter-waw.

Instructed to "ascertain the causes of the dissatisfaction" reported to exist among the Klamath reservation inhabitants, Fort Ter-waw's soldiers, after a week in camp, were convinced that those Indians indigenous to the region were "perfectly contented." The problem lay with the Tolowa. In response to Crescent City's clamor, they had been moved

---

[14] Henley to Clarke, Aug. 10, 1857; and Mackall to Henley, Aug. 15, 1857; and Citizens of Del Norte County to Commander, Pacific Div., Sept. 8, 1857; and Mackall to Crook, Sept. 11, 1857, RG393; Schmitt, *Crook*, p. 48.

to the Klamath reservation from their Smith River environs.

On the reservation the Tolowa were understandably upset. They had been displaced from their traditional territory, where they had once expected their own government reservation. After they moved to the Klamath, the six hundred Tolowa found insufficient food. They were on lands inhabited by other Indians of different languages. The newly arrived reservation Indians were further agitated by "misrepresentations of ill disposed whites" from the coast who wanted them closer to Crescent City, where they could be exploited as cheap labor.[15]

Crook followed a policy of "firmness united with prudence." Despite the soldiers' friendly presence, tension heightened. Learning of various Tolowa plots to start trouble, Fort Ter-waw went on alert early in November and sent guards to strategic spots. By November 14, agency employees found it unsafe to travel beyond sight of their offices. Nobody attempted to work on November 16. Violence hit on November 17. Knives flashed. Musket shots echoed up and down the river.

Agent H. P. Heintzelman and an employee had gone to the Indian residences when they received a call for medical assistance. On the way back they were attacked by Tolowa armed with knives, bows, and arrows. A rush by Regular Army sentries saved their lives; two or three volleys from the military drove off the attackers.

Responding with the rest of the Fort Ter-waw garrison, Crook crossed the river and joined the fray. Troops fired shots into the underbrush, killing ten Indians. Confused,

---

[15] Mackall to Crook, Sept. 11, 1857; and Crook to Mackall, Oct. 21, 1857, RG393; Henley to Denver, Dec. 19, 1857, M234, R36; PR, Camp on Klamath, Sept. 1857; and Ft. Ter-waw, Oct. 1857, M617, R1262,1517.

many Tolowa withdrew from the vicinity of Fort Ter-waw. Remaining some distance from the troops, the Tolowa watched. Soon three unarmed travelers happened into the Tolowa group, who made them captives. With no tradition of organized warfare, the next day the Tolowa brought their three prisoners, unharmed, to the Indian reservation.

Crook anticipated further disturbances but remained confident that he could repel any Tolowa raids on the reservation. There were a few false alarms. For example, one large group of Tolowa positioned themselves on the Smith River, where they challenged soldiers to come and kill them. But soon twenty-six Tolowa men from the riled group joined women and children and returned to the Klamath reservation, resigned to living near Fort Ter-waw.

In San Francisco, Superintendent Henley criticized Heintzelman for moving the Tolowa to a reservation against their wishes, something that Henley himself had belittled the Army for not acceding to in other situations. Henley blamed his own agent for the violence on the Klamath, terming it "unnecessary" and "unfortunate." In his own assessment of the situation around Fort Ter-Waw, Crook took a more charitable view of Heintzelman than Henley had. Crook blamed the November violence on "low, unprincipled whites about Crescent City and vicinity who have been living with squaws and subsisting off the Indians." These agitators had convinced the Tolowa that they were mistreated on the reservation and promised them a more comfortable life away from the Klamath.[16]

---

[16] Crook to Mackall, Nov. 24 and Dec. 11, 1857, RG393; Henley to Denver, Dec. 19, 1857, M234, R36; Report of Labor, Klamath Reservation, 4th Quarter 1857, M234, R35; PR, Ft. Ter-waw, Nov. 1857, M617, R1262; Schmitt, *Crook*, pp. 56–57.

Crook's disgust with some of his fellow citizens grew. He wrote that the same crowd who pretended sympathy for the Tolowa were in reality their worst enemies. Crook termed this set of Americans "true depredators." They were persons who blamed their own unruly acts on Indians, then volunteered as militia to punish the unruly savages, and finally put in large monetary claims against the federal government for such services in defense of the country.

Estimating the number of Indians who had fled the reservation at six-to-seven hundred out of some two thousand, Crook worried that without their winter food supply they must either steal or starve. Crook and Agent Heintzelman believed that only force could move the main Smith River group back to Fort Ter-waw. General Clarke exercised caution and consulted Henley. Reversing his previous denegration of the Army's refusal to use power to move Indians to reservations, Henley decided to forego force against the Tolowa. Fort Ter-waw settled into a frontier routine.

Crook's command received twenty-seven recruits from New York. Limited to protecting the Indian agency's employees, Crook disbursed $12.50 from Company D funds for Christmas refreshments. At Fort Humboldt eighteen recruits joined Company B, 4th Infantry, but morale and disciplinary problems between August and December had caused seventeen more desertions.[17]

No mass desertions occurred at Fort Crook; discipline remained steady despite hard work and isolation. Mail

---

[17] Crook to Mackall, Nov. 24, Dec. 11 and 25, 1857; and Crook to Rains, Dec. 11, 1857; and Mackall to Crook and Proceedings of Company Council, Fort Ter-waw, Dec. 31, 1857, RG393; PR, Ft. Ter-waw and Ft. Humboldt, Dec. 1857, M617, R993, R1262.

sustained morale. Captain Gardiner had hired a mail rider, salaried at $125 a month, to get letters through during the bad weather. Installation of a library and a bowling alley at Fort Crook offered soldiers recreation unusual for northern California in the 1850s.

Gardiner was saddled with all the administrative duties at the new post when Lieutenant Sanders transferred to another regiment. Gardiner appointed himself post quartermaster and post administrative officer, personally needled supply and subsistence officers at headquarters to speed up funds, and then hired a civilian supply clerk at one hundred dollars per month. As garrison administrative officer, Gardiner supplemented the hired civilian quartermaster clerk's salary by an extra twenty-five dollars per month and gave him the additional task of keeping ration records. Fort Crook's civilian payroll swelled in November 1857 with the employment of a teamster at sixty-five dollars per month to supervise heavy hauling, and a herder at sixty dollars per month to assist Company A with the care of animals. The dragoon captain also complied with Ordnance Department requirements and inventoried Fort Crook's sixty-nine percussion rifles, ten Sharp's rifles, sixty-six percussion pistols, eighteen Colt pistols, and eighty-four cavalry sabres.[18]

Southeast of Fort Crook, settlers in the Honey Lake Valley sought a military post to defend against Indians. Henley added his weight to their request by urging General Clarke to station twenty-five soldiers there during the coming winter. Resorting to former practices, Henley told

---

[18] Gardiner to Lt. Col. J. M. Ripley, Oct. 12, 1857; and Return of Company Fund of Company A, 1st Dragoons, Jan. and Apr. 1858, RG393; PR, Ft. Crook, July-Nov. 1857, Jan. and Mar. 1858, M617, R271.

his superiors in Washington, D.C., that a real need for troops existed in Honey Lake Valley to protect overland immigration and to aid the "progressive settlement of the country." He expected no action from the Army without a direct order from the War Department.[19]

At Red Bluff on the Sacramento River, 215 petitioners wanted a cavalry company to protect them from murder and pillage blamed on Indians. They complained that they had to stay awake nights guarding their houses and barns. Red Bluff's citizens, hinting that a legalized Indian hunt might solve their problems, offered to "gladly cooperate in subduing the enemy."

Adding to the chorus of demands for troop detachments all over northern California, Humboldt County chimed in with thirty-seven petitioners. They asked for a military unit in the Bald Hills, just fifteen miles from Fort Humboldt. According to their view, soldiers were needed to foster agriculture and stock raising, unimpeded by Indians.[20]

Driblets of reinforcements continued to arrive for California garrisons. At Fort Jones, Captain Judah's Company E, 4th Infantry, received thirty men. In contrast to the first winter at the post, when the Army ran out of food, Fort Jones had received with government rations 848 pounds of ham, 64 pounds of tea, and 256 gallons of whiskey by December 1857.

The Army also continued to supplement the diet of the Shasta under protection at Fort Jones. Officers furnished

[19] Henley to Clarke, Oct. 29, 1857; and Henley to Denver, Oct. 30, 1857, M234, R35; J. Williams et al. to Clarke, Nov. 7, 1857, RG393.

[20] Petition, Citizens of Red Bluffs [sic] to Clarke, June 29, 1857; and Rains to Mackall, Sept. 20, 1857, RG393.

the Indians with tons of fresh beef, flour, and hard bread during the cold months of 1857–1858. Earlier, in August 1857, Agent Stevenson had visited the post and praised Judah's efforts, but he noted that the Shasta had resorted to drinking and prostitution.[21]

The expense of operating Fort Jones displeased the Department of the Pacific. Settlement had rapidly expanded through the valleys around the fort, and Clarke thought about abandoning it, as had been done earlier at Fort Reading. Nevertheless, Henley had plans for the Army in 1858. Finding eastern Mendocino County Indians more attached to their lands than anticipated, Henley asked for troops to tour the area in the coming summer. A show of the flag by the military would restore peace and order and, in the superintendent's opinion, save many lives.[22]

----

[21] 1st Lt. George P. Andrews to Mackall, Sept. 4, 1857; and Lee to Mackall, Mar. 31, 1858, RG393; Henley to Denver, Nov. 23, 1857, M234, R35; PR, Ft. Jones, Dec. 1857, M617, R560.

[22] Henley to Denver, Oct. 27, 1857, M234, R35; Henley to Clarke, Mar. 6, 1858, RG393.

Chapter 6

March and Countermarch

This want of troops to give reasonable security to our citizens in distant settlements, including emigrants on the plains, can scarcely be too strongly stated. . .

Annual Report of the Secretary of War (1858)

While Army officialdom pondered closing Fort Jones and shifting the soldiers to salve some other sore spot, in 1858 John B. Weller, the fifth governor of California, complained of Indian hostilities. He wanted U.S. Army troops to suppress Indians who were committing "numerous outrages" south of Fort Jones in Shasta, Tehama, and Colusa counties. The inhabitants were in a "helpless condition" for want of troops. With the closure of Fort Reading two years earlier, Fort Jones, which was already short of troops, drew the task of sending forces to the troubled area. Faced with the prospect of marching all over the Sacramento River Valley, eleven privates deserted the Scott Valley post in the spring of 1858.

The outcome of missions assigned to Fort Jones that spring did not support the governor's allegation of an Indian menace. After receiving orders to ascertain the facts of reported violence, Captain Judah marched to the site of old Fort Reading, found no war in progress, and returned to Fort Jones.[1]

Another Fort Jones mission resulted from the claims of citizens in the area of Antelope Creek in Tehama County. They said that a group of Indians, formerly employed by local citizens, now possessed modern firearms. Superintendent Henley of the Indian Office promised to cooperate in solving the alleged problem. Judah sent 1st Lieutenant Hiram Dryer to the affected area east of Red Bluff. Dryer's detachment carried the new Army rifle instead of the older musket, and Dryer planned to put the new weapons to good use in protecting settlers. Leading two dozen men from Fort Jones, he awaited the arrival of a federal Indian agent and established his command of Regulars at Antelope Mills.[2]

On May 21 and 22, 1858, Dryer marched up Battle Creek in response to unfounded reports that Indians had stolen and killed cattle only the night before. Three days later the soldiers scouted along Antelope Creek after aroused settlers expressed fears that the canyon was full of Indians. Dryer could find neither Indians nor Henley's promised agent. In Dryer's opinion no Indians had encamped in the area for many months. Constant marching by Company E, 4th Infantry, accomplished little beyond the waste of shoe

---

[1] Weller to Clarke, Mar. 24, 1858; and Mackall to Judah, Apr. 6 and 21, 1858, RG393; PR, Ft. Jones, Mar.-May 1858, M617, R560.

[2] Mackall to Judah, Apr. 27, 1858; and Clarke to Henley, Apr. 27, 1858, RG393.

leather. The men's shoes were worn to the point where several of Dryer's soldiers were nearly barefoot.

The absence of hostile Indians appeared immaterial to Tehama County citizens, some of whom seemed bent on killing any Indian that came into sight. Dryer informed this segment of the population that the Regular Army's presence in no way legitimized an extermination policy in California. With Judah's backing, Dryer warned settlers that the Regulars would withdraw if "such barbarity" persisted. His statements went unheeded. Disgusted with civilians and convinced that no Indian agent was on the way, Dryer marched his men out of Tehama County and back to Fort Jones on May 18. In Dryer's wake, a number of county residents warned citizens who employed Indian laborers to send them to Nome Lackee or see them killed.[3]

Unknown to Dryer, the Department of the Pacific had already decided that the detachment should return. The entire garrison was to be sent to Washington Territory. The Army had decided that Fort Jones had outlived its usefulness as a military post. Siskiyou County counted thirteen thousand acres under cultivation, four grist mills in operation, and a population in the thousands. Settler relations with Indians had become a matter of Siskiyou County law enforcement that did not require Army intervention.

Judah got the news of his projected move on June 17, 1858. Reacting swiftly, he prepared equipment for transport north and sold off immobile government property.

3 Judah to Mackall, May 8, 1858; and Dryer to Judah, May 28, 1858; and Judah to Dryer, June 1, 1858; and Judah to Mackall, June 1 and 17, 1858; and Dryer to Judah, June 9, 1858, RG393; PR, Ft. Jones, May 1858, M617, R560; Giles, *Shasta County*, p. 41.

The last commander of Fort Jones completed all necessary arrangements in a week. On June 23, 1858, the Regular Army, seventy-nine strong, left Fort Jones for Fort Vancouver on the Columbia River.[4]

In addition to closing Fort Jones, the Army also withdrew the detachment from the Nome Lackee Indian reservation for the second and final time. No real need for a small, permanent military presence at Nome Lackee had been proven. The twenty-two Regulars closed camp and returned to their parent unit in April 1858.[5]

What the Army needed in northern California was some means of showing nervous settlers and distraught aborigines that a strong federal arm existed in the redwoods and river valleys. With Fort Reading and Fort Jones gone, Fort Crook stood as the only Regular Army post in all of northeast California. Fort Crook was well suited to the role, having cavalry. The horse soldiers could cover distance more quickly than the improvised, mule-mounted expeditions or foot-slogging marches made by the 4th Infantry and 3d Artillery.

Gardiner's 1st Dragoons responded to the need for covering the upper reaches of the Sacramento Valley. Dragoons from Fort Crook went out in April 1858 in reaction to reports of trouble on Hat Creek. An Indian had allegedly run off with a settler's ox. Gardiner knew that the animal's owner was a respectable man who never harrassed Indians. After identifying the culprit, Gardiner thought

---

[4] Mackall to Dryer, June 9, 1858; and Judah to Mackall, June 17 and 22, 1858, RG393; PR, Ft. Jones, June 1858, M617, R560; Mrs. Warren Nelson, *History of Scott Valley* (publisher and date unknown), p. 5. At least one Fort Jones enlisted man, James Bryan, chose to remain as a settler.

[5] PR, Nome Lackee, Mar. 1858, M617, R867; 35th Cong., House Ex. Doc., No. 93, Feb. 15, 1859, p. 23.

that he might stave off alienation between Hat Creek Indians and settlers if he could have the ox returned or bring the thief to Fort Crook.

Gardiner selected an experienced noncommissioned officer, Sergeant Charles F. Gillies, to head a ten-man detachment. Several months earlier Sergeant Gillies had met the Hat Creek Indians (who were probably Atsugewi) on friendly terms; he had successfully demonstrated the Army's desire to offer them protection. Thereafter, many Hat Creek Indians visited the garrison, where they received gifts of food. Unfortunately, Gillies's fresh attempt at mediation turned into disaster.

He approached the Hat Creek settlement with discretion on April 5, 1858. Seeing Indians flee at his approach, the sergeant halted and dropped off part of his detachment to reassure the Indians of his peaceful intentions. He decided to cross Hat Creek alone to give confidence to his apprehensive watchers. Careful to remain under the cover of his men's rifles, Gillies showed the band's leader evidence that one of their number had taken a settler's ox. After receiving no satisfaction, the sergeant told the Hat Creek leader to return with him to Fort Crook, where they could discuss the case with the post commander.

Gathering his own escort, the Hat Creek leader started for the Army post with the soldiers. As they crossed the stream, the leader and another of his band abruptly turned back. Indians reached for their weapons and one swung to seize Gillies's rifle. Gillies knocked him into the river. Rifles barked. Shots hummed. One Indian was dead, another bleeding. Those to the rear ran off. Gillies's shaken detachment sped to Fort Crook after an absence of only thirty-six hours.

Captain Gardiner was satisfied with Gillies's forbearance under difficult circumstances, and he assured his superiors that the situation was under control.[6] Gillies returned to the field in May, accompanied by a corporal and thirteen privates. Their three-day reconnaissance ended with no bloodshed.

Four days after the detachment's return, twenty-five recruits arrived at the riverside post. The recruits were accompanied by 1st Lieutenant Milton T. Carr, an experienced cavalry officer who was four years out of the Military Academy. These reinforcements strengthened Gardiner's ability to mount strong reconnaissance from Fort Crook across the pine-covered north of California.

In August the complement at the fort doubled as Company F, 1st Dragoons, reported for duty. The garrison stood at 121 soldiers and 116 government horses. Post Surgeon Hollenbush described the new troopers as "fine healthy young men." With Company F came 2d Lieutenant John T. Mercer, a West Point classmate of Lieutenant Carr's. Like Carr, he was a Southerner. Mercer was pleased to see that at Fort Crook good care was expected for government mounts. Horses of the 1st Dragoons traditionally received gentle treatment. Sergeants enforced "ironclad rule" and forbade abuse of horses—including cussing, kicking, jerking, or unnecessary spurring.[7]

---

[6] Gardiner to Mackall, Apr. 5, 1858, RG393; PR, Ft. Crook, Apr. 1858, M617, R271. Other Army records incorrectly listed Gillies as "Gillis."; Ltr., George R. Stammerjohan, Cal. Dept. of Parks and Recreation, Oct. 5, 1990.

[7] Hollenbush to Surgeon General Thomas Lawson, July 1, 1858, RG112; PR, Ft. Crook, May and Aug. 1858, M617, R271; Percival G. Lowe, *Five Years a Dragoon* (Norman: Univ. of Oklahoma Press, 1965), p. 118; San Francisco *Daily Alta California*, May 28, 1858. Surgeon Hollenbush also reported that among older soldiers at Fort Crook, "intemperance is still prevalent."

Doubling the riding strength of Fort Crook proved timely. There were repeated demands for Regulars in the Honey Lake Valley far to the southeast of the post. One of Lassen County's earliest settlers, Isaac Roop, petitioned the Army for protection. Indians were blamed for stock theft, which disrupted crop cultivation and cattle raising. Indian Superintendent Henley added his weight to Roop's request. He repeated his contention that until United States troops demonstrated their presence, no civil order seemed possible around Honey Lake.[8]

In San Francisco General Clarke assured settlers that the Army, aware of their anxiety, would send soldiers. Orders went to Fort Crook for a scouting detachment to cover not only Honey Lake Valley, but also adjoining Indian Valley. The detachment commander was given a twofold mission: to make his presence obvious to any Indians, and to remain in each valley long enough to assure the settlers' safety.

Quickly acclimated to Fort Crook, Lieutenant Carr led a column of thirty-eight dragoons to Honey Lake. Assistant Surgeon Hollenbush and a frequently employed civilian guide, Dick Pugh, accompanied Carr when he marched from the fort on June 9, 1858.

Covering eighty-five miles on horseback, Carr found what an Army officer considered a remarkably refined lot of 130 settlers around Honey Lake. They were "very quiet, orderly, and gentlemanly persons, different from what one would expect to find on a newly settled frontier." He suspected that either Indians from the Pit River or

---

[8] Mackall to Isaac Roop, May 4, 1858; and Henley to Clarke, May 1 and 10, 1858, RG393; Henley to Charles E. Mix, May 1, 1858, M234, R36; Olmsted, *Hutchings' California*, pp. 323–25. Honey Lake already had a sawmill and a flour mill.

the Shushanie Indians were responsible for the disappearance of the stock that belonged to the law-abiding citizens. Although Carr's theory lacked evidence, the thievery caused some settlers to leave their new homesteads in discouragement.

Carr discussed valley problems with residents and fed his men on locally purchased beef. Satisfied that he had accomplished all that the Army desired for the time being, Carr returned his column to Fort Crook on July 2. He told Gardiner that a permanent military camp near Honey Lake would be useful.[9]

No further scouting expeditions for Honey Lake left Fort Crook during the summer of 1858. The Department of the Pacific turned to a second piece of unfinished business, the Indian Office's concern over the Nome Cult farm. Occupied by one of Superintendent Henley's agents in 1856, the embryo reservation was in the Round Valley in Mendocino County. The Indian Office worried that the Eel River Indians, their lands pierced by settlers, threatened the Nome Cult project. Friendly treatment and small gifts to Indians by the Indian Office bore no results, and Indian hostility made the trail between Round Valley and the Mendocino Indian reservation near Fort Bragg unsafe for small groups. Reports arrived that lives had been lost on the Eel. Henley wanted troops to restore peace and order.[10]

At Fort Humboldt, Lieutenant Collins, an old hand on the Pacific coast, prepared a detachment of Company B, 4th Infantry, for the 150-mile march to Round Valley.

[9] Mackall to Gardiner, May 11, 1858; and Gardiner to Mackall, July 8, 1858, RG393; PR, Ft. Crook, June and July 1858, M617, R271.

[10] Henley to Clarke, Mar. 6, 31 and Apr. 24, 1858, RG393; S. P. Storms to Godard Bailey, Aug. 14, 1858, M234, R36.

Lieutenant Rundell, who was also experienced in dealing with Indian-settler problems; Assistant Surgeon La Fayette Guild; and thirty-eight soldiers departed Fort Humboldt with Collins on May 12.

Collins was determined to make a positive impression in the Eel and Matole river valleys by a show of numbers, firearms, and discipline. Meanwhile, he kept alert to the danger of ambush—one blunder would ruin their mission. No civilian guides knew the trail from Humboldt Bay to Round Valley, so Collins explored pathways personally. Only once did a wrong bearing force him to countermarch.

Ordered to "treat the Indians with kindness but with firmness," Collins initially succeeded in communicating with various small bands. He described the native inhabitants of the rough, mountainous territory as inoffensive and dressed in deerskins. The bands spoke different languages, and Collins observed that each band was reluctant to venture into another Indian group's territory. That fear, plus the fact that their weapons were limited to bows and arrows, caused Collins to predict no Indian alliance against settlement. The terrain seemed so difficult that he reported that "many parts of it will not I think ever be settled."

Fortunately for troops and packtrain, the timbered path from the coast to Round Valley provided an abundance of water and grass. One member of a small group of Indians on Van Duzen's fork of the Eel River voluntarily guided the soldiers safely over twelve miles of the intricate territory. Later, another Indian group gave Collins two guides who showed him a blazed trail that led directly to Round Valley.

In general, tensions eased as the Regulars progressed

through the forest. Only when they neared Round Valley did the mood change. Apprehensive Indians watched the soldiers from hills above the trail. All declined to come within conversation range.

After a twenty-five–day march, the troops from Fort Humboldt appeared in Round Valley on June 6. Collins thought that Nome Cult provided enough cultivated ground to feed the inhabitants, all of whom seemed to be content on the federal lands. He noted that comfortable houses had been built for the partly acculturated Indians at Nome Cult and added sardonically about reservation quarters: "indeed I have seen much worse [quarters] in this country occupied by our officers and men."

Nome Cult reservation agent S. F. Storms was delighted with the Regulars' presence but found their effect slightly overwhelming. The Indians were intimidated by the sight of so many armed men and voluntarily moved onto the reservation in numbers greater than Storms could handle. He summarized what he termed the good effects of the Regulars' passage by writing to Henley: "The mountain as well as the valley Indians are decidedly opposed to powder and ball."[11]

The show of force in Round Valley was made at the expense of the garrison at Fort Humboldt. The commander of the fort, Major Rains, now had just seven soldiers on post. Moreover, Regulars were needed in Washington Territory, too. Indian Office officials had expected that Collins would remain at the edge of the redwoods all summer, hiking along the Eel River with his soldiers.

---

[11] Mackall to Rains, Apr. 29, 1858; and Collins to Mackall, May 24, June 8 and 9, 1858, RG393; Henley to Mix, June 19, 1858; and Storms to Henley, June 11, 1858, M234, R36; PR, Ft. Humboldt, May 1858, M617, R497.

Despite Henley's praise for the success of Collins's detachment and his request that they remain along the Eel, the troops returned to Fort Humboldt on July 2.[12]

The next day, hard-marching Company B under Collins added five new recruits to the ranks. Moving companies of the 4th Infantry around on a chessboard of conflicting priorities, the Department of the Pacific decided to send Lieutenant Crook's Company D from Fort Ter-waw to the campaign in Washington Territory. Company D was fresher and stronger than Company B. Collins, in turn, left for Fort Ter-waw with thirty-one men on July 8. The garrison at Fort Humboldt dropped to three officers and eleven enlisted men.

The prospect of duty at isolated Fort Ter-waw failed to excite every soldier in Company B; four deserted after dark on the first day of the journey from Fort Humboldt. After arrival, Collins was dissatisfied with the upkeep of the buildings at the military post and hired a civilian carpenter. He complained about the lack of a physician and laundresses.[13]

As Collins's group moved into quarters recently vacated by Crook's company, Del Norte citizens from the area around Fort Ter-waw complained about Crook's departure. A petition from them with 118 signatures asked department headquarters to keep Crook's Company D at Fort Ter-waw. The petition said the men of Company D knew the Klamath country well and the "terror in which they are held by the Indians" made them best suited for

[12] Henley to Clarke, June 19, 1858, RG393; Henley to Mix, June 19, 1858, M234, R36; PR, Ft. Humboldt, July 1858, M617, R497.

[13] Collins to Mackall, July 12 and Aug. 1, 1858, RG393; PR, Ft. Humboldt, July 1858, M617, R497; PR, Ft. Ter-waw, Sept. 1858, M617, R1262.

operations along the Klamath. While Collins fretted over laundry, Crook worried about the potatoes, onions, and parsnips that his command had planted. They had used company funds to cultivate a garden of fresh vegetables to supplement government rations.

At Fort Vancouver later in the summer, Crook found an opportunity to reassert his request that Company D be returned to California before the troops' garden was ruined. His effort was successful. Crook's command, seventy-five strong, returned to Fort Ter-waw on October 16.[14]

Collins turned the post over to Crook and left with his men for Humboldt Bay on October 21. Lieutenant Crook's command was increased by the arrival of a second officer, 2d Lieutenant Thomas E. Turner. Fort Humboldt also received more replacements. Newly promoted to captain, Underwood returned to Fort Humboldt, where he had been stationed several years earlier. Because of his seniority in military grade, Underwood took command of Company B from Collins.

Additional manpower seemed timely because relations between citizens and Indians around Fort Humboldt were on the decline. In an attempt to improve rapport with the settlers, the post commander, Major Rains, journeyed to Hydesville to deliver the Fourth of July speech. The effect was inconsequential; the situation worsened.[15]

---

[14] Proceedings, Company Council, Ft. Ter-waw, Apr. 20, 1858; Petition, Citizens of Del Norte County to Clarke, July 4, 1858; and Crook to Mackall, July 29, 1858, RG393; PR, Ft. Ter-waw, M617, R1262; Schmitt, *Crook*, p. 58, 68; Crescent City *Herald*, July 7, 28 and Aug. 4, 1858.

[15] PR, Ft. Ter-waw, Oct. 1858; and PR, Ft. Humboldt, Aug.-Oct. 1858, M617, R497,1262; *Weekly Humboldt Times*, July 10 and Oct. 9, 1858. During the return from Fort Ter-waw to Fort Humboldt, Collins's party was hit by several ocean waves while crossing a lagoon near Trinidad. Mrs. Collins, aided by her husband and another soldier, was able to remain in her saddle. A civilian packer drowned.

Throughout the summer California volunteers attacked Indians in Humboldt County. Worry about retaliation caused state authorities to consider the trail from Humboldt Bay to Weaverville dangerous. Citizens petitioned Governor Weller for help. In September a mass meeting of Matole River Valley residents resulted in formation of a twenty-man armed party with authority to kill Indians. Townspeople from Eureka and Union called for war on Indians regardless of state or federal action. Moreover, Superintendent Henley had little doubt that he needed troops to protect his employees in Mendocino County.[16]

In response to the turmoil in Humboldt County, Major Rains sent Underwood with what men the garrison could muster to the vicinity of Pardee's ranch. The ranch was east of the fort, halfway to the south fork of the Trinity River, and bordering on Wintu lands. From this point Underwood could guard the Weaverville trail, escort packtrains, and protect stock. He marched for the redwoods with a portion of Company B, 4th Infantry, on October 6. Collins, returning from Fort Ter-waw, set out with men on November 3 to catch up with Underwood.

Although local volunteers had antagonized Indians throughout southern Humboldt County, the Hoopa, farther north, had remained quiet. The Department of the Pacific decided to shift Underwood from Pardee's ranch

[16] Weller to Clarke, Sept. 1, 1858; and Mackall to Rains, Sept. 6, 1858; and Mackall to Weller, Sept. 6, 1858; and Henley to Clarke, Oct. 21 and Nov. 29, 1858, RG393; Browne to Mix, Sept. 29, 1858, M234, R36; *Weekly Humboldt Times*, July 17, Aug. 17, Sept. 18, and Oct. 30, 1858; Millard Brown, "Indian Wars in Trinity, 1858–1865," *Trinity, Yearbook of the Trinity County Historical Society*, (Trinity Co. Hist. Soc., 1969), pp. 36–38. Criticism of Indian reservation administration reached public print. The *Weekly Humboldt Times* said: "If there is any one branch of our government from which more money is stolen than the Custom House, it is from the Indian Department."

into Hoopa territory. The Hoopa were concentrated in a six-mile–long valley along the Trinity River. A dozen Hoopa villages, numbering at least eighty-eight houses, lay close to one another below a line of evergreen forests. Underwood marched Company B, 4th Infantry, to the west bank of the Trinity River, fourteen miles above the junction with the Klamath. His unit of eighty-three soldiers was to protect local inhabitants and the Weaverville trail. General Clarke expected "energy and prudence" from him in the Hoopa Valley.

Underwood, Collins, and Company B were destined to winter on the Trinity under government canvas. Underwood named the post Fort Gaston in honor of a lieutenant killed during the spring campaign in Washington Territory. Because of the isolation of the fort, he instructed Lieutenant Rundell to organize a resupply system by packtrain from Fort Humboldt. Despite temperatures that dipped to 23 degrees Farenheit, Rundell's detail of enlisted men shifted supplies from Fort Humboldt with regularity. [17]

The situation east of the redwoods at Fort Crook was slightly better. Spared any killings between settler and Indian, the all-cavalry garrison sent out a scouting party in October from Company F, 1st Dragoons. Led by Lieutenant Mercer, the party returned in early November without incident.

At Fort Crook Captain Gardiner was ailing, and Lieutenant Carr replaced him as post commander. Carr was concerned over the presence of several hundred Indians

[17] Mackall to Rains, Oct. 20, 1858; and Underwood to Mackall, Dec. 14, 1858 and Feb. 5, 1859, RG393; PR, Ft. Humboldt, Aug. and Nov. 1858; and PR, Ft. Gaston, Jan. 1858, M617, R396, 497; *Weekly Humboldt Times*, Oct. 9, 16, 30 and Dec. 11, 1858.

who had assembled in the vicinity, which was devoid of Indian Office supervision. He issued flour, meat, and salt to the Indians while Superintendent Henley steadfastly refused support unless Carr moved them to Nome Lackee. Once at Nome Lackee, Henley assured the Army, the Indians would be received and provided for by reservation agents. At an impasse, Carr fed the Pit River band as best he could through the winter of 1858–1859.[18]

Fort Crook benefited from the presence of two companies of the 1st Dragoons, but other northern California posts faced a grim manpower shortage. Fort Bragg was bare of troop units. Half of the 4th Infantry from Fort Humboldt was in the Hoopa Valley. The single company at Fort Ter-waw lacked the soldiers necessary to move to troubled areas.

Contentious feelings continued in northwestern California, where Indians were considered "wards of the Federal Government." Despite the vague federal status of Indians, state volunteers took to the field, and State Adjutant General W. C. Kibbe managed the effort. No Regulars participated. In the "Wintoon War," named after local Indians, Kibbe's volunteers killed some one hundred Indians and took several hundred prisoners, most of them women and children.

Discussions with Superintendent Henley yielded the decision to send Indians to the Mendocino reservation. To handle the influx of arrivals, U.S. Treasury Agent J. Ross

---

[18] Mackall to Carr, Nov. 11, 1858; and Mackall to Henley, Nov. 11 and 17, 1858; and Henley to Clarke, Nov. 12 and Dec. 8, 1858; and Carr to Mackall, Sept. 30, 1858, RG393; PR, Ft. Crook, Oct. and Nov. 1858, M617, R271. In addition to feeding Indians, Carr had problems with deserters, holding six in the post guardhouse.

Browne appealed to the Department of the Pacific (which had been redesignated as the Department of California) for troops at vacated Fort Bragg.[19]

In partial response, an entire regiment of Regular Army Infantry was diverted to California. The 6th Infantry, ten companies strong, marched overland from Wyoming and reported for duty at Benicia in November 1858. Troops of the newly arrived regiment were sent on assignments throughout California. Two companies deployed north to the redwood coast. Five companies of the 6th Infantry remained in the San Francisco Bay area. Three others deployed to southern California.[20]

At Fort Humboldt a steamer put ashore Company B, 6th Infantry, on December 18. Captain Charles S. Lovell and 2d Lieutenant Aaron B. Hardcastle, both 6th Infantry officers since receiving their commissions, joined Major Rains in performing garrison duties. Major Rains saw no reason to keep a military post in Hoopa Valley. The county treasurer and other settlers disagreed with Rains. Department Adjutant William W. Mackall assured the group that there was no intention of removing Fort Gaston troops so long as protection of Hoopa Valley proved necessary. In fact, plans had already been made for still another Army post in northern California.[21]

---

[19] J. Ross Browne to Denver, Jan 18, 1859, M234, R37; *Weekly Humboldt Times*, Jan 1 and 29, 1859; Brown, "Indian Wars," pp. 37–39; Heizer, *Indians*, p. 325; Sacramento *Union*, Oct. 16, 1858.

[20] Returns from Regular Army Infantry Regiments, 6th Infantry, Aug.-Nov. 1858, M665; Eugene Bandel, *Frontier Life in the Army, 1854–1861* (Philadelphia: Porcupine Press, 1974), pp. 228–243. The 6th Infantry marched 1,017 miles from Fort Bridger to California in less than two months, thus avoiding a time-consuming sea voyage and the sickness and death suffered by the 4th Infantry and 3d Artillery when they moved to California by ship.

On December 13, 1858, Captain and Brevet Major Edward Johnson marched Company D, 6th Infantry, from Suisun Bay on a journey to the Round Valley of Mendocino County. Johnson, who was twice breveted for gallantry after graduation from West Point, brought twenty years of military experience to his mission, which was to protect employees at the Nome Cult reservation and the lives and property of settlers in Round and Eden valleys.

Heavy storms that rolled in from the Pacific mired Johnson's march. Near the headwaters of the Russian River, Johnson concluded that he was "as far as wagons can possibly go." The nineteen army wagons were unloaded. Continuing personally to test trail conditions to Round Valley, Johnson decided that positioning a Regular Army company at the Nome Cult reservation was impractical because of the inclement winters on the California coast. Accepting Johnson's estimate, the Department of California instructed him to get Company D sheltered. Johnson established a fort at the spot where he had halted his wagons and named the new Army post Fort Weller after the governor, Democrat John B. Weller.

Military administration kept Major Johnson and his two subordinates, 1st Lieutenant William P. Carlin and 2d Lieutenant Edward Dillon, busy. Orders called for an officer-commanded detachment at the Round Valley reservation. On January 3, 1859, Johnson set out for Round Valley with thirty-one men to supervise the placement of a detachment under Dillon, which he planned to supply by packtrain from Fort Weller. His initial trip to Round Valley was too late. According to press reports, settlers had

<hr>

[21] PR, Ft. Humboldt, Dec. 1858 and Jan. 1859, M617, R497.

killed forty Indians on New Year's Day for stealing livestock.

On Johnson's return he learned that the garrison at Fort Weller would be further depleted; he was to send a detachment to partially regarrison Fort Bragg. Given the option of assigning command of the second detachment to a commissioned officer or a noncommissioned officer, Johnson, with only Lieutenant Carlin left, chose a corporal to take charge of the twenty privates earmarked for the redwood coast. They left Fort Weller and, with a civilian guide, marched overland to Fort Bragg.

Johnson's command — two lieutenants, three sergeants, three corporals, a pair of musicians, and seventy-one privates — stood divided in three locations. Company D had not been paid since June 1858. Johnson stated the obvious: "The men are much in need of money". He requested that they be paid before the next muster formation.[22]

Irregular receipt of authorized pay complicated bachelor and family life at northern California garrisons. A number of wives joined their husbands at the isolated posts. By 1860 a total of seventeen Army wives lived at military posts in northern California. The wife of Lieutenant Underwood accompanied him to Fort Humboldt as part of the original post complement in 1853. Mary Underwood gave birth in a floored tent to the first Army child at Fort Humboldt. The following year Assistant Surgeon Potts's wife joined him at the fort.

Two years after Fort Jones had been established, Mrs. Collins, a "good cook" and the wife of Lieutenant Collins,

---

[22] Mackall to C.O., Company of 6th Infantry (undated); and Mackall to Johnson, Jan. 10, 1859; and Johnson to Cooper, Jan. 28, 1859; and Johnson to Mackall, Feb. 7, 1859, RG393; PR, Ft. Weller, Jan. 1859, M617, R1409. *Alta California*, Jan. and 20, 1859.

came to the post. In a ten-year period, Mrs. Collins would live at five Pacific Coast forts. Later, post commander Captain Judah raised his child at the primitive fort. As a rule, Army wives made do with bare necessities and crude furniture, although the occasional luxury sometimes appeared. In 1855 Harriet Simpson of Fort Humboldt received what was probably the first melodeon in the county.[23]

Among the hardy Army families who braved the journey to northern California forts were those of Fort Crook. Captain Gardiner brought his family to the post soon after it was established. Before summer was out in 1857, Army wives were at Fort Crook in sufficient number to object at the sight of the near-naked Indian woman accompanying Lieutenant Crook and Indian Agent Stevenson. The Army women combined resources to attire her in a white dress and convert her to a "fashionable belle." None of the Army ladies could subdue their prejudices sufficiently to care for an Indian baby that was abandoned at Fort Crook, however.[24]

At Fort Bragg on the coast, the sole military caretaker after the departure of the 3d Artillery in 1858 had been Sergeant William G. Lee. He occupied one of the newly constructed buildings with his wife. When troops of the 6th Infantry regarrisoned Fort Bragg in 1859, families began to appear. By December 1860 the families of enlisted

---

[23] Buchanan to Townsend, Aug. 18, 1853; and Judah to Mackall, Feb. 8 and Apr. 14, 1857; and Fort Humboldt Special Order No. 5, Apr. 16, 1854, RG393; Chad L. Hoopes, *Fort Humboldt, Explorations of the Humboldt Bay Region and the Founding of the Military Post* (Provo: Brigham Young Univ., 1964), p. 150; Alden, "Letters of B. R. Alden," p. 207; Charles Ellington, "Charles Peter Deyerle at Fort Humboldt," *Journal of the West*, vol. 20, no. 4 (Oct. 1981), p. 28.

[24] Gardiner to Mackall, July 18, 1857, RG393; Henley to Denver, Nov. 23, 1857, M234, R35.

men included a total of eight children. The number was sufficient for the post commander to request employment of a chaplain—a request that was not granted.

Children abounded as more officers brought their families to California at their own expense and an enlisted man occasionally married a laundress. Fort Gaston was home to four Army offspring in 1860. There were nineteen at Fort Humboldt, and five at Fort Crook. At Fort Ter-waw two of the enlisted men had married.[25]

Army families and bachelor soldiers needed housing. Construction materials, often scarce, proved dear in northern California, because expensive transportation was often required. To reduce costs, enlisted men cut trees, sawed boards, made shingles, and built fireplaces. Despite frequent use of troop labor, construction and repairs at Forts Reading, Jones, Humboldt, Bragg, Crook, and Ter-waw and the Nome Lackee facilities had cost the Army seventy-five thousand dollars by mid-1858 (see table). Major Johnson added to this sum by hiring a carpenter at Fort Weller for two months and paying him five dollars per day.[26]

Changes ordered by the War Department brought additional costs for uniforms. In 1858 it modified the pattern of the dark blue Army coat to omit the pleats. The color of trousers changed from sky blue to dark blue. Instead of a cap, General Orders called for a black felt hat, hardly an item fit for frontier wear. Infantry and dragoon officers were to wear two black ostrich feathers on the left side of the

[25] Lee to Mackall, July 29, 1858; and Dillon to Cooper, Dec. 3, 1860, RG393; *Eighth Census of the United States, 1860,* M653, R58,59,66.

[26] 35th Cong., 2d Sess., House Ex. Doc., No. 93, Feb. 15, 1859, pp. 16, 17; PR, Ft. Weller, Feb. and Mar. 1859, M617, R1409.

Construction and Repair Costs at
Northern California Military Posts*

Fort	1853	1854	1855	1856	1857	1858	Total Cost
Fort Reading	24,081	12,025	119	91	—	—	36,316
Fort Jones	354	5,363	196	10,561	2,963	528	19,965
Fort Humboldt	4,956	5,771	209	550	134	425	12,045
Nome Lackee	—	—	—	165	—	344	509
Fort Bragg	—	—	—	—	74	535	609
Fort Crook	—	—	—	—	—	6,083	6,083
Fort Ter-waw	—	—	—	—	—	292	292

* Costs are cited to the nearest dollar per fiscal year, which ended June 30. Through General Order No. 7 (April 11, 1859), the War Department halted all construction and repair except by troop labor.
Source: 35th Cong., 2d sess., House Exec. Doc. No. 93, Feb. 15, 1859.

hat. Enlisted men were limited to one feather. Such changes in Army uniforms resulted in supply and transport problems at relatively isolated northern California forts. Over a year after the new uniforms became standard, a War Department inspector duly noted that at Fort Humboldt soldiers wore "mixed uniforms" and "light & dark blue pants." At Fort Ter-waw and Fort Crook all the men still wore the old uniform. At Fort Gaston the men lived in tents and cooked "in the open air"; in addition to an entirely new set of uniforms, the men needed new individual equipment.[27]

Despite costs for facilities and uniforms, plus problems with Indians and settlers, headquarters expected post commanders to conduct routine military training. The commander at Fort Weller, for instance, was notified to provide formal instruction based on Captain Heth's system of rifle target practice and Captain McClellan's bayonet exercises. How Major Johnson, who had some forty raw recruits and soldiers scattered all over Mendocino County, was to assemble and drill his company was left to his imagination. Lieutenant Crook at Fort Ter-waw received the same orders. Before target practice could begin, he had rusty weapons and wet cartridges to overcome. In truth, commanders set their own priorities. They conducted little or no military drill at northern California army posts.[28]

The Army had incurred this cost and confusion in response to civilian requests for military presence. The garrisons had pushed columns over rugged terrain to Red Bluff, Honey Lake, Round Valley, and back again. The Army established detachments at Pardee's Ranch and Round Valley and added two new posts, Fort Gaston and Fort Weller. But for all the hundreds of miles marched and countermarched by the Regular Army, relations between civilians and the military would grow more tense.

[27] "Mansfield Reports" (unpub. manuscript), James Hutchins, ed. (Washington, D.C.: Smithsonian Inst.); Salvador A. Ramirez, *Fort Gaston, California: A Brief Sketch* (Encinitas, Calif.: Mustang Press Club, 1985), pp. 6, 8, 10; War Dept., Gen. Orders, No. 3, Mar. 24, 1858.

[28] Crook to Mackall, Nov. 21, 1858, RG393; PR, Ft. Weller, Jan. 1859; and PR, Ft. Ter-waw, Jan. 1859, M617, 1262, 1409.

Chapter 7
1859–1860

Separating Settlers
and Indians

> *. . . it has been obviously impossible to give that ample and
> perfect protection to our whole frontier which our citizens
> have a right to expect, and which it is the duty of government
> to afford.*
>
> *The sudden calls to which our troops are constantly liable,
> the length of marches to be made, the amount of real and
> severe fatigue, privation, and hardship to be endured by
> them, are not exceeded in any service, nor at all equaled on
> any peace establishment whatever. The cheerfulness, alac-
> rity, and efficiency with which they have performed their
> duties entitle them to the commendation of the country.*
>
> Annual Report of the Secretary of War (1859)

Major Johnson, commanding Fort Weller, jangled local
nerves. Johnson took a hard view of settlers who molested
Indians on federal reservations. Beating or maltreating an
Indian called for arrest and confinement as far as he was
concerned. Regardless of California law or custom, Johnson
expected action from his men in fulfilling their protective
mission. Johnson and the commander of his Round Valley
detachment, Lieutenant Dillon, showed no hesitation in
speaking to any white seen physically abusing Indians.

In February 1859 Dillon arrested a settler for clubbing a reservation Indian. The reservation agent advised Dillon that the arrest could cause trouble. Regardless, Dillon confined the man as a prisoner. Fifteen to twenty-five citizens soon approached, asked that they be allowed to explain the arrested man's actions, and offered to post bail. Dillon rebuffed them. Dissatisfied by Dillon's attitude, the group left him an ultimatum: release the prisoner by 10:00 the next morning or they would release the man themselves. Dillon warned them that they would first have to fight the U.S. Army.

The next day the group, fully armed, reassembled and prepared resolutions against Dillon and the Army. Cool heads prevailed, and a party of three went to Dillon with the group's resolutions. Himself calmer than the day before, Dillon provided a written reply to the agitated settlers. He expressed his regrets over the circumstances of the incident, hoped that they would allow a legal settlement in place of violence, and assured them of his wish to avoid a battle. In the meantime, he kept his prisoner. Three men from the armed band left Round Valley on horses to find a judge who might intervene. During his second night of captivity, Dillon's prisoner providentially escaped, defusing the situation.

Major Johnson approved Dillon's actions. Realizing that animosity existed between soldiers and settlers over the Round Valley incident, Fort Weller's commander told Dillon to make no attempt to imprison his escaped suspect. Soldiers would make no further arrests unless requested to do so by a federal Indian agent and then only when sufficient troops were present to hold prisoners. Dillon was to seek support from Round Valley's law-abiding citizens. Johnson started for Round Valley himself, hoping to stem the tide of recriminations. He was too late.[1]

Superintendent Henley complained to Washington, D.C. about the 6th Infantry's conduct in Round Valley. Two of his sons who had business interests in the area became involved in the Round Valley incident with Dillon. Henley warned both Interior and War Department officials that only the escape of Dillon's prisoner had prevented a fight between soldiers and civilians at Nome Cult. Military headquarters in San Francisco admonished Johnson to take instant measures and preclude any confrontations between Regular Army troops and California citizens.[2]

Passing on the new instructions to Dillon, Johnson told him to continue to give Nome Cult's federal agent and Indians all possible protection. Whenever force became necessary, Dillon was to operate strictly within reservation territory. Johnson advised Dillon to keep his diminished authority confidential. Word that Regulars lacked power to separate contentious settlers from reservation Indians might encourage more attacks on Nome Cult. The new orders also prohibited Dillon from confining citizens to the guardhouse, but Johnson interpreted them to mean that Dillon still had the right to remove from the reservation anybody who molested the government charges.

Johnson obeyed orders in a soldierly manner and made

---

[1] Dillon to M. Corbet et al., Feb. 10, 1859; and G. Henley to T. Henley, Feb. 12, 1859; and Henley to Denver, Mar. 19, 1859, M234, R37; Johnson to Dillon, Feb. 21, 1859, RG393; PR, Ft. Weller, Feb. 1859, M617, R1409; Legislature of the State of Calif., "Majority and Minority Reports on the Mendocino Indian War," (Sacramento: 1860), p. 59. The Mendocino Indian "War" was investigated by the California legislature, which filed majority and minority reports.

[2] Mackall to Johnson, Feb. 25, 1859, RG393; Henley to Denver, Mar. 19, 1859, M234, R37.

sure that his command understood the ground rules. Then Major Johnson told department headquarters of his objections to the lack of policy for arresting lawless frontier citizens. He complained that it was impossible to protect Indians without arresting irresponsible whites. Johnson accused the citizens of Round Valley and nearby Eden Valley of slaughtering some 240 Indians. In his opinion, they were determined to kill all Indians in their locale. Under such circumstances, protection of Nome Cult was feasible only when troops happened to be in the immediate vicinity of sudden incursions and possessed power to arrest perpetrators.[3]

Local Californians complained to Fort Weller that Indians were stealing livestock. In response, Johnson spread his command still thinner by posting a five-man guard at Eden Valley. He told Dillon to patrol, secure property, and punish those found stealing.

Dillon tried. When a settler complained that Indians had stolen hogs, Dillon searched for them. Approaching a rancheria, one of Dillon's men received an arrow wound. The soldiers returned fire, and two Indians died. Later in the spring, Dillon sent soldiers to investigate the death of a settler's cows. The troops arrested three Indians, one of whom they turned over to the Indian Office. The other two escaped.

Realizing that the only effective way of preventing the disappearance of cattle was to get Indians onto a reservation where they might obtain proper diets, Johnson sent Dillon to confer with Indians. He was to discuss the advantages of living at Nome Cult. At the same time, Dillon was to induce Nome Cult employees to feed the Indians well.

---

3 Johnson to Dillon, Mar. 7, 1859; and Johnson to Mackall, Apr. 10, 1859, RG393.

Dillon found few Indians willing to consider Nome Cult in place of the mountains. Without rifles, they justifiably feared approach by any whites. Their aversion to reservation life could be attributed to the scarcity of food at Nome Cult, the prevalence of disease, and the lack of protection. Despite military vigilance, a renegade citizen entered the reservation and raped a child in broad daylight. The Regulars' rage increased when a Fort Weller corporal came upon a group of citizens hanging an Indian.[4]

In Sacramento, Governor Weller wrote to the Army in San Francisco, asking that more Regulars be sent to protect Round Valley and Eden Valley. Superintendent Henley bypassed San Francisco and wrote directly to Washington, D.C. He had visited Round Valley, noted the general state of hostilities there, and called attention to "the indisposition of the military there to give necessary protection to property."[5]

Unaware of Henley's letter, General Clarke at the department headquarters told Governor Weller that the military commander at Round Valley had investigated reports of killing. He had determined that not a single citizen had been killed there by an Indian in 1859. Clarke coolly informed the governor that Round Valley enjoyed "reasonable protection"; he felt unauthorized "to add to the public expense" with troop transfers. To ensure that headquarters kept abreast of the facts, it sent the governor's letter and a memorandum attached to it by certain Round Valley and Eden Valley settlers to Johnson for comment.[6]

---

[4] Johnson to Dillon, Apr. 12, 1859; and Johnson to Mackall, Apr. 10, 1859, RG393; Legislature of the State of Calif., "Mendocino Indian War," pp. 56–57.

[5] Weller to Clarke, Apr. 29, 1859, RG393; Henley to Mix, May 5, 1859, M234, R37.

Irked by allegations in the memo, Johnson wrote a twenty-five hundred word essay. He stated that settler claims of attacks by Yuka Indians were false. He ridiculed their request for added protection and a call for state volunteers. Johnson accused his fellow Americans of slaughtering over six hundred Indian men, women, and children during the previous two years. He asserted: "The Indians and not the whites require protection."

Johnson produced two more documents from Mendocino County that countered the information contained in the memorandum. These two documents were transmitted with Johnson's "history of the present condition of Indian affairs." Johnson reported that the two countermemos were from true Round Valley residents while the first memo had in reality been signed by employees of an absentee rancher.[7]

Johnson's volley had little effect in Sacramento. Regulars watched in frustration as California's governor authorized formation of an armed volunteer company in Mendocino County. Fort Weller apprised San Francisco that the volunteers, under W. S. Jarboe, planned to sweep all Indians from Round Valley.

The U.S. Army, employing Indian guides, tried to warn the Yuka of what to expect. Assured of protection by Lieutenant Dillon, fifteen Indians went from Eden Valley to Nome Cult. Fearing whites, Eel River Indians avoided all attempts at contact. Reports arrived at Fort Weller of five Indians killed by ranch employees and one girl

---

[6] Clarke to Weller, May 18, 1859, RG393; PR, Ft. Weller, May 1859, M617, R1409.

[7] Johnson to Mackall, June 1, 1859, RG393; Legislature of the State of Calif., "Mendocino Indian War," pp. 29–30.

"appropriated" as a servant. Soldiers of the 6th Infantry continued their efforts to protect Nome Cult and guard Eden Valley.[8]

Skeptical of accusations that Indians had again stolen stock in Round Valley or that they were responsible for the disappearance of hogs, Johnson personally surveyed the area for evidence. He found none. Jarboe's state volunteers diligently killed Indians, claiming seventy-four deaths by mid-September. Yuka fled in fear to inaccessible upland regions where, Johnson surmised, subsistence was impossible. The Indians would be forced to kill any loose, unherded stock to satisfy hunger.

Food was scarce at Nome Cult, too. Johnson's command had helped collect several hundred Indians at the Round Valley reservation, only to see eight to ten die each day from dietary problems or syphilis. Frustration increased with reports of Indian women and children being kidnapped. Summarizing the situation, the commander of Fort Weller reported: "I believe it to be the settled determination of many of the inhabitants to exterminate the Indians, and I see no way of preventing it."

Johnson also wrote to the department adjutant in wonderment at the continued killings by Jarboe's state-authorized volunteers: "Can it be that the Governor is aware of the activities committed by this man and his followers? Can not the Executive of this state be induced to stay the hands of this Jarboe and his assassins?"[9]

The Army prepared for a long stay in Round Valley.

---

[8] Carlin to Mackall, July 22, 1859; and Johnson to Mackall, Aug. 2, 1859, RG393.

[9] Johnson to Mackall, Aug. 21, Sept. 16, and Oct. 22, 1859; and Johnson to Dillon, Sept. 18, 1859, RG393.

Fort Weller sent a packtrain to Dillon with supplies for six months to preclude any shortages should bad weather isolate his detachment.

Compared to the situation in Round Valley, the situation at Fort Bragg seemed quiet. There were problems, however. When Johnson visited Fort Bragg in the summer months, he expected to find Indian Office employees supervising reservation farming. Instead, he found that Superintendent Henley had allowed fifty Indians to be hired out to an agriculturist in Sonoma County. Worse, several Indian children from the Mendocino reservation were indentured to California citizens at their homes in the Russian River region.[10]

At Fort Humboldt Major Rains worked on the Army's public image. He accepted an invitation to speak about the Pacific Railroad project at the Eureka Lyceum in March 1859. In May, Lieutenant Rundell was a guest lecturer in Union. By then people were calling for the troops that were "lying idle" at Fort Humboldt to help protect property on Yager Creek, where Indians were charged with killing cattle. Rains felt compelled to send Regulars to the field only to learn shortly thereafter that twenty-five volunteers from Hydesville had decided to act on their own.[11]

Captain Lovell, Lieutenant Hardcastle, and half of Company B, 6th Infantry, went to Yager Creek in mid May 1859. The soldiers thrashed about the redwoods for six weeks, encountering no Indians. After refitting at Fort Humboldt, Lovell returned to the field for a two-month

[10] Johnson to Mackall, Jan 10, Feb 6, and Aug. 25, 1859; and Johnson to Sumner, Mar. 9, 1859, RG393; *Humboldt Times*, Mar. 5 and 19, 1859.

[11] Ft. Humboldt, Orders, No. 31, May 11, 1859, RG393; *Humboldt Times*, Mar. 19, 26, Apr. 23, 30, May 21 and 28, 1859; Bledsoe, *Indian Wars*, pp. 162–63.

Colonel and Mrs. Charles S. Lovell
He served at pre-Civil War Fort Humboldt,
where one of their five children was born
Courtesy of U.S. Army Military History Institute

swing along the stream valleys. He tried to restore calm and a degree of mutual trust. By the second week of August, Indians along the Van Deusen and Eel began visiting the military column. The Indians showed no apprehension. They assured the soldiers that they were guiltless in allegations of stock killing.

Lovell's optimism was marred by two incidents. Early on the morning of August 9, Indians from the direction of the Mad River attacked some two dozen Indians who were encamped near Lovell. Before the soldiers comprehended what was happening, the intruders killed seven Indians, five of them women. In September, four enlisted men deserted Lovell's field detachment. During their unauthorized movements, Indians fired on the four deserters and one soldier was killed. Lovell returned to Fort Humboldt with his remaining troops on September 30.[12]

Further inland at Fort Gaston and Fort Ter-waw, Regular Army efforts at defusing settler animosities and Indian fears ended on a small note of success. Waxing complimentary over establishment of Fort Gaston on the Trinity River, a local newspaper informed that "[where] before, alarm and apprehension existed in the minds of the community, business checked, property depreciated, and families removed from a scene of prospective danger; since the arrival of the company [Underwood's Company B, 4th Infantry] confidence has been re-established, prices have risen and families are returning to their deserted homes."

At Fort Ter-waw Lieutenant Crook continued his efforts to build confidence in the Army as a peace keeper. He

---

[12] Lovell to Rains, Aug. 22 and Sept. 11, 1859, RG393; PR, Ft. Humboldt, May, June, and Sept. 1859, M617, R497.

received a quantity of old surplus military clothing and distributed the textiles to local Indians on the Klamath as gifts from the federal government.[13]

False alarms of Indian violence caused Fort Gaston and Fort Ter-waw to send detachments to the field in the summer of 1859. A guard had already been sent to the Trinity Road from Fort Gaston. Fort Ter-waw dispatched a detachment some seventy miles to the junction of the Klamath and Salmon rivers. Travelers were unhampered throughout the summer. Movement of troops away from Fort Ter-waw brought formal objections from Crescent City citizens. Lieutenant Crook visited his detachment in September, doubted reports that Indians were responsible for gunshots heard near Orleans Bar, and drew his detachment back to Fort Ter-waw before winter rains arrived to drench them.[14]

Before the end of 1859, affairs of the federal and state governments complicated the Army's performance of duty in northern California. Mismanagement of federal Indian reservations and Indian deaths caused special federal agents to investigate expenditures at Indian reservations. The investigators accused Superintendent Henley of fraud and mismanagement; he lost his job with the Indian Office.

Henley fought back through the newspapers. Branding past assertions from Major Johnson as falsehoods, he denied year-old reports from the Army that he had led citizens

---

[13] Rains to Mackall, Jan. 27, 1859, RG393; PR, Ft. Ter-waw, Aug. 1859, M617, R1262; *Humboldt Times*, July 9, 1859. The tranquility of Fort Gaston was broken after the man who had manufactured a wooden cannon for the garrison's Fourth of July celebration was killed when the device unexpectedly exploded.

[14] Mackall to Underwood, July 2, 1859; and Mackall to Crook, July 2 and Sept. 26, 1859; Citizens of Klamath Vicinity to Mackall, July 21, 1859; and Crook to MacKall, Sept. 23, 1859, RG393; PR, Ft. Gaston, June and July 1859, M617, R1262.

against Indians in Round Valley. Henley said that he had never carried a weapon or killed an Indian. He then ridiculed Johnson:

> [Johnson] too, is perfectly guiltless of ever having killed an Indian, though stationed in a country where, within the past two years, fifteen or twenty white men have been killed by the Indians, and where thousands of dollars worth of stock has been destroyed, he has never shed the blood of a single one of those innocent and amiable people. And whilst he heroically forbears to kill Indians, he is equally determined that they shall not kill him, and when he rides the trail between his post and the Reservation, where a schoolboy would go whistling along without a thought of fear, he is generally protected by ten or fifteen of his brave and impetuous soldiers.

Meanwhile, Governor Weller's sanctioned volunteers had slaughtered Indians in Mendocino and Humboldt counties and earned the distaste of Army field commanders and the fear of Indian groups. Sensing problems, the Army shifted troops in northern California.

In Mendocino County Major Johnson received orders to close Fort Weller and to move Company D, 6th Infantry, to Fort Bragg. Near the end of August 1859, Lieutenant Carlin took the post's extra government animals back to Benicia. Carlin then returned to Fort Weller and moved the garrison west to Fort Bragg. The detachment remained in Round Valley, and Major Johnson stayed at Fort Weller with three enlisted men into October, closing out Army affairs at the site. Johnson had been unable to use his military office to prevent mistreatment of Indians. He sought a leave of absence to the eastern states. His leave approved, Johnson left California forever.[15]

Fort Weller had been of little use to the small, over-extended Regular Army. It was situated without regard for proximity to Indian or settler. Manned by a conventional infantry company, Fort Weller could in no way be pictured as the vanguard of American civilization in Mendocino County. The garrison obtained little success in defending Yuka Indians. In the soldiers' opinion, local stockmen needed no protection from the Yuka—the situation was just the reverse. Officers and men saw the problem but devised no lasting solution.

Company D moved into Fort Bragg on September 9, 1859, minus Major Johnson. Command of Fort Bragg devolved to the senior lieutenant, Carlin. Carlin was an experienced professional who had served in campaigns against the Sioux and Cheyenne. Now that his orders were to protect Indians, he would be as firm as Major Johnson had been in Mendocino County.

Reservation supervisor H. L. Ford was the first to feel the blast of Carlin's convictions. Some drunken, off-duty soldiers were bothering reservation Indians. Ford's clerk sent a note to Carlin to remove the soldiers. The note instructed Carlin to maintain discipline in accordance with Ford's standards. Failure to do so would be reported to Carlin's military superior.

Carlin gave the federal Indian agent written notice: "You are totally mistaken in thinking that I am in any manner subject to your orders." He reminded Ford that the U.S. Army had garrisoned Fort Bragg to protect citizens against Indian attacks and Indians against citizen

15 Mackall to Johnson, Sept. 14, 1859; and Johnson to Mackall, Oct. 22, 1859; RG393; PR, Ft. Weller, Aug. and Sept. 1859, M617, R1409; Returns from Regular Army Infantry Regiments, 6th Infantry, Oct. 1859, M665, R68; *Alta California*, Feb. 10, 1860.

attacks. Carlin advised Ford that he would receive requests for assistance from the agent but act only on his own military judgment. He also advised Ford's clerk that on his own volition he had sent a file of troops to remove any drunken soldiers from the reservation.[16]

Several weeks later, in February 1860, Carlin again faced problems at the Indian reservation. A California citizen had reportedly abducted an Indian teamster's wife. Ford was temporarily absent. His subordinates requested military assistance.

Responding quickly, Carlin arrested the man. He explained to him the reason for his action, turned the woman over to reservation employees, and stated that any further action was Ford's responsibility. Agent Ford reappeared. He told his employees that they had erred in calling on Fort Bragg for support. After examining the sequence of events, Ford decided that the arrested man had been within his legal rights in taking the woman off the reservation.

Carlin released the arrested man and told Ford that he thought all the federal employees at the reservation should be fired. Carlin also told department headquarters that the Indian Office's boat was being used to land whiskey on the coast.[17]

Whiskey was on Carlin's mind. Learning that one Frank Warren might be appointed the local postmaster, Carlin asked the Army to inform the Postmaster General that Warren's abode was "a low whiskey shop . . . the resort of

---

[16] Carlin to H. L. Ford, Dec. 27, 1859, RG393; David M. Goodman, *J. Ross Browne* (Glendale: The Arthur H. Clark Co., 1966), pp. 106, 140–41, 146, 148.

[17] A. W. McPherson to Carlin, Carlin to Simpson, and Carlin to Mackall, Feb. 6, 1860, RG393.

all the Drunkards, Gamblers and Loafers in the neighborhood." Warren lived just south of the Noyo River. If a post
office was necessary, Carlin reported that there were respectable citizens north of the Noyo who could serve as postmaster. Carlin doubted the need for a post office; a hired
expressman had proven satisfactory. [18]

Newly elected California governor John G. Downey
thought many things were unsatisfactory in Mendocino
County. In a letter to General Clarke, he requested
that more government troops be sent there immediately.
Downey told Clarke that, particularly in the Round Valley,
the Indians were "exceedingly hostile . . . murdering and
robbing the settlers." Clarke ordered Lieutenant Dillon to
send him a direct report.

Dillon bluntly termed the governor's assertions as
"emphatically incorrect." Dillon said that during his year
of duty at the Round Valley reservation, the only citizen
killed by an Indian had been trying to kidnap an Indian
woman. With the exception of this incident, Indians had
killed no settlers or stock. Dillon reported that Downey's
electorate needed no troop protection. Indeed, "the Indians
stand infinitely more in need of protection than the whites."
In Dillon's view, certain parties in Round Valley wanted
nothing more than an excuse to exterminate all Indians in
order to increase grazing lands for their livestock. Previous
motives for killing Indians in California's northern counties were seemingly limited to extralegal punishment for
theft, prevention of supposedly looming attacks, and main-
tenance of the sanctity of mining claims.

---

[18] Carlin to Mackall, Jan. 18, 1860, RG393. Francis M. Warren became postmaster during the four months that Noyo River had a post office.

Carlin backed Dillon's claim that Mendocino County Indians were inoffensive. Because the Nome Cult employees of the Indian Office cared little for invoking state law or assisting Indians, Carlin recommended that Dillon's detachment be pulled back from Round Valley. At Fort Bragg, Carlin reported that Indian reservation employees regarded Army officers as spies. He said that the Indian Office personnel "dread only the presence of Indians and Army officers." Carlin's outlook for the Indians' future in Mendocino County was gloomy.[19]

Dillon's detailed report on Round Valley and a steady stream of supporting information from Carlin calmed Governor Downey. At the same time, Dillon confided to Carlin: "I am so sick of it all that I would do anything conscientiously to get away from this place. . . ." Still, Dillon added that he truthfully recommended to Carlin that the detachment stay at Round Valley despite the soldiers' low opinion of California settlers and federal Indian agents. In Dillon's view only the presence of Regulars kept some modicum of peace in the valley.[20]

Carlin continued to bicker with officials at the nearby Indian reservation. He accused them of condoning prostitution and liquor sales and allowing squatters on land reserved for Indians. Carlin's reports to San Francisco helped convince the newly appointed superintendent of Indian Affairs, James Y. McDuffie, that somehow Agent

[19] Downey to Clarke, Jan. 18, 1860; and Dillon to Mackall, Jan. 27, 1860; and Dillon to Carlin, Feb. 3, 1860; and Carlin to Mackall, Jan. 25, Feb. 9, 13, and 29, 1860, RG393.

[20] Downey to Clarke, Feb. 8. 1860; and Dillon to Carlin, Feb. 23, 1860; and Carlin to Mackall, Feb. 29, 1860, RG393.

Ford must go. McDuffie recommended that the Mendocino reservation agent be removed.[21]

Another incident needed Carlin's energy. Carlin hurried north some fifty miles in April 1860 to investigate an alleged Indian attack. Arriving at Shelter Cove, the scene of the incident, the Regulars heard one story from local stockmen and quite another from the Indians. According to the stockmen, who had notified the Mendocino reservation of the attack, an Indian leader had haughtily ordered one of their number to remove cattle and horses from grazing lands adjacent to the Indian settlement. Sensing danger, the herder withdrew temporarily, obtained weapons for protection, and headed for the Indian village. There he was surrounded by Indians who severely wounded him with arrows. Only the timely intervention of other herdsmen saved him. They chased off the attacking Indians, killing one in the process.

The Indians, who lived in Shelter Cove because mussels were available, told another version. They said that the whites had demanded women, a demand their spokesman rejected. Lending heavy credence to the Indians' claim was the absence of dead livestock and the awful reality of six dead Indians, all scalped by whites.

With little legal authority, Carlin sought a peaceful solution. He got the stockmen to agree that Indians could continue to live at Shelter Cove without molestation. In their turn, the Indians promised peace and friendship with all persons "passing through their country." Carlin remained in the area an extra couple of days to assure

---

[21] J. Y. McDuffie to Mackall, Feb. 17, 1860; Carlin to McCall, Feb. 29, Mar. 6, and Apr. 3, 1860; Carlin to Dr. Ames, Mar. 2, Apr. 6 and 9, 1860, RG393.

himself that calm prevailed. He placed blame for difficulty on the "misconduct of the whites." Returning to Fort Bragg, Carlin reported to military authorities that Mendocino reservation Indians suffered from poor food and bad medical care. He recommended dismissal of most of the reservation employees, including the medical officer, Dr. Ames.[22]

Carlin saw a way out of his frustration: his years of service qualified him for recruiting duty. He applied for that duty and received official orders to report for recruiting service in the eastern states. Like Major Johnson, Carlin used military procedures to escape unpleasantness in California.[23]

Lieutenant Dillon took command of Fort Bragg on May 8, 1860, leaving the Round Valley detachment in charge of one of the "intelligent and trustworthy" sergeants. Aware of the notoriety accorded Dr. Ames by Army officers, Dillon requested that a military doctor be sent to the coastside post. He objected to being forced to trust the health of his command to the "incompetent and otherwise disqualified" local doctor. The department sent Assistant Surgeon Pascal A. Quinan to Fort Bragg in June.[24]

Dillon checked the Round Valley situation. He found an increased number of Indians on the Nome Cult reservation and ascribed the change to better management. Surprisingly, he described Indian Office employees in Round

[22] Carlin to Ford, Apr. 14, 1860; and Carlin to Mackall, Apr. 25, 1860; and Carlin to Hamilton and Oliver, Apr. 25, 1860, RG393.

[23] Carlin to Mackall, Mar. 27, 29 and May 3, 1860, RG393; PR, Ft. Bragg, Apr. 1860, M617, R138.

[24] Carlin to Mackall, Mar. 27, 1860; and Dillon to Surgeon Charles McCormick, May 17, 1860, RG393; PR, Ft. Bragg, May and June 1860, M617, R138.

Valley as "zealous, kind hearted and faithful." The settlers' persistence in killing Indians continued to trouble him, however. The protracted violence may have been a reaction to the fact that settlers knew the federal government intended to reserve all of Round Valley as Indian land. Dillon doubted the veracity of the settlers' sworn claim of losing one hundred thousand dollars in property to Indian destruction. The lieutenant cross-checked the data and reported that all the taxable property in the valley had a combined value of only thirty thousand dollars.[25]

Army observations on the miserable state of Indian reservations were seconded by California superintendent McDuffie. Journeying to the Mendocino reservation, he learned first-hand from the Indians that they were "much dissatisfied with their condition." He reported to the commissioner of Indian affairs in Washington that at Round Valley, the "killing of Indians is a daily occurrence."

In July 1860 Dillon received an unexpected opportunity to obtain deeper insight on Mendocino reservation affairs. Agent Ford had accidentally killed himself with his own pistol. Superintendent McDuffie had no other federal officials of stature on the Mendocino coast; he asked Dillon to take charge. The Army officer was to supervise the Mendocino reservation until a successor to Ford arrived from the Indian Office.[26]

Dillon did not shirk his new burden. He fired all but four of the reservation employees. Among those dismissed was Dr. Ames. Fort Bragg's military doctor, Surgeon

[25] Dillon to Mackall, May 16, 1860, RG393; PR, Ft. Bragg, June 1860, M617, R138.

[26] McDuffie to Dillon, July 6, 1860, M234, R38; Rogers, "Bear Flag Lieutenant," p. 168; Ex. Doc. 46, Senate, 36th Cong., 1st Sess., pp. 7, 30.

Quinan stepped in to attend reservation Indians. "Out of humanity,"[27]

Taking advantage of his temporary position, Dillon communicated directly with the Commissioner of Indian Affairs in Washington, D.C. He told him that Mendocino reservation agents had condoned the encroachment of money-making businessmen on reservation lands, the presence of "lawless, unprincipled" persons on or near the reservation, and the introduction of "ardent spirits" among the Indian peoples. The effect, said Dillon, had been disastrous. The new agent, J. H. Smith, faced the situation when he assumed his duties and inventoried government property with Dillon in October.[28]

By October Dillon had caused a new round of complaints at Army headquarters in San Francisco. Dillon had let his opinion of California Senator William Gwin be known in Mendocino County. Gwin came to California from Mississippi. Dillon also called Mississippi home. Common origin did not lead to like thought. Gwin charged that Dillon had been "grossly assailing" him. In addition, he said that Dillon had threatened to cause his soldiers to vote in an upcoming primary election, "which is calculated to bring on collisions between them and . . . citizens in that vicinity." According to Gwin, Dillon's continued presence at Fort Bragg disrupted the "peace and harmony of that neighborhood."

Dillon's latest outburst brought an official investigation

---

[27] John G. Dreibelbis to Alfred B. Greenwood, Nov. 22, 1860, M234, R37. The purview of the California Indian Office was split in 1860. McDuffie became supervisor for southern California and John A. Dreibelbis supervised northern California.

[28] Ibid., Dillon to Commissioner, Indian Affairs, Aug. 6, 1860, M234, R37.

by the Army. Artillery captain Joseph Stewart proceeded to Fort Bragg and ascertained that Gwin's charges were correct. Stewart thereupon delivered a letter from General Clarke pointing out Dillon's impropriety and telling him to stay out of California politics. Properly admonished, Dillon retained command of Fort Bragg.[29]

In comparison to the continual Indian Office–Regular Army friction at Fort Bragg, the problems at Fort Ter-waw garrison seemed small. A liquor dealer suddenly set up a nearby shop in the late summer of 1859, and some of the troops could not resist it. Lieutenant Crook quickly responded. He built a new guardhouse on the military post and placed nine soldiers under arrest. Crook determined that Regulars would boycott unscrupulous citizens.[30]

The settlers southwest of Fort Ter-waw had more pressing troubles than Crook. After removal to the Mendocino Indian reservation by California state authorities, groups of Humboldt County Indians made their way back to their traditional grounds. When they returned to the north in the winter months, they were starving and looked to the settlers' livestock. Some forty settlers fled their homesteads ten miles east of Fort Humboldt when Indians attacked cattle. Seeking the protection of numbers, the settlers assembled at a prominent citizen's house in the Bald Hills. Somewhat in a quandry, Major Rains accepted the need to do something. He sent a sergeant and nine infantrymen to the Bald Hills, where they remained through Christmas of 1859.[31]

---

[29] Gwin to W. B. Dameron, Sept. 30, 1860; and Mackall to Captain Joseph Stewart and Mackall to Dillon, Oct. 5, 1860, RG393.

[30] Crook to Mackall, Aug. 30, 1859, RG393; PR, Ft. Ter-waw, Sept. and Oct. 1859, M617, R1262.

During previous episodes of "Indian trouble," Rains had seen state volunteers kill Indians and draw state pay for their acts. The experience had led him to observe sarcastically that "volunteering was considered a good business." Even after thirty-three years in the Army and service in the bitter struggle against the Seminole in Florida, however, Rains was unprepared for what occurred in Humboldt County near the end of February 1860.

New reports reached Fort Humboldt of unrest in the Bald Hills. Rains once more ordered a squad of Regulars out to scout the area. A fresh company of local volunteers formed around Humboldt Bay, a mobilization that Rains blamed on the editor of the *Humboldt Times*. The volunteers headed for the south fork of the Eel River, killed thirty to forty Indians, and waited for reaction from Sacramento. They expected to be mustered into state service for the purpose of putting down the latest locally defined Indian uprising. To their surprise, the state refused to authorize their services or salaries.

The volunteers continued their attacks. On the night of February 25, 1860, they killed nine men and forty-seven women and children at Indian residences on the shores of Humboldt Bay. Crossing to an island in the bay before daylight, they extinguished the lives of an additional three men and fifty-seven women and children. Unopposed, the volunteers swept on to Eagle Prairie and killed another thirty to thirty-five persons. Major Rains described those

---

31 Rains to Mackall, Dec. 16, 1859, RG393; Rains to Hendricks, Apr. 30, 1860, M234, R37; PR, Ft. Humboldt, Dec. 1859, M617, R497; *Humboldt Times*, Dec. 17, 1859, Jan. 7 and 21, 1860. The void in government services was shown when Fort Humboldt troops had to march to the wreck of the civilian steamship *Northerner* in January 1860 to bury bodies and conduct a funeral.

Major Gabriel Jones Rains in his pre-Civil War uniform
Courtesy of Mrs. Jane Tupper Hilliard

who had been killed as "inoffensive" Indians who had "killed nobody, troubled nobody, and nobody's cattle." The Indians had been killed, he wrote, "for no crime whatever," and he underlined the phrase.

Disturbed over the mass murder, the Army moved troops. After traveling by steamer from Benicia, Company H, 6th Infantry, reinforced Fort Humboldt. Two companies of Regulars temporarily garrisoned the post. Under Lieutenant John McCleary, Company H took the field near the end of March 1860.[32]

Major Rains's difficulties were compounded because of a misunderstanding with D. E. Buel, the federal agent on the Klamath reservation. Buel was instructed by his department to remove Indians from Humboldt Bay to the Klamath. Rains, meanwhile, harbored and fed survivors of the Indian massacres. The two government officers conferred on April 9. Buel believed that Rains was both willing and eager for local Indians to go to the Klamath but was concerned over any involuntary displacement. Rains had repeated the often expressed Army policy that soldiers would not use force to move Indians to reservations.

The next morning Rains, to Buel's surprise, announced that he would not allow Indians under asylum at Fort Humboldt to be compelled to move. Should the Indians decline to move to the Klamath, the Army would allow none to starve.

Buel took 124 Indians who had been protected by sympathetic citizens outside the bounds of Fort Humboldt and

---

[32] Rains to Hendricks, Apr. 30, 1860, M234, R37; PR, Ft. Humboldt, Jan. and Mar. 1860, M617, R497. Among critics of the Indian massacre was aspiring editorial writer Bret Harte, who lost his job on the *Northern California* in Union for his stand.

headed for the Klamath. He wrote to Rains of his willingness to transport and feed the Indians who still remained at the Army post. Rains considered that Buel had forcibly and illegally moved the Indians.

Watching the Fort Humboldt scenario, local publisher Austin Wiley sneered that the garrison, unable to protect citizens, might be able to "take care of a few squaws and Indians." Later the same sheet said it was well known "that the Indians readily distinguish U.S. troops from volunteers" and recognized the blue coats as "friends." Major Rains, the editor said, was "better fitted to command a lunatic's cell in Stockton than a military post in Indian country."

Picturing himself as protector of the Indians who remained in the area outside the fort, Rains tried to convince them to go to the reservation. He presumed that he had successfully induced 322 more to move. Buel was sure that his own actions had led to the Indians' decision; he had been unsure of how to handle Rains.

Rains appointed Lieutenant Hardcastle of Fort Humboldt to command a Regular Army escort for the Indians as they traveled to the Klamath. Hardcastle was to "protect them from assassination."

Hardcastle and some 180 Indians reached the mouth of the Klamath River on April 26, 1860. He had been forced to leave behind approximately one hundred aged and infirmed Indians at Redwood Creek under soldiers' protection and with rations for about four days. Nearer to Fort Humboldt another forty Indians awaited assistance to move to the reservation. Hardcastle was in the unexpected position of having to protect three separate groups, and he sent a message to Buel explaining his predicament. Buel collected boats and convoyed Hardcastle's refugees to the Klamath reservation. He sent animals to help transport the Redwood Creek group. After delays caused by gross misunderstandings between Indian agent and Army officers, most of the Indians affected by the February massacre were on the reservation. Buel was busy through September, denying Rains's accusations of forcibly moving Indians. By then, Rains had been transferred from California to another Army post.[33]

Captain Lovell, who had served a year at the post, took command of Fort Humboldt. Company H, 6th Infantry, had returned to San Francisco Bay at the end of May. Lovell, in addition to commanding the fort and Company B, 6th Infantry, also undertook to supply Fort Gaston. For this he employed four civilians, a packmaster, and three packers.

Stock losses, blamed on Indians, continued in the countryside. Lovell, long on the frontier, had a practical solution. He cut a trail from the bay to the Bald Hills to quicken the armed response to settler problems. The trail was not enough for Bald Hills residents, who wanted Regular Army detachments permanently stationed in the vicinity of their dwellings.

Lovell judged such static defenses ineffective and foresaw problems arising from tiny, dispersed detachments without the supervision of an officer or sergeant. Lovell, who had risen from the ranks, thought that in such

---

[33] Hardcastle to Buel, Apr. 26, 1860; and Rains to Hendricks, Apr. 30, 1860; and Buel to McDuffie, Aug. 1, 1860; and McDuffie to Greenwood, Sept. 7, 1860, M234, R37; PR, Ft. Humboldt, Apr. 1860, M617, R497; *Humboldt Times*, Mar. 3, Apr. 28, and May 19, 1860.

situations loose liquor posed a greater danger to his troops than angry Indians. He would husband his command for the time being.[34]

Many of the Indians removed to the Klamath reservation during the spring of 1860 were rumored to have returned to Humboldt Bay. On a Sunday evening in September, a citizen reported to Lovell that forty to fifty Indians were lurking near his dwelling on the opposite side of the bay from the Army post.

Lovell formed a small party of Regulars. Through good fortune, the small steamer *Shubric* was available to transport the soldiers across the water before sunset. Searching the sand hills, Lovell after some time came upon two male Indians. He explained to them the "very great risk" of returning to the Humboldt Bay area from the Klamath reservation. Lovell asked the pair to advise all the other Indians in the strictest terms to go back to the Klamath reservation for safety. While obtaining promises to do just that, the Army officer supposed that the Indians would evade his observation and turn south to the Eel River.

Danger to Indians was real, on and off the reservation. Fifty-five local petitioners beseeched Lovell to use the force at his command and return Indians to the Klamath. They expected the Army to "teach them that they *must* stay at the Reservation." Meanwhile, a newspaper reported food shortages at the Klamath reservation.[35]

How the Army was to enforce compliance was a matter of debate. In the spring of 1859 Inspector General Colonel

34 Lovell to Mackall, July 18 and Aug. 1, 1860, RG393; PR, Ft. Humboldt, May–Aug. 1860, M617, R497.

35 Lovell to Mackall, Oct. 3 and 5, 1860, RG393; PR, Ft. Humboldt, Nov. 1860, M617, R497.

Joseph K. F. Mansfield again toured military posts in northern California and raised concerns about enforcement ability in general. Although he was impressed by the discipline and youthful appearance of Company B, 6th Infantry, at Fort Humboldt and pleased with the "excellent" bread at the post bakery, he noted several practical problems that limited the effectiveness of the troops. The infantry at Fort Humboldt, for example, was short of canteens. At Fort Ter-waw the troops still carried the musket that the Army had taken out of service in 1855. The most crippling problem did not relate to equipment, however. According to Mansfield, the posts were hampered by the shortage of officers, and he showed particular concern about the shortage at Fort Crook. Without more officers, Mansfield saw no means of sending patrols any distance from the post. The men, he said, needed training; "some . . . have never fired a pistol from a horse." Mansfield recommended that more officers be sent to Fort Crook. He looked to West Point graduates to train the garrisons of California.[36]

---

[36] "Mansfield Reports" (1859).

Chapter 8
1859–1860

Troubles and Triumphs
East of the Redwoods

*The positions held by our troops . . . are, in the main,
. . . the best to secure the peace of our territories and to
give protection to our frontiers and the overland routes
to the Pacific.*
Annual Report of the Secretary of War (1859)

Captain John Adams, an energetic West Point graduate
who had been breveted for actions in the Mexican War,
took command of Fort Crook on California's Fall River in
January 1859. He assumed the dual role of managing the
post and leading Company F, 1st Dragoons. Lieutenant
Carr also held twin functions; he fulfilled post supply
duties, with the assistance of Lieutenant Mercer, and
commanded Company A, 1st Dragoons.

Supply problems sent Carr south in February to chide
quartermaster and subsistence officers at headquarters for
better support. Lieutenant Mercer also rode out of Fort
Crook in February. His mission was to take an armed
detachment and sweep the road to Red Bluff. Once in

Red Bluff, Mercer was to pick up ammunition con-
signed to Fort Crook. Snow ten feet deep slowed travel.
Mercer returned to post on March 23 and Carr on
March 29, 1859.[1]

Before the snow melted, Governor Weller once more
complained over supposed Indian outrages in Tehama
County. He sent a petition bearing twelve signatures to
department headquarters, asking for immediate protection. The petitioners claimed that Indians were burning
their dwellings and driving them from their homes.

Not wishing to deploy Fort Crook's precious cavalry
resource, headquarters dipped into the department's
infantry units. Company A, 6th Infantry, was ordered
north from Benicia. Commanded by Captain Franklin F.
Flint, Company A was to establish Camp Cass across the
Sacramento River from Red Bluff.[2]

Flint's expedition turned into a fiasco. While the troops
were on a riverboat en route to Red Bluff, at a cost of
$1,685, one of the enlisted men fell overboard, disappeared,
and was presumed drowned. Shortly after Flint arrived in
Red Bluff, the unit's trouser supply proved to be insufficient.
In addition, the reception the company received from the
locals was unenthusiastic. On May 27, 1859, the day after
arriving at the site, Flint met with prominent citizens and
surmised that they would have preferred the governor's
authorization of state volunteers to the presence of the
Regular Army. The Army, the citizens believed, would
not go far enough. Citizens had already hired "scalp

---

[1] PR, Ft. Crook, Jan.-Mar. 1859, M617, R271.

[2] Weller to Clarke, May 18, 1859, RG393; PR, Camp Cass, June 1859, M617,
R1501. Among the petitioners to Governor Weller was Henley, the deposed superintendent of the Office of Indian Affairs.

hunters," despite the criticism of the Red Bluff newspaper, and the settlers around Camp Cass favored similar action. They asked Flint if he was authorized to commence a war of extermination against their alleged tormentors. Flint gave them a copy of his official orders and stated that he had no instructions for such a campaign. The citizens were dissatisfied with Flint's orders and even more dissatisfied with Flint's personal opinion that lawless whites were responsible for the recent burning of a settler's house.[3]

Flint sent small scouting parties into open terrain and around settlements. They found nothing. The lack of progress prompted State Adjutant General Kibbe to offer the Regulars help. Flint informed Kibbe that he deemed his company of the 6th Infantry "sufficient to check the hostile incursions of any Indians in this vicinity." Disease proved more dangerous to Camp Cass than Indians. Illness struck nine of the forty-eight men and then Flint himself.[4]

Second Lieutenant Archibald I. Harrison joined Flint's command at Camp Cass. The camp finally mounted a major scouting expedition on June 28. Under Harrison's leadership, a sergeant, two corporals, and twenty privates scoured the hills. This expedition, like the one before it, found nothing. Harrison reinforced Flint's belief that the reported Indian depredations were exaggerations designed to provide certain Tehama County elements with an excuse to eradicate any remaining Indians.

Harrison left fourteen men in the hills to watch for

<hr>

[3] Flint to Mackall, May 27 and June 1, 1859, RG393; Heizer and Almquist, *The Other Californians*, p. 29.

[4] Ibid.; PR, Camp Cass, June-July 1859, M617, R1501; Adjutant Gen. W. C. Kibbe, *Report of Expedition Against the Indians in the Northern Part of the State* (Sacramento: 1860), pp. 7, 26.

Indian movement. He returned to Camp Cass with the remainder of his scouts on July 12. Flint went to Benicia, seeking medical care, while Harrison took command of Camp Cass until the last day of August. Apparently convinced that gyrations through Tehama hill country offered little in a military career, Harrison resigned from the Army.[5]

While citizens around Camp Cass knew the contents of Flint's orders, Indians around Fort Crook were unaware of new orders received by Captain Adams. The fort had provisioned Indians during the winter of 1858–1859. Army-wide cuts in military appropriations demanded economy, however, so headquarters instructed Adams to reduce food for Indians. The orders also reminded him to avoid hostile feelings with local Indian bands—an order that conflicted with other instructions. Farther north other Indians, the Modoc, attacked a wagon train.

In Washington, D.C., and San Francisco, Army officials agreed that any savings that resulted from administrative economy would be negated by warfare. Somehow, Adams was to keep the peace. The captain did placate Indians somewhat by using troops to intervene in a murder case involving Indians. His efforts were poorly rewarded by the Army. In July orders for even stricter economy arrived from headquarters. At Fort Crook the War Department wanted Army rations for Indians "*restricted* to occasional and very limited quantities, in individual cases."[6]

---

[5] PR, Camp Cass, June-Aug. 1859; and Camp Taylor, Sept. 1859, M617, R1501, 1545.

[6] Mackall to Adams, May 20 and 21, 1859; and Adams to Mackall, June 23 and July 16, 1859, RG393; Murray, *Modocs*, p. 32. Adams's initial orders were to stop feeding local Indians, but these directions were quickly modified.

Confederate Brig. Gen. John Adams
As Captain he commanded Fort Crook, 1859–61
Courtesy of Tennessee State Library and Archives, Nashville

In addition to maintaining calm in the Pit and Fall river valleys, Fort Crook once again received the task of restoring a measure of tranquility to the Honey Lake area. Citizens there called for troops in June 1859, claiming a need for protection. Fort Crook housed 108 serviceable government horses and a garrison trained as cavalry. The men from Fort Crook could move across northern California faster than any other garrison when troops were needed. By good fortune, thirty-four cavalry recruits arrived at Fort Crook in July 1859, just in time to join the Honey Lake excursion. Although the officer-escort had lost the recruits' military records, Adams parceled the new men out to Companies A and F.[7]

On July 8 the fifty soldiers of Company A, led by Lieutenant Carr, departed Fort Crook for an eighty-mile march. Adams wanted Carr to report on the necessity of stationing troops at Honey Lake. Carr arrived at his destination on July 21. He established a temporary bivouac and named it Camp Mackall, in honor of the adjutant general of the Department of California. The camp was on the Susan River, downstream from the outlet of Honey Lake. Carr selected an ideal site, one that commanded the Emigrant Road from the Humboldt River, the Willow Creek trail, and two key passes used by Indians. In the dragoons' five supply wagons were enough rations for two months.

Information about emigrants, not Indians, passed back to Fort Crook from Honey Lake. Carr advised Adams that large numbers of emigrants were reported to be on the trail to California from Salt Lake. Seeking to ease the journey

---

7 Mackall to Adams and Mackall to John H. Neal, June 23, 1859, RG393; PR, Ft. Crook, May and July 1859, M617, R271.

A View of Mount Lassen in 1855
From the Pacific Railroad Surveys publications

of their fellow Americans, soldiers improved a crossing of the Susan River between Honey Lake and Pillow Creek and not far from their camp. Their work became known as Dragoon Bridge, or Soldier Bridge. Of Indians they saw none.[8]

While Company A, 1st Dragoons, enjoyed the peace of Honey Lake, trouble struck closer to Fort Crook. At Hat Creek Station Indians killed a settler in August. A twenty-man detachment led by a newly assigned, Maryland-born lieutenant, Richard H. Brewer, scouted for tracks, picked up a trail, and pursued the murderers. After twice encountering a group of some forty to sixty Indians armed with modern rifles, Brewer attacked. Two Indians died. Settlers seeking revenge for the murder also attacked Indians. They struck on Beaver Creek, mistakenly hitting a rancheria of innocents. The sudden deaths of settlers and Indians upset the delicate balance of peace.[9]

Aware of the approaching emigrants' wagon trains and sensitive to local threats, Adams sent parties out to protect the most-traveled trails. One group of soldiers patrolled the road along Hat Creek; another group protected the Oregon Trail north of Fort Crook. Already in position, the Honey Lake detachment guarded the California Trail, where during the summer twelve hundred wagons passed into California from the east.[10]

Looking for ways to reinforce Adams's thinly spread

---

[8] Ft. Crook Orders No. 280, July 7, 1859; Carr to Adams, July 28, 1859; "Map of Honey Lake," Lt. J. Hamilton, 3d Artillery 1860, RG393.

[9] PR, Ft. Crook, Aug. 1859, M617, R271; Headquarters of the Army, Gen. Orders, No. 5, Nov. 10, 1859; Heizer, *Indians*, p. 243.

[10] PR, Ft. Crook, Sept. and Dec. 1859, M617, R271; Asa Merrill Fairfield, *Fairfield's Pioneer History of Lassen County, California* (San Francisco: H. S. Crocker Co., 1916), pp. 157, 180.

Fort Crook garrison, department headquarters decided that Captain Flint's command had accomplished little in Tehama County. Flint agreed and hoped to return to Benicia. Instead, his orders sent him on a 110-mile march to the Pit River.

Headquarters expected Flint to cooperate with Captain Adams to protect the Red Bluff–Yreka road. They planned no indiscriminate warfare against the Pit River Indians, but any attacks on public roadways or on settlements would receive an instant reaction. If the ground called for cavalry tactics, Adams's men were to ride out and members of Company A, 6th Infantry, were to take up their guard duties. Similarly, when the ground was more suitable for infantry, Flint's men were to pursue and the 1st Dragoons were to cover the camp on the Pit. [11]

Flint arrived at the Pit River on September 15 and set up camp five miles southeast of Fort Crook near the Fall River–Pit River junction. He posted a half dozen men at the bridge and the ferry crossing. Having complied with military orders, Flint immediately made plain his desire to be far south of the Pit before winter. [12]

Before Flint's pleas reached headquarters, Indians attacked again and California State Adjutant General Kibbe and state volunteers entering the area vastly complicated the situation. Adams was displeased. He wanted cool, consistent heads, not volunteers. Despite the presence of Captain Flint, Adams dismounted twenty of his dragoons

---

[11] Mackall to Flint, Sept. 1, 1859, RG393; PR, Camp Taylor, Sept. 1859, M617, R1545.

[12] Flint to Mackall, Sept. 17 and Oct. 6, 1859; and Mackall to Flint, Sept. 26, 1859; and Carr to Adams, Oct. 14, 1859, RG393; PR, Ft. Crook, Sept. 1859, M617, R271.

and sent them under command of Lieutenant Carr into the network formed by Beaver, Canoe, and Hat creeks.

Long-time civilian guide Pugh went with Carr. Two friendly Indians joined the reconnaissance party as guides and interpreters. To gain firepower, Carr swung by Flint's camp and picked up a sergeant and nine infantry privates. By then, Kibbe's volunteers already had done their damage. The Regulars encountered no Indians, friendly or unfriendly; all had fled into hiding before the California volunteers. On September 28 Lieutenant Carr halted his men, who were weary from slogging in damp terrain for ten days. They dried out wet blankets and cleaned weapons. Carr resumed his march, covered 137 miles on foot, and returned to Fort Crook on October 4.

Carr's uneventful tour was good news for Flint. If Adams thought that the 6th Infantry was not needed on the Pit, Flint would be allowed to return to barracks at Benicia. Adams was probably weary of Flint's uninspired contingent and complaints of sickness. He decided that his 1st Dragoons could protect the Yreka road. By the end of October, Company A, 6th Infantry, was gone from the Pit.

Kibbe's complement of state volunteers had gone too. The resentment caused by the volunteers around the Pit remained. Kibbe summarized the ill will on both sides in a report to Sacramento: "[The] citizens are prejudiced against the officers at Fort Crook and vice versa." On his part Lieutenant Brewer had allegedly stated that only two of the sixty to eighty citizens in the Pit River Valley were decent Americans. Kibbe admitted that local settlers had exacted revenge on Indians. Of the actions by his volunteers he wrote that "no children were killed, and but one woman."

The volunteers had killed two hundred males and sent twelve hundred prisoners to Round Valley.[13]

The approach of winter brought two field detachments of dragoons in from the trails where they had been on guard since August. Lieutenant Carr transferred to a new assignmènt. Fellow Southerner and West Point classmate Alfred B. Chapman replaced him at Fort Crook. Horses also needed replacing. Seven in Carr's company were classified as unserviceable.[14]

In November the chief commissary officer of the Department of California learned to his surprise that Fort Crook was short of rations. The inventory at Fort Crook contained enough beans and soap for only two months, pork and salt for one month, and but a half-month supply of sugar. Colonel Thomas Swords discovered that although he had turned over a year's subsistence to the department's quartermaster for movement during the summer months, the food reposed at Red Bluff with the quartermaster's agent, awaiting transportation.

An infantry officer who specialized in quartermaster's duties, Captain Treadwell Moore, arrived at Fort Crook in December 1859 to give Adams technical assistance. Another new member of the post commander's staff, Assistant Surgeon Edward P. Vollum, reported for duty, too late to help Adams with a new problem. For the first time since its founding, disease had taken a toll in the garrison; three men had died.[15]

---

[13] Kibbe to Weller, Sept. 30 and Nov. 29, 1859, Calif. State Ārchives.

[14] PR, Ft. Crook, Oct.-Nov. 1859, M617, R271.

[15] Captain M.D.L. Simpson to Swords, Nov. 21, 1859, RG393; PR, Ft. Crook, July, Sept., Oct., and Dec. 1859, M617, R271. Moore probably carried instruc-

Vollum's scientific interests extended beyond the limits of medicine. His assignment to Fort Crook brought him to an Army post that enjoyed strong but unofficial ties with the Smithsonian Institution in Washington, D.C. The original post commander, Captain Gardiner, had maintained a long-standing relationship with the assistant secretary of the Smithsonian, Spencer F. Baird. From Fort Crook, Gardiner had shipped examples of Indian fishnets to him for the institution's collection.[16]

At Fort Crook, Vollum eagerly set about testing atmospheric conditions with materials supplied by Baird. Seeing a breed of grasshopper that destroyed local gardens, a strange sight to his New York eyes, Vollum captured some of the insects in a glass enclosure. He scientifically observed their habits and reported the results regularly to Baird, who in January 1861 deemed Vollum's notes worthy of publication.

Vollum, like other officers at Fort Crook, quickly grew to admire Sergeant John Feilner of the 1st Dragoons. A German-born enlisted man, "indefatigable, enthusiastic and sagacious," Feilner was also the Smithsonian's champion bird collector at Fort Crook. He sent one large collection to Baird before Vollum taught him how to use a camera. Pleased with the steady stream of material to the Smithsonian from Fort Crook, Baird mailed Vollum two books to aid the garrison in identifying specimens during their off-duty pursuit of natural science: Zantus' *Collection*

---

tions to restore proper accounting procedures. The post staff of Fort Crook had been criticized for its handling of surplus flour (see Proceedings of F Company Council, Fort Crook, Dec. 31, 1859, RG393).

[16] *Annual Report of the Smithsonian Institution* (1859), (Washington, D.C.: Thomas H. Ford, Printer, 1860), p. 74.

of Birds and Cooper's *Distribution of Forests and Trees of North America.*[17]

Vollum advised Baird that Sergeant Feilner "is willing to face any danger to gratify his taste for Natural History." Feilner met danger when he set out for Klamath and Rhett lakes in the spring of 1860 to collect birds, eggs, and nests for the Smithsonian. Captain Adams authorized the sergeant a military leave of twenty days to collect ornithological specimens for the national museum. Concerned about his sergeant traveling alone in northern California, the post commander allowed a second enlisted man to accompany Feilner. They collected several specimens before reaching the Klamath River on May 19. Smoke from an Indian settlement warned Feilner of possible danger. The next day an Indian leader, unimpressed by the sergeant's scientific endeavors, told him to get out of Klamath territory.

Heading south, Feilner fortuitously met and joined a group of local stockmen. Assuming that there would be safety in numbers, Feilner and the herders tried to mollify distrustful Indians by talking with them. Feilner and the three other would-be peacemakers ended up fleeing for their lives.

The four holed-up in a deserted cabin and beat off some thirty to forty attackers. They shifted to a second cabin, where the other herders and Feilner's soldier-companion joined them. The group counterattacked and drove the Indians out of the valley. Feilner returned to Fort Crook on May 27 with but five specimens. He told Vollum that if

[17] Vollum to Baird, Dec. 14, 1859, Mar. 28 and Nov. 28, 1860; and Baird to Vollum, Jan. 5, 1861, Smithsonian Inst. Archives. Vollum told Baird that he had sent him a photograph of Feilner. It was not found during a search at the Smithsonian in 1979.

left unmolested at the lakes, "he could fill a canoe with eggs in an hour."[18]

Other soldiers at Fort Crook collected for the Smithsonian as well. The enlisted man detailed to chop firewood for the garrison gathered specimens of tree bark. A member of the Honey Lake detachment took along material with which to conduct atmospheric tests there. Apprised of Vollum's interest, several Indians brought "quite a number" of birds and eggs to the doctor.

Nearer to hand, Vollum's own assistant, Hospital Steward David F. Parkinson, showed interest in the garrison's scientific program. Intelligent, industrious, and "a prime shot," Parkinson amassed the skins of some ninety different bird species plus those of several animals for the Smithsonian. In the spring of 1861, he switched to collecting plants. In a subtle attempt to renew Parkinson's interest in bird eggs and nests, Baird sent the hospital corpsman an egg drill.[19]

Several years before the burst of scientific collecting activity at Fort Crook, another Army doctor gathered specimens for the Smithsonian at Fort Reading. Assistant Surgeon John F. Hammond collected bats, hare, fish, predatory birds, crickets, grasshoppers, moths, and samples of mollusks from the Sacramento River. Hammond, who was used to the heat of his native South Carolina, told Baird that in "summer the sun is as hot as it is at Sierra

---

[18] Vollum to Baird, May 29, 1860, Smithsonian Archives; *Annual Report, Smithsonian* (1864), pp. 421–24. Feilner's Klamath adventure is told in Donald K. Smith, *Sergeant Feilner's Furlough* (Chico, Calif.: Assoc. for Northern California Records and Research, 1977).

[19] Vollum to Baird, May 21, Nov. 3 and 28, 1860 and Apr. 20, 1861, Smithsonian Archives; *Annual Report, Smithsonian* (1862), p. 66.

Leon! [*sic*]" Despite swampy conditions, Hammond collected well. Before the end of the summer of 1855 he had preserved squirrels in alcohol and sent them to Baird.[20]

From his faraway military post, Hammond also corresponded with the Army's surgeon general in Washington, D.C., on scientific matters. The phenomena of communicable diseases especially interested Hammond. Studying the latest in published medical books and weighing them against his own military experience, Hammond remained unconvinced that cholera was a contagious disease. He so informed the Army's surgeon general.

When Williamson's Pacific Railroad Exploring Party assembled at Fort Reading in the summer of 1855, Hammond's scientific bent proved of great value. To help Williamson increase the accuracy of altitude computations along the route to be explored, Hammond volunteered to make a series of barometric observations at Fort Reading while Williamson was away. Using a barometer left behind by Williamson, the post doctor compiled statistics as requested.[21]

Barometric observation came naturally to Hammond in his military routine. Like all post medical officers, he was supposed to render monthly reports on local meteorology. At northern California Army posts, surgeons routinely registered the temperatures, measured rainfall, and noted wind direction and cloud cover. At Fort Humboldt the surgeon recorded 266 fair days and 99 cloudy days in 1854. The cloudy days included fifty-five with rain and

[20] Hammond to Baird, June 21, Aug. 7, Sept. 18 and Oct. 14, 1855, Smithsonian Archives; *Annual Report, Smithsonian* (1862).

[21] Hammond to Lawson, June 1, 1855, RG112; *Reports of Explorations*, vol. 6, p. 58.

two with snow. The War Department consolidated the surgeons' nationwide findings and shared the data with the Smithsonian.[22]

Lieutenant George Crook, who served over most of northern California for more than eight years, directed his spare-time interests to ethnology. Crook compiled vocabulary lists for the Yurok, Kurok, Hoopa, and Tolowa languages. His list of Hoopa and Tolowa terms totaled 180 words each.[23]

The Topographical Engineers sent Lieutenant Joseph C. Ives from Washington, D.C., in 1860 to help determine the location of the eastern boundary of California. Ives expanded his role by becoming one of the first astronomers in the state.[24]

While scientific inquiry continued, disorders spilled over into Honey Lake Valley again. Rumors of animosity between citizens of what would soon be Nevada and Paiute resulted in orders to Fort Crook. Dragoons were to go to Honey Lake to prevent trouble between settlers and Indians.

Lieutenants Chapman and Brewer started for the valley with Company A, 1st Dragoons on May 16, 1860. The

[22] Crane to Surgeon General, Feb. 2, 1853; and Hammond to Lawson, June 1, 1855; and Henry to Lawson, Jan. 23, 1856, RG112; *Sickness and Mortality in the Army*, vol. 2, pp. 557–58, 589, 601–02.

[23] Buchanan to Townsend, Aug. 18 and Oct. 1, 1853, RG393; Catalog to manuscripts at the National Anthropological Archives, National Museum of Natural History (Washington, D.C.: Smithsonian Institution), p. 471; Heizer, *Indians*, p. 729.

[24] Ives to Major Hartman Bache, Aug. 1, 1861, LR; Topographical Bureau, War Dept., 1824–65, M506, R31; *ARSW* (1860), vol. 2, p. 300; *ARSW* (1861), vol. 2, p. 127; Francis D. Uzes, *Chaining the Land* (Sacramento: Landmark Enterprises, 1977), p. 75; James W. Hulsa, "The California-Nevada Boundary: History of Conflict," *Nevada Hist. Soc. Quarterly*, vol. XXIII (Summer 1980), no. 2, pp. 94–95.

wagons mired in deep mud. Chapman left a guard detail with them and pushed ahead. After a forced march Chapman and Company A reached Honey Lake on May 22. They encamped at Dragoon Bridge.

No bloodshed had occurred in the Honey Lake Valley, but across the state boundary whites had taken the law into their own hands by abusing Paiute Indians. Nevadans paid a high price when the Paiute struck back.

A sergeant and nine men from Company F, 1st Dragoons, had started from Fort Crook to reinforce Chapman's group. Their hard ride was wasted. Using a new civil telegraph line to help transmit orders, headquarters recalled the dragoons to Fort Crook. Half of Company A journeyed to the Carson River Valley while the others closed down company operations at Fort Crook. On August 8 Company A, 1st Dragoons, was formally transferred from Fort Crook to Carson River. In the opinion of Honey Lake residents, Chapman had accomplished nothing. He left them "unprotected."[25]

The 3d Artillery as before turned out a detachment to act as infantry, this time for Honey Lake. Selected for duty on the Sierra flank, 1st Lieutenant John Hamilton led his men from the Presidio of San Francisco. After a laborious uphill march of 148 miles from Marysville, the cannoneers descended into the Honey Lake Valley on July 3, 1860. On the Fourth of July, valley residents hosted Hamilton and presented him with eggnog, dinner, and salutes.

---

[25] Mackall to Adams, Mar. 22, 1860; and Chapman to Mackall, May 16, 1860, RG393; Vollum to Baird, May 29, 1860, Smithsonian Archives; PR, Ft. Crook, May-Aug. 1860, M617, R271; Fairfield, *Lassen County*, p. 216.

Hamilton found Dragoon Bridge a perfect tactical location. Practically, though, Hamilton wondered how useful he could be at the site without scouts. Checking local informants, he discovered that no Indians had lived in the valley since the previous year, when one was brutally whipped by a settler for a supposed theft.

Hamilton judged that the area was overstocked with cattle. Neglected stock became lost and often the loss was charged to Indian theft. The settlers expressed much alarm over the Paiute. Some citizens even evacuated the eastern portion of the valley. The artillery officer saw no sign of warring Indians. In Hamilton's opinion, Company I, 3d Artillery, served at Dragoon Bridge only to calm settlers. Moreover, an Interior Department road builder had joined Carson Valley and Honey Lake residents in pursuit of Indians and concluded a truce with organized Paiutes.

Uncharmed by Honey Lake, Hamilton complained, "I have never seen snakes so plentiful." He killed three scorpions in his tent and termed mail service "worse than poor." Receiving word that the expedition was to remain at Honey Lake throughout the coming winter, he pleaded for a lower-ranking lieutenant to take his place.[26]

Hamilton's desires were met. On September 13, 2d Lieutenant Edward R. Warner arrived at Hamilton's camp with orders to take command of a twenty-man detachment at Dragoon Bridge. Four days later Hamilton left for San Francisco with twenty-seven of his men. A sergeant, two corporals, and seventeen privates remained with Warner in the mountains.

[26] Hamilton to Mackall, July 13, 1860, RG393; PR, Dragoon Bridge, Aug. 1860, M617, R1508; Fairfield, *Lassen County*, p. 230; W. Turrentine Jackson, *Wagon Roads West* (Lincoln: Univ. of Nebraska Press, 1979). pp. 216–17; San Francisco *Alta California*, July 17, 1860.

Cadet Edward R. Warner.
On graduation from West Point, he commanded at Dragoon's Bridge, 1860–61

Warner got an extra twenty rifles before Hamilton departed for San Francisco, enough with which to arm a sizable body of local volunteers if necessary. Such potentially drastic action deviated from normal procedures, but Warner's snowbound isolation warranted unusual precaution. Headquarters instructed Warner to act with great prudence. Orders restricted him from attacking Indians except in defense of lives or property. Warner moved into winter quarters, appointed a sutler, and arranged for medical service from a civilian.[27]

The strength and mobility of the garrison at Fort Crook had been halved by the transfer of Company A, 1st Dragoons, out of California. Fort Crook's remaining soldiers were still responsible for protecting emigrant groups and highway travel between California and Oregon. Cavalry reinforcements were unavailable. A company of the 6th Infantry was ordered to Fort Crook from Benicia as a partial solution to the manpower shortage. Infantry could free the horse soldiers for long-distance security and, during their absence, take care of garrison duties.

Captain Adams must have been relieved to see Company E, 6th Infantry, under West Point graduate Lieutenant James A. Smith rather than Company A and the complaining Captain Flint. Company E, with only forty-seven men, arrived at Fort Crook on August 5, 1860. Before the end of the year, more foot soldiers joined the infantry company, including 2d Lieutenant John J. Upham and thirty-two recruits.[28]

---

[27] Mackall to Hamilton, Aug. 20, 1860, RG393; PR, Dragoon Bridge, Sept.-Oct. 1860, M617, R1508. Warner, ten years junior to Hamilton and sent on duty that Hamilton found disagreeable, survived the Civil War as a brigadier general of volunteers. Hamilton finished the war one grade lower, as a brevet colonel.

The infantry held the fort at the end of September, when Lieutenant Mercer conducted a scouting party from Company F, 1st Dragoons. Returning in October, Company F saw one of its own former enlisted men promoted from the ranks. A board of officers at higher echelons approved the commission of Sergeant Henry S. Pearce to second lieutenant. He became the first non–West Point officer assigned to Fort Crook.

Mercer rode out again in December to reconnoiter better routes for reaching Red Bluff from Fort Crook. Despite reports to the contrary, Mercer found both the Dobbins Road and the McElroy Road unsuitable for wagons. The Dobbins cutoff had a steep, mile-long hill. The McElroy Road ran through deep sand and deeper mud. Fort Crook wagons, he concluded, would be better off going by Thomas Ferry and along the Oak Run to reach Red Bluff.[29]

Seven years after Colonel George Wright first spanned the upper Sacramento with troops, the Army still sought peace between settlers and natives in northeastern California. Captain Adams fed Indians at Fort Crook. His men patrolled public thoroughfares. At Honey Lake, soldiers had become a permanent fixture.

While Company E settled in at Fort Crook, Company D, 6th Infantry remained on station at Fort Bragg under Lieutenant Dillon. The only officer present at Fort Bragg, Dillon had multiple administrative duties. He commanded

---

[28] *ARSW* (1860), p. 110; PR, Ft. Crook, Aug., Nov., and Dec. 1860, M617, R271.

[29] Mercer to Pearce, Dec. 5, 1860, RG393; PR, Ft. Crook, Sept.-Nov. 1860, M617, R271. Pearce lost his commission after Captain Adams determined that the ex-sergeant was an alcoholic; Ltr., George R. Stammerjohan, Calif. Dept. of Parks and Recreation, Oct. 5, 1990.

the post and supervised one or more detachments in the field. In December 1860 help arrived; freshly graduated from West Point, 2d Lieutenant James P. Martin joined Dillon's force. Martin came with thirty enlisted recruits to strengthen Company D.

Dillon put Martin temporarily in command of Fort Bragg on the day after Christmas. Despite the season, Dillon set off for Shelter Cove, a perennial trouble spot. Satisfied that there were no new problems, he returned to Fort Bragg and sent Lieutenant Martin on a march to Long Valley. Martin returned after thirteen days in the countryside without incident.[30]

Farther north at Fort Humboldt, forty-seven soldiers were added to the ranks of Company B, 6th Infantry. Daniel D. Lynn, a West Point classmate of Lieutenant Martin of Fort Bragg, joined Captain Lovell's command. Anxious to check reports of Indian hostility in the Bald Hills, Lovell ordered Lynn out with a reconnaissance force of thirty men. They left Fort Humboldt four days before Christmas, but heavy rain and snow drove the party back into the post before the end of the month.[31]

While Company B awaited favorable weather, Lovell continued morale-building efforts. Sensitive to the fact that his men were far from home, Lovell subscribed to newspapers from Washington, D.C., New York, Cincinnati, and New Orleans, plus a Humboldt County paper, *Northern Californian.* He also saw to it that the fort received *Harper's Monthly, Knickerbocker Monthly,* and several temperance publications. Special twenty-five–pound purchases

---

[30] PR, Ft. Bragg, Dec. 1860 and Feb.-Mar. 1861, M617, R138; Legislature of the State of Calif., "Mendocino Indian War," p. 7.

[31] PR, Ft. Humboldt, Nov.-Dec. 1860, M617, R497.

of pepper enlivened Company B's meals. All these purchases came about from Lovell's able administration of the company fund. A long-standing American Army tradition, the company fund sought to improve the enlisted men's comfort and morale.[32]

Other northern California posts followed similar procedures. Fort Ter-waw purchased garden seeds, hops, and potatoes, as did the Regular Army at Fort Bragg. An extra $11.50 supplemented Christmas rations at Fort Ter-waw in 1859; two years earlier the company at Fort Jones had spent $36.90 to enliven Christmas. Athletics were not overlooked. Fort Ter-waw allocated $3.50 for a football and Fort Crook spent $40.00 for ten-pin bowling balls. The post expenditures of the cavalrymen at Fort Crook were unsurpassed; the men spent six hundred dollars for books.[33]

While Lovell and Lynn waited for clear skies, mail to Fort Humboldt was delayed for two weeks. Official correspondence finally reached Lovell on January 18, 1861, informing him that the Department of California and the Department of Oregon had once again been merged into the single, unified Department of the Pacific. In San Francisco, Brigadier General Albert S. Johnston assumed command of the department.[34]

---

[32] Fund Account of Company B, 6th Infantry, Dec. 31, 1858, Dec. 31, 1859, and Apr. 30, 1860, RG393.

[33] Company Fund Proceedings of Company D, 4th Infantry, Dec. 31, 1858, Aug. 31 and Dec. 31, 1859, and Apr. 30, 1860; and Company D, 6th Infantry, Apr. 30 and Dec. 31, 1859; and Company E, 4th Infantry, Dec. 31, 1857; and Company A, 1st Dragoons, Dec. 31, 1857 and Apr. 30, 1858, RG393.

[34] PR, Ft. Humboldt, Jan. 1861, M617, R497.

Chapter 9
1861

Out of The Redwoods

It does seem to me that in the 'Cotton States' & especially in South Carolina reason has been dethroned and her place usurped by the Demon of fanaticism.

Lieutenant James B. McPherson, San Francisco, December 18, 1860

The Regular Army started its tenth year in the northern counties of California hurt by severe logistics problems. Treasury Department funds for the Army were below needs. General Albert Sydney Johnston described his command as in "a state of pauperism." At Fort Bragg barracks construction was halted to save money.

Potential food shortages threatened two northern posts. Rations at Fort Humboldt would be exhausted in thirty days; subsistence at Fort Bragg was provided for only another two months. At other Regular Army posts north of Sacramento, sufficient rations were on hand until summer, but there were other problems. Fort Crook, for example, was garrisoned by an infantry company and a cavalry company, and each was armed with weapons of different caliber. Captain Adams required rifle musket cartridges for his 6th Infantry troops, but his own 1st Cavalry troops needed Sharp's carbine cartridges and primers plus Colt pistol cartridges and percussion caps.[1]

Johnston reported the situation of the Department of the Pacific to Washington. Closer to San Francisco, the governor of California, John G. Downey, compounded Johnston's immediate problems. Downey complained over "continued outrages of the Indians" in Mendocino, Humboldt, and Trinity counties. He needled Johnston, pointing out that previous commanders had taken prompt measures against marauders. Downey threatened to send state-hired volunteers into the northern counties if the Regular Army lacked sufficient force to protect lives and property.[2]

Forces from northern California posts had actually been in the field weeks before Downey's complaint. After receiving rumors of Indians blocking routes to Red Bluff, troops at Fort Crook mounted a show of force in January 1861. The cavalrymen found over one hundred Indians near McElroy's Bridge, but no hint of disorder existed. A pair of residents at the bridge felt no apprehension over Indians. Likewise, no citizen complained of the several hundred Indians closer to Fort Crook. Stories of the Pit River Indian groups holding cattle seemed farfetched when nobody had reported missing livestock.

Captain Adams wrote that "the white inhabitants of this

---

[1] Dillon to Mackall, Nov. 20, 1860; and Quarterly Return of Ordnance and Ordnance Stores, Mar. 31, 1861, 1st Lt. J. A. Smith, Capt. J. Adams, RG393; *Official Records of the Union and Confederate Armies* (Washington: Gov. Printing Office, 1897), vol. L, part 1, pp. 432–33; Charles P. Roland, *Albert Sidney Johnston* (Austin: Univ. of Texas Press, 1964), p. 242. The 1st Dragoons were redesignated as the 1st Cavalry on August 3, 1861.

[2] *OR*, pp. 452–53, 456–58.

section are more than anxious to be at war with these Indians." He commended the Indians for not stealing food despite their hunger. In disputing allegations about Indian hostility, Adams reminded military headquarters that the corral at Fort Crook held fifty-five horses but that there were only twenty-six cavalrymen. He asked that replacements for his understrength command be speeded to Fort Crook.[3]

South of Fort Crook at Honey Lake, the 3d Artillery detachment heard from settlers about stolen cattle. Loss of some fifteen head of stock was attributed to a renegade band that responsible Indian leaders had renounced. Lieutenant Warner said the band consisted of Pit and Paiute malcontents and that Paiute chief Winnemucca had promised to punish the thieves.[4]

At Fort Humboldt the situation appeared more ominous. Captain Lovell received disturbing reports that recounted retaliatory killings by Indians on the south fork of the Eel River. The report resulted from a reconnaissance party led by Lieutenant Lynn, who encountered the same difficulties that his predecessors had experienced when trying to communicate with Indians in the redwood forests. Afraid for their lives, most of the Indians around Humboldt Bay had scattered into the hills. Some Indians had indeed committed "a few depredations," according to Lynn. Lynn's attempts to gain information were hindered by the fact that the Indian who had helped Lovell in the course of operations in 1859 had been tied to a tree and shot by a white resident.

---

3 Adams to Mackall, Jan. 23, 1861, RG393; *OR*, pp. 451–52.

4 *OR*, p. 459.

Lynn described Downey's Eel River constituents as a scrubby lot, "vagabonds from society," who through practice had long forgotten the art of telling the truth. Listening to their extravagant claims against Indian stock stealers, the Army officer offered to attack the thieves if the victims would but show him where they were. Assuring him that two specific rancherias housed the culprits, settlers guided Lynn and his soldiers on a fruitless chase. The volunteer guides could locate no rancheria. One guide mistook a fellow American for an Indian and shot and killed him.

Lynn dismissed the Eel River guides. Resupplied, his twenty-nine–man expedition traveled the river valleys for two months, but he saw no organized Indian groups. After an endurance contest with weather and terrain, the soldiers returned to Fort Humboldt on March 25, 1861.[5]

Shortly after Lieutenant Lynn returned to Fort Humboldt, the commander of Fort Gaston moved to calm settlers and head off trouble in his area. Captain Underwood doubled the guard and bluffed the Hoopa into surrendering a number of rifles to him. Unappeased by the Army's action, some thirty citizens of Hoopa Valley built a private blockhouse for self-defense. Two sizable Hoopa groups, fearful of harm to themselves, moved out of the valley and into the safety of the hills.[6]

Lieutenant Dillon had scouted Mendocino County in January and found no trouble. Snow-flooded streams made travel difficult. Dillon decided to divide his Round Valley detachment to quiet citizens in neighboring Long Valley who claimed that Indians had stolen property. Four sol-

---

[5] *OR*, pp. 6–12; PR, Ft. Humboldt, Mar. 1861, M617, R497; *Humboldt Times*, Feb. 21, 1861.

[6] *OR*, pp. 466–67.

diers positioned themselves at the forks of the Eel River, where they enjoyed a peaceful spring and collected overdue military pay.[7]

Moving to silence citizen petitions and complaints, the Pacific Department ordered a concentrated effort. Captain Lovell would focus on southern Humboldt County. Lovell was best situated to coordinate actions and resupply, because he was closer to valley trails. A captain for fifteen years, Lovell was senior to the commanders of Forts Bragg and Gaston.

Lovell warned that stories of Indian attacks were greatly exaggerated. Unprovoked killing of Indians by a certain strata of Californians, a group that a Fort Humboldt officer derisively described as "the buckskin gentry," perpetuated violence in the countryside.

The department acknowledged Lovell's advice. Orders cautioned against "indiscriminate slaughter of the guilty with the innocent" but proffered no guidance about how to attain such worthy goals.

Soon after assuming command of the department, General Johnston asked Governor Downey for thirty state volunteers to act as guides for Lovell's Regulars. Johnston viewed the volunteer guides as an experiment. They would be paid from federal funds instead of by California. For the first time since 1853, an organized body of Californians accompanied the Regular Army on field operations. Previously, field commanders declined the use of state volunteers. The policy reversal brought dire consequences.

Lovell followed a headquarters plan to encircle the troubled area and squeeze it with fast-moving detachments. A

---

[7] Dillon to Sgt. J. Dowling, June 10, 1861, RG393; *OR*, pp. 464–65. The sergeant in charge of the detachment received $63.65 in back pay.

party from Fort Humboldt would strike east from the Eel River. Sweeping up from the south, a Fort Bragg detachment was to work in tandem with Fort Humboldt troops. Sergeant-led patrols supplied by Fort Gaston would come in from the west to complete the circle. Each group had common missions: to patrol, to protect settlers and their property, and to attack any Indians who committed depredations in the valleys of the Eel or Trinity.[8]

Moving out in mid April 1861, probably unaware that in South Carolina rebels had fired on Fort Sumter, the column from Fort Humboldt followed Lieutenant Collins into the forest. They carried their own provisions to eliminate the noise of packtrains and assure stealth. Often marching at night to achieve surprise, they skirmished with Indians on nine different occasions before the end of June. Accompanied by the sanctioned volunteers recruited by Downey, the troops fought Indians desperate enough to face firearms with bows and arrows. One soldier and two civilians received arrow wounds. Collins did not fire on Indians presumed innocent; still, the expedition exacted a terrible toll. Ninety-seven Indians fell to the detachment's rifles, an unprecedented number of casualties for the Army in northern California. In all the violence associated with the early history of northern California, the Regular Army had accounted for fewer than fifty Indian deaths between 1852 and 1860.[9]

Fort Gaston's patrols, totaling twenty-nine Regulars and eight volunteers, set out several days after Fort Humboldt had initiated action. Highlighted by a hand-to-hand melee

---

[8] Downey to Johnston, Mar. 26, 1861, RG393; *OR*, pp. 9, 451, 453, 456–59, 464.

[9] PR, Ft. Humboldt, Apr. 1861, M617, R497; *OR*, pp. 12, 17–19.

on Boulder Creek in May, Fort Gaston's assault resulted in six Indian deaths. After twice engaging Indians, the soldiers encountered them a third time. One soldier received a gunshot wound; eight additional Indian lives were lost.[10]

Last to take the field, the sixty-man detachment from Fort Bragg headed after a band accused of stealing cattle. Commanded by relatively inexperienced 2d Lieutenant James P. Martin, the combined Fort Bragg–volunteer group killed fifty-two Indians during eight separate occasions, a number unheard of for the Regular Army in Mendocino County. Reaching the Eel's south bank, Martin explained to Captain Lovell with "regret" that among those killed in the semidarkness of an early morning fight on June 4 were three women. Later Martin reported that another two women were "killed through mistake."[11]

Martin failed to admit his inability to control the civilian volunteers. He possessed "no means of finding out whether those that we may come upon are guilty or innocent. . . . Circumstantial evidence goes to show that they are all guilty." Apparently unreported by Martin was the act of a volunteer who dropped back out of the lieutenant's sight, tied an Indian child to a tree, and shot him or her. Mixing volunteers with Regulars proved to be an unwise decision.

Other signs showed that the Regular Army's relations with Indians were deteriorating. From the Mendocino coast, Lieutenant Dillon of Fort Bragg alerted Captain Lovell that several parties of Californians were following in the wake of troops "for the purpose of obtaining children." Despite the presence of Regular Army troops,

[10] PR, Ft. Gaston, Apr.-June 1861, M617, R396; *OR*, pp. 472–73.
[11] PR, Ft. Bragg, May 1861, M617, R138; *OR*, pp. 19–21.

Dillon estimated that the "brutal trade" of kidnapping and selling Indian children to citizens had resulted in some fifty youngsters being taken from their parents. Such "infamous acts" only invited retaliation by upset Indian families.[12]

On the eastern seaboard, drastic political events tore apart families. South Carolina and five states bordering the Gulf of Mexico seceded from the United States. Braxton Bragg, for whom Fort Bragg was named, assumed command of the military forces of Florida. General Johnston resigned from the Regular Army. As the southern states organized the Confederacy, the federal government blocked Confederate ports. Brigadier General Edwin V. Sumner rushed by ship from New York to San Francisco to replace Johnston. He took over command of the Department of the Pacific on April 25, 1861.

Ordering post commanders to protect U.S. property at all costs, Sumner directed instant discharge of any civilians in Army employ who were known to oppose the Union. With no artillery batteries, Fort Humboldt and Fort Bragg were somehow to capture or sink any rebel ships spotted. Concerned over reports of Confederate sympathizers in the populated areas of the Pacific Coast, Sumner looked for more troops.

Sumner felt the importance of war was more vital than the expectations of emigrants in wagon trains. He ordered the infantry company at Fort Crook to move to Benicia, and the company complied on May 28. The troop transfer left Fort Crook with only one company of cavalry. The men were experienced field soldiers, but the company

---

[12] Dillon to Lovell and Dillon to Buell, May 31, 1861, RG393; *OR*, pp. 20, 835.

lacked sufficient numbers to watch trails. Trails southeast of Fort Crook would also be left unguarded. Herders, miners, and emigrants east of the Sierra in California would have to fend for themselves. Sumner ordered the Honey Lake detachment back to San Francisco. The two troop moves positioned a handful of disciplined Regulars for service in regions deemed critical in a civil war.[13]

While preparing for war between Union and Confederate partisans, Sumner also sensed that he possessed faulty information about Indian attacks. He dispatched his own, pro-Union adjutant, Major Don Carlos Buell, to get a firsthand look at the northern counties. Buell was to report personally on the actual condition of Indian affairs, a situation that threatened to tie down Regular Army troops north of San Francisco when events demanded their presence elsewhere. Buell sought an accurate estimate of the situation along the Eel River where parts of three Regular Army garrisons were deployed. Arriving at Fort Humboldt, he hastened to visit various field detachments. Next he checked Fort Bragg and then inspected Fort Gaston on July 11–14.

Combining personal discretion with the prestige of his San Francisco staff position, Buell talked to soldiers, looked at the land, and drew his own conclusions. A witness to death in the Mexican War, Buell disliked the killing that he saw in northern California. He found allegations by Lieutenant Dillon and others regarding California citizen-volunteers to be true. That the Regular Army was engaged in combat against pro-slave states while accompanied by volunteers who sold Indians for a similar

---

13 PR, Ft. Crook, May 1861, M617, R271; *OR*, pp. 486–87, 494, 518.

purpose was an irony that was probably not lost on Buell.

Buell ordered a halt to any attacks against Indians except in reaction to new hostilities. Taking Indian women and children as prisoners was prohibited. Indians were to be reassured that Regular Army troops would pursue them only if settlers had been attacked. For that reason Lieutenant Martin of Fort Bragg was to shift his operations to Shelter Cove, where two whites had been killed.

Buell sent back to their respective forts all other Eel and Trinity River expeditions. Orders went out to pay interpreters and packers and to discharge volunteers. Long a sore point with the 6th Infantry and judged useless by Buell, the Round Valley detachment was to return to Fort Bragg.[14]

When the Round Valley detachment arrived back at the fort, Lieutenant Dillon was gone. Branded with harboring "treasonable designs," Dillon had left for the Confederacy. A newcomer, 1st Lieutenant Orlando H. Moore, commanded Fort Bragg. Taking charge on June 25, 1861, Moore, as the senior officer present, promptly asked that the name of Fort Bragg be changed "for patriotic motives." Occupied by other matters, headquarters overlooked Moore's request. Moore was promoted and ordered to a regiment destined for Civil War battlefields. Command at Fort Bragg devolved to Lieutenant Martin.

At Fort Crook command also changed. Twenty years after he had entered West Point, Captain Adams, unable in good conscience to wear his Regular Army uniform, turned the post over to Lieutenant Josiah H. Kellog. Adams left

---

[14] PR, Ft. Humboldt, June 1861; and Ft. Gaston, July 1861, M617, R497,396; *OR*, pp. 518, 527–28, 530–32.

California to lead Confederate cavalry at Memphis. Kellog and Martin, West Point classmates who were equally inexperienced, now commanded forts.[15]

Post commanders at Fort Humboldt and Fort Gaston remained steadfastly loyal to the Union, but both post medical officers, Assistant Surgeons La Fayette Guild and Nathaniel Crowell, resigned. Informed that the owner of the sutler shop at Fort Gaston advocated the Confederate cause, Underwood suspended his privileges at the post and closed his business. He also sent a military escort with the Weaverville mail carrier, who had reported an Indian attack while performing his service.

In Eureka patriotic sentiment was high. Lieutenant Lynn participated in the town's Fourth of July celebration, which featured a toast to the Army and Navy. Many could not be swayed by displays of Union sentiment. A number of the officers who had previously served in northern California sided with the Confederacy.[16] (See Appendix B.)

Concerned over "active and zealous" secessionists in Nevada and southern California, General Sumner decided to close Fort Ter-waw and redeploy the troops. He ordered Lieutenant Crook to abandon the post and get his men on the next steamer to San Francisco. Moving swiftly, Crook evacuated the fort and boarded a ship at Crescent City on June 8.[17]

Less sanguine about conditions on the Klamath than

---

[15] Moore to Capt. H. C. Drum, June 25, 1861; and Martin to Asst. Adj. Gen., Dept. of the Pacific, September 9, 1861, RG393; PR, Ft. Bragg, June, Aug., and Sept. 1861, M617, R139.

[16] Underwood to Simon Cameron, Aug. 11, 1861, RG393; PR, Forts Humboldt and Gaston, May 1861, M617, R497,396; *Humboldt Times*, July 6, 13 and Aug. 24, 1861.

[17] Returns of the 4th Regiment of Infantry, June 1861, M665; *OR*, pp. 472, 494.

federal authorities, Del Norte County protested the closing of Fort Ter-waw. Del Norte voters sent a petition
directly to General Sumner instead of to the governor.
They warned that citizens would be forced to arm themselves against "numerous and treacherous" Indians and
requested return of Regulars to Fort Ter-waw as soon
as possible.

Persuaded by civilian fears of Indian attacks, the
Department of the Pacific relented. It ordered Captain
Lewis C. Hunt's company of the 4th Infantry to reoccupy
Fort Ter-waw. Traveling from San Francisco to Crescent
City by ship, some sixty Regulars of Company C, 4th
Infantry, regarrisoned Fort Ter-waw on August 28.
Although troops had been absent for nearly three months,
Captain Hunt reported that the "Indian population are
quiet and well disposed."[18]

The population around Fort Crook was far from quiet.
After commanding the post for only a month, Lieutenant
Kellog, notified that Indians had attacked a group of California prospectors, sent Lieutenant Feilner, newly promoted from sergeant, to the northeast with a detail. Feilner
met two survivors of a fight with Indians. He learned that a
nineteen-man party of cattle drivers, not gold prospectors,
had collided with Indians near the head of the Pit River.

Told that two of the cattlemen had been killed, Feilner's
detachment covered sixty-seven miles in three days. Spot-
ting Indians driving cattle, Feilner "took after them." He
then saw butchered cattle and needed to ask no questions.
Hit by two arrows, Feilner killed one Indian, and the other
Indians fled.

---

[18] PR, Ft. Ter-waw, Aug. 1861, M617, R1262; *OR*, pp. 522, 525, 558, 597–98.

Feilner's men buried the two cattle owners. Then, accompanied by the eight surviving drovers, the expeditionary force rounded up scattered cattle. After following telltale tracks, Feilner engaged a second group of Indians on August 9, this time without casualties. Burdened by some 350 head of repossessed cattle and believing the cattle thieves to be dispersed, Feilner returned to Fort Crook on August 12.

Kellog sent Feilner out a second time on August 15. With twenty-nine enlisted men, the follow-up party left to look for more stray cattle and to punish those who stole stock. The soldiers collected only forty-two cattle. They exchanged long-range rifle fire with Indians who were mounted on horses. After covering some 300 miles, Feilner headed home. The party returned to Fort Crook on August 22.[19]

Displeased with the reduction of the Fort Crook garrison, Pit River settlers resorted to petitioning the Department of the Pacific, just as Del Norte citizens had done. Twenty-seven petition signers complained that Indians plundered "with impunity from their knowledge of the smallness" of the complement at Fort Crook. They asked that troop strength at the post be restored to at least two Regular Army companies. East of Yreka an equal number of petitioners laid claim to Army protection after they were warned by Indians to abandon their Butte Valley homes or see their livestock taken. All along the northern border of California, relations with Modoc and other groups worsened. Chasing Confederate phantoms further south, the Army's senior officer in San Francisco said,

---

[19] PR, Ft. Crook, Aug. 1861, M617, R271; *OR*, pp. 21–23, 25–27; William S. Brown, *California Northeast* (Oakland: Biobooks, 1951), pp. 22–24.

"I doubt very much these Indian reports." The Army
took no action. [20]

Indian problems continued in the Eel River region.
Captain Lovell, at Fort Humboldt, received a petition
from seventy-two law-abiding citizens pleading that he
take under his protection various Indians on the lower Eel.
Describing the Indians as peaceful, the petitioners feared
another Indian massacre by unprincipled whites. They
offered to assist soldiers in gathering up Indians prior to
moving them to the Klamath reservation. Lovell protected
some 130 Indians who assembled at Fort Humboldt. He
wrote to the Klamath reservation agent while citizens fed
the Indians as best they could.

General Sumner closed Fort Humboldt in 1861. His
headquarters directed Lovell to establish a new Army post
near the Humboldt–Mendocino County line. Although
Lovell doubted the wisdom of the orders, he moved out of
Fort Humboldt. He took with him not only the soldiers,
but the door locks and window sashes as well. Arriving at
the new location on September 21, 1861, and naming it
Fort Seward, Lovell raced to build barracks, storehouses,
and stable before winter. He expected mountain trails to be
blocked by December. After that, packtrains were out of
the question until April.

Lovell lost his race against time. While he rushed
construction, the War Department in Washington, D.C.,
reacted to Union disasters by ordering all California Regulars east. Desperate for trained soldiers, the Army would
allow but four companies of artillery to remain on the
Columbia River and San Francisco Bay.

---

[20] *OR*, pp.507–508, 613–14, 631.

Also in response to the national emergency, California raised regiments of blue-uniformed Volunteers for the Union. In federal service the California Volunteer units, unlike previous state volunteers, would be under the strict direction of the Department of the Pacific. The regiments were accorded numerical designations and subject to Army regulations. They wore Army uniforms and received Army pay.[21]

Immediate pullout of the Regular Army proved unfeasible. The Volunteer regiments needed to reach some semblance of organization. Lovell was to stay at Fort Seward until relieved by Californians mustered into the Department of the Pacific. Meanwhile, Governor Downey passed on new petitions about Indians, these signed by citizens of Mendocino and Napa counties.

After only a month of skimpy military training, the 3d California Volunteer Infantry received word to send companies by ship to Forts Seward, Bragg, Gaston, and Terwaw. A company of the 2d California Volunteer Cavalry, marching overland, also went to Lovell at Fort Seward. Another company of the 2d California Cavalry moved north to take over Fort Crook from the Regulars.

Events in the Regular Army regiments picked up speed. At Fort Bragg Lieutenant Martin asked for two copies of *McClellan's Bayonet Exercises* to assist with bayonet drill. The Regular Army promoted Underwood of Fort Gaston to major despite his poor health. Lovell read in a newspaper that he, too, had been promoted to major. Perhaps sensing a clarion call to duty, eleven Regular Army deserters

---

[21] PR, Ft. Seward, Sept. 1861, M617, R1542; *OR*, pp. 558–60, 562, 584, 613, 620–21; 633–34.

turned themselves in at northern California forts. In San Francisco, Colonel George Wright, who had commanded Fort Reading nine years earlier, took command from Sumner in November 1861. Sumner was ordered east.[22]

Regulars at Forts Seward, Gaston, Crook, and Ter-waw greeted their replacements early in November. Ordered to hasten to the coast where they were to take passage to San Francisco, the Regulars inventoried government property, turned over posts to Volunteers, and quickly departed. Time permitted no terrain orientation for the newcomers. Gone with the Regular garrisons was a wealth of local knowledge accumulated by officers, sergeants, and corporals. They also took with them years of garrison discipline and field experience, assets that paid dividends at Antietam and Gettysburg.[23]

Only at Fort Bragg was there hesitation. Pondering over the legality of the transfer order brought to the Mendocino post by Company B, 3d California Infantry, Lieutenant Martin wondered if he had sufficient documentation to turn over federal grounds and property to the Volunteers. Two weeks elapsed while Martin resolved his doubts. Satisfied that all papers were legitimate, he led his Regulars to a steamer on November 23. The last units of the 4th Infantry, 6th Infantry, and 1st Cavalry were out of the redwoods.[24]

---

[22] Martin to Asst. Adj. Gen., Dept. of the Pacific, Sept. 9, 1861, RG393; PR, Ft. Gaston, July 1861, M617, R396; *OR*, pp. 602–03, 650–52, 666, 691, 693–94; Aurora Hunt, *The Army of the Pacific* (Glendale: The Arthur H. Clark Co., 1951), pp. 40, 186–87.

[23] PR, Forts Crook, Gaston, Seward, and Ter-waw, Nov. 1861, M617; *OR*, p. 743.

[24] Drum to Martin, Oct. 12, 1861; and Martin to unknown, Nov. 11, 1861, RG393; PR, Ft. Bragg, Nov. 1861, M617, R138; *OR*, pp. 652, 694, 731, 735.

Without contacts in the local population and unable to move due to an overabundance of rain and a dearth of food and forage, the California Volunteer regiments faced a perilous situation. They struggled to survive at northern California forts and suspended military operations for several months. In the absence of troops, physical abuse and killing within civilian and Indian populations continued. Adding to the loss of momentum caused by floods and food shortages at California posts, three different commanders directed the Department of the Pacific in 1861. Their attention had been deflected from the northern counties to rumors of Confederate threats and the need to protect overland mail service.[25]

The reassembled 4th and 6th Infantry reached Washington, D.C., in December 1861. On the day after Christmas they were joined by the 1st Cavalry. The massed Regulars guarded the defense works of the nation's capital against the Confederacy. On the other side in a gray uniform was the ex-commander of Fort Weller, Edward Johnson, a Rebel brigadier general.

Before the sad split of North and South, the Regular Army had accomplished much during ten years in the redwoods. Their presence in troubled areas had maintained calm when agitated civilians contemplated taking matters into their own hands. The Army was not always popular. If a family member was killed by Indians or a settler's life savings were eroded because Indians had stolen livestock, Regular Army policies of restraint went unappreciated. Military-civil relations had reached such a state in 1860

---

[25] *OR*, pp. 792, 803, 805, 812–13, 834, 836, 966–67; Leo. P. Kibby, *California, the Civil War, and the Indian Problem,* (Los Angeles: Lorrin L. Morrison, 1968), pp. 50–51; *Mendocino Herald,* Dec. 27, 1861.

that the same story of Army officers hoping that Indians would kill all the cattle and then their owners circulated in both Mendocino and Humboldt counties.[26]

Popular or not, the U.S. Army provided security to public thoroughfares. Soldiers ranged beyond the forts to protect wagon trains, roads, trails, and ferry crossings and to escort mail riders. Army doctors responded to the needs of humanity by providing emergency medical care to emigrants, settlers, and Indians.

To the extent possible, military security also served to bar the extermination of long-established Indian communities. On more than one occasion disciplined ranks of federal soldiers stood between California citizens and local Indians. In the absence of Indian Office officials or when Army commanders judged the efforts of Indian agents lax to the point of inhumanity, Army officers acted as unofficial Indian agents. In fact, Dillon served as the official agent at the Mendocino reservation for several months.

Army officers twice gave legal support to Indians. On countless other occasions, however, Regulars advanced the Indians' cause by reporting to San Francisco how miners, ranchers, and farmers were destroying traditional Indian food sources. On Indian reservations Regulars readily aired their views about what they saw as mismanagement or malfeasance by federal appointees.

The Army overcame obstacles to accomplish what it did. Manpower shortages were rife, yet the Regulars built shelters—largely with their own hands. Post commanders used unconventional tactics to make up for inherent organizational problems. Always short of cavalry, they

---

[26] Legislature of the State of Calif., "Mendocino Indian War," p. 30; *Humboldt Times*, Mar. 17, 1860.

improvised "mule cavalry" by putting infantry and artillery troops on garrison animals. Knowing that their few hundreds were unable to blanket all the wooded terrain, the Regulars employed civilian guides, Indian guides, and, on occasion, Indian allies.

The Regulars left their mark in California. The towns of Fort Jones, Fort Bragg, and Fort Seward grew from former Army posts. After building barracks, tending post gardens, and handling horses and mules, some Army men took honorable discharges and settled in nearby valleys of the "further West." Dr. Sorrel of Fort Jones, for example, left the Army, made his residence in Siskiyou County, and was elected to the state legislature.[27]

Government contracts made an economic impact. Troop movements by chartered ships were expensive. Government animals always needed hay and barley, and there were civilian payrolls of at least $39,000 over a period of years.[28]

The Regulars who remained in military service fought each other in a long civil war. Former hunting partners from Fort Jones, George Crook and John B. Hood, survived on opposite sides as generals. Bird collector John Feilner was killed while serving the Union. His commander at Fort Crook, John Adams, died for the Confederacy.

After the war Captain Lovell of Fort Humboldt com-

---

[27] U. S. Grant, *Personal Memoirs of U. S. Grant* (New York: Charles L. Webster & Co., 1885), vol. 1, p. 210; Wells, *Siskiyou History*, p. 112–13; Ellington, "Deyerle at Fort Humboldt," *Journal of the West*, p. 28; Yreka *Weekly Journal*, Oct. 4 and Nov. 1, 1860 and June 1, 1861.

[28] Survey of incomplete post returns and Quartermaster General Office, Register of Contracts, No. 12, 1852–1859, RG92, showed the Army's payroll in the northern counties totaled $39,000 between 1854 and 1861. At Fort Crook the bill for locally procured hay between 1858 and 1860 was $12,400.

manded the 14th Infantry as a colonel with headquarters at Fort Yuma. San Francisco feted General George Crook in 1875. Brevet Brigadier General Michael R. Morgan, former lieutenant at Nome Lackee, served as a staff officer for the Department of California in 1882.

Service in and about the redwoods brought some soldiers to a new home. Others gained experience that served them in later life as civilians or military men. In return Regular Army troops contributed to our knowledge of the peoples and lands of the far west, saved settlers and Indians, and gave their lives.

Epilogue

I would respectfully suggest for the consideration of Congress the propriety of transferring the Indian bureau from the Interior to the War Dept.

U. S. Grant, general and former captain of Fort Humboldt, *Annual Report of the Secretary of War* (1868)

The Regular Army returned to the redwoods on November 8, 1865, at Fort Humboldt. Six months after Appomattox, one officer and forty-nine enlisted men of Company E, 9th Infantry, were all that the Army could spare to ship north. More months would expire before the Regular Army relieved units of California Volunteers farther inland from the ocean.[1]

Some things had changed in four years. Proving the accuracy of Captain Lovell's dire predictions, Fort Seward had been difficult, if not impossible, to resupply. War-enlisted volunteer soldiers brought out the last government property from Fort Seward in March 1862, abandoning the post. Likewise, Fort Ter-waw was evacuated in June

[1] PR, Ft. Humboldt, Nov. 1865, M617, R497; Allan R. Millet and Peter Maslowski, *For the Common Defense* (New York: The Free Press, 1984), p. 233.

1862, after extensive flood damage. On the last day of September 1864, the Army closed Fort Bragg as a military post.

Other aspects of life in California remained the same, however, particularly the unsettled state of Indian affairs. Constrained against his wishes from joining fellow Regulars in pursuit of battlefield honors, Brigadier General George Wright, the wartime commander in California, gave his prognosis for post–Civil War Indian matters. Writing to the U.S. Congress from Sacramento in June 1865, he plainly stated his belief that the only way to prevent total Indian extinction was to place Indians on military reservations. Under exclusive Army jurisdiction, far removed from the evils of white settlements, each Indian family could cultivate land, attend school, and be inspired by Protestant ministers. Wright's words went unheeded.[2]

Command in San Francisco had gone to Brevet Major General Irving McDowell, the Union's less-than-successful commander at Bull Run. Pressured to muster out the California Civil War Volunteer regiments as fast as possible, McDowell hesitated when it came to northern California. He was convinced of the genuine need for keeping a recognizable troop force near the redwoods to ensure peace. The Pacific coast was devoid of Regular Army cavalry. McDowell kept certain California Volunteer units on duty until Regular Army garrisons arrived to substitute for them, in 1866. Reinforcing McDowell's caution, citizens of the northern counties asked for more military protection.[3]

[2] OR, part 2, pp. 1268–70.

[3] Ibid., pp. 1214–15, 1222–23, 1265–68, 1288–89.

To speed the rebuilding of the Regular Army from the shambles of the Civil War, Congress authorized more cavalry. The federal government recruited soldiers in populous California and selected Fort Reading as a site to train peacetime cavalry. In December 1866 Company G of the newly constituted 8th Cavalry of the Regular Army reoccupied the post. The parade ground thudded with the hoofbeats of Regular cavalry for the first time in nine years. By May 1867, however, forty-seven new enlistees had deserted, a 2d Lieutenant had drowned in Cow Creek, and the War Department ordered the entire 8th Cavalry to Arizona. Fort Reading closed again.[4]

Regulars returned to Fort Gaston on April 15, 1866, replacing a company of the 4th California Volunteer Infantry, which finally left federal service. Two companies of the 9th Infantry, double the pre–Civil War strength of Fort Gaston, settled into quarters in Hoopa territory. At Fort Humboldt Company E, 2d Artillery, joined the garrison. Major Andrew W. Bowman, possessor of an undistinguished Civil War record, became Fort Humboldt's first Regular Army commander since the departure of Captain Lovell in 1861.

During the Civil War years, Round Valley had been regarrisoned with the establishment of Camp Wright. Company A, 9th Infantry, took over Camp Wright on April 13, 1866, relieving men of the 2d California Infantry Volunteers. The following month Company C, 9th Infantry, paused briefly at Fort Crook to relieve California Volunteers. Then the company continued to Fort Bidwell to the northeast. Federalized California volunteers established

---

4 PR, Ft. Reading, Dec. 1866, Mar.-June 1867, M617, R993.

Fort Bidwell in the Surprise Valley and Camp Lincoln near Crescent City as a result of settler-Indian struggles while the Regulars fought the Civil War. The Regular Army was installed in the forts before the summer of 1866.[5]

In the southern states the Civil War was over. East of the redwood coast, cultural animosity between settler and Indians continued. The Regular Army stayed in Northern California another twenty-five years.

[5] PR, Camp Lincoln, Nov. 1865; and Forts Gaston, Humboldt, and Wright, Apr. 1866; and Forts Crook and Bidwell, May 1866, M617, R627, 396, 497, 1467, 271, 112.

Appendices
Bibliography
Index

Appendix A
POST COMMANDERS, 1852–1861

Fort Bragg
> 1st Lieutenant Horatio G. Gibson, June 1857-June 1858
> 1st Lieutenant William P. Carlin, September 1859-May 1860
> 2d Lieutenant Edward Dillon, May 1860-June 1861
> 1st Lieutenant Orlando H. Moore, July-August 1861
> 2d Lieutenant James P. Martin, August-November 1861

Camp Cap-El
> 2d Lieutenant Hezikiah H. Garber, January-March 1856
> 2d Lieutenant Charles H. Rundell, March 1856-April 1857

Camp Cass
> Captain Franklin F. Flint, May-July 1859
> 2d Lieutenant Archibald I. Harrison, July 1859
> Captain Franklin F. Flint, August-September 1859

Post at Crescent City
> Captain DeLancey Floyd-Jones, January-March 1856
> 2d Lieutenant Hezikiah H. Garber, March-October 1856

Fort Crook
> Captain John W. T. Gardiner, July 1857-July 1858
> 1st Lieutenant Milton T. Carr, July 1858-January 1859
> Captain John Adams, January 1859-July 1861
> 1st Lieutenant Josiah H. Kellog, July-November 1861

Fort Gaston
    Captain Edmund Underwood, December 1858-August 1861
    Captain Joseph B. Collins, August 1861-November 1861
Post at Honey Lake (Camp Mackall, Dragoon Bridge)
        1st Lieutenant Milton T. Carr, June-July 1858 and July 1859
        1st Lieutenant Alfred B. Chapman, May-July 1860
        1st Lieutenant John Hamilton, July-September 1860
        2d Lieutenant Edward R. Warner, September 1860-June 1861
Fort Humboldt
    Major and Brevet Lieutenant Colonel Robert C. Buchanan,
        January 1853-February 1856
    1st Lieutenant Francis H. Bates, February-June 1856
    Major Gabriel J. Rains, June 1856-July 1860
    Captain Charles S. Lovell, July 1860-September 1861
Fort Jones
    Captain and Brevet Major Edward H. Fitzgerald, October
        1852-January 1853
    2d Lieutenant Charles H. Ogle, January-March 1853
    1st Lieutenant Richard C. W. Radford, March 1853
    Captain and Brevet Major Edward H. Fitzgerald, April-May
        1853
    1st Lieutenant Richard C. W. Radford, May 1853
    Captain Bradford R. Alden, June-August 1853
    1st Lieutenant Joseph B. Collins, August-September 1853
    Captain and Brevet Major George W. Patten, October-
        November 1853
    1st Lieutenant John C. Bonnycastle, November-December 1853
    Captain Henry M. Judah, January 1854
    1st Lieutenant John C. Bonnycastle, February-October 1854
    2d Lieutenant George Crook, October-December 1854
    Captain David A. Russell, December 1854-June 1855
    Captain Henry M. Judah, June-September 1855
    Assistant Surgeon Francis Sorrel, September-October 1855
    2d Lieutenant George Crook, November-December 1855
    Captain Henry M. Judah, December 1855-April 1856

Captain and Brevet Major Francis O. Wyse, April-August 1856

Captain Henry M. Judah, August 1856-June 1858

Detachment at Nome Lackee Reserve

2d Lieutenant James Deshler, January 1855-June 1855

1st Lieutenant John Edwards, June 1855-August 1856

1st Lieutenant and Brevet Captain John H. Lendrum, June 1857

1st Lieutenant Michael R. Morgan, June 1857-March 1858

Fort Reading

1st Lieutenant Nelson H. Davis, May-September 1852

Major and Brevet Colonel George Wright, September 1852-May 1855

Captain and Brevet Major Francis O. Wyse, May 1855-April 1856

Fort Seward

Captain Charles S. Lovell, September-November 1861

Fort Ter-waw

1st Lieutenant George Crook, October 1857-July 1858, October 1858-June 1861

1st Lieutenant Joseph B. Collins, July-October 1858

Captain Lewis C. Hunt, August-November 1861

Fort Weller

Captain and Brevet Major Edward Johnson, January-October 1859

Camp Wool (Camp Strowbridge)

Captain Henry M. Judah, March-April 1855

Captain DeLancey Floyd-Jones, April-August 1855

2d Lieutenant Hezikiah H. Garber, August-October 1855

Appendix B

Fort Bragg
> Brigadier General USA and Major General Volunteers William
> P. Carlin

Fort Crook
> Brigadier General Volunteers William P. Sanders

Fort Humboldt
> Brevet Major General Robert C. Buchanan
> Brigadier General Volunteers Lewis C. Hunt
> General USA Ulysses S. Grant

Fort Jones
> Brigadier General USA Charles H. Crane
> Brigadier General Volunteers Henry M. Judah
> Major General USA David A. Russell

Nome Lackee Detachment
> Brigadier General USA Michael R. Morgan

Fort Reading
> Brigadier General USA Nelson H. Davis
> Brigadier General USA and Major General Volunteers William
> B. Hazen
> General USA Philip H. Sheridan
> Brigadier General Volunteers George Wright

Fort Ter-waw
   Major General USA George Crook

OFFICERS WHO SERVED AS GENERALS IN THE CONFEDERATE STATES ARMY

Fort Crook
   Brigadier General John Adams
   Brigadier General James A. Smith
Fort Humboldt
   Brigadier General Gabriel J. Rains
Fort Jones
   General John B. Hood
Nome Lackee Detachment
   Brigadier General James Deshler
Fort Weller
   Major General Edward Johnson

Bibliography

MANUSCRIPTS

National Archives. Washington, D.C. Records of U. S. Army Continental Commands, Record Group 393. Div. and Dept. of the Pacific. Letters Received, 1852–1861; Letters Sent, 1852–1861.

Records of the Office of the Surgeon General. Record Group 112. Letters Received, 1852–1861.

Records of the Office of the Quartermaster General. Record Group 92. Register of Contracts, 1852–1860.

NARS Microcopy No. 234. Records of the Bureau of Indian Affairs. Letters Received 1849–1880.

NARS Microcopy M506. Letters Received by Topographical Bureau, War Dept., 1824–1865.

NARS Microcopy No. 617. Returns from U.S. Military Posts, 1800–1916.

NARS Microcopy 661. Historical Information Relating to Military Posts and Other Installations, ca. 1700–1900.

NARS Microcopy No. 665. Returns from Regular Army Infantry Regiments, June 1821-December 1916.

NARS Microcopy No. 711. Register of Letters Received by the Office of the Adjutant General Main Series, 1812–1899.

NARS Microcopy M727. Returns from Regular Army Artillery Regiments, June 1821-January 1901.

NARS Microcopy M744. Returns from Regular Army Cavalry Regiments, 1833–1916.

Federal Archives and Records Center. San Bruno, Calif. NARS Microcopy M653. Federal Population Census. Eighth Census of the U. S., 1860.

Smithsonian Institution. Washington, D.C. Smithsonian Archives.

Spencer Baird correspondence.

National Museum of Natural History. Catalog to Manuscripts at the National Anthropological Archives.

California State Archives. Sacramento. Indian War Papers.

Bancroft Library. Berkeley, Calif. Rosborough Papers. Alexander Madison Rosborough. Notes and Accounts as Special Indian Agent.

DOCUMENTS

U.S. Congress. House. *Report of Explorations and Surveys to Ascertain the Most Practicable and Economical Route for a Railroad from the Mississippi River to the Pacific Ocean.* Ex. Doc. No. 91, 33d Cong., 2d sess., 1857. 13 vols.

U.S. Congress. House. *Expenditures for Barracks and Quarters.* Ex. Doc. No. 93, 35th Cong., 2d sess., 1859.

U.S. Congress. Senate. *Correspondence between the Indian Office and the present superintendents and agents in California, and J. Ross Browne, Esq.* Ex. Doc. No. 46, 36th Cong., 1st sess., 1860.

U.S. War Dept. Secretary of War. Annual Report. 1851–1861.

Statistical Report on the Sickness and Mortality in the Army of the United States. 1855.

The War of the Rebellion: A Compilation of the Official Records of the Union and Confederate Armies. Series I, Vol. L.

U.S. Dept. of the Interior. Commissioner of Indian Affairs. *Annual Report. 1856–1862.*

U.S. Air Force Academy. Seventh Annual Military History Symposium. *The American Military on the Frontier.* 1978.

Smithsonian Institution. *Annual Report of the Board of Regents of the Smithsonian Institution. 1855–1864.*

California. Adjutant General W. C. Kibbe, *Report of Expedition Against the Indians in the Northern Part of the State.* 1860.

California Legislature. *Majority and Minority Reports of the Special Joint Committee on the Mendocino War.* 1860.

BOOKS AND ARTICLES

Abbot, Brig. Gen. Henry L. "Reminiscences of the Oregon War of 1855," *Journal of the Military Service Institution of the United States,* 45, (Nov. 1909), 436–42.

Alden, Capt. Bradford R. "The Oregon and California Letters of Bradford Ripley Alden," *Calif. Hist. Soc. Quarterly,* XXVII (Sept. and Dec. 1949), 199–232, 351–59.

Anderson, Mary. *Backwoods Chronicle: A History of Southern Humboldt, 1849–1920.* Redway, Calif.: SoHumCo Press, 1985.

Arnold, Mary Ellicott and Mabel Reed. *In the Land of the Grasshopper Song.* Linclon: Univ. of Nebraska Press, 1980.

Bandel, Eugene. *Frontier Life in the Army 1854–1861.* Glendale: Arthur H. Clark Co., 1932; rpt., Philadelphia: Porcupine Press, 1974.

Barns, George C. *Denver, The Man.* Wilmington, Ohio. NP. 1949.

Bledsoe, A. J. *Indian Wars of the Northwest.* Oakland: Biobooks, 1956.

————*History of Del Norte County.* Privately published reprint, 1971.

Boggs, May H. B. *My Playhouse Was a Concord Coach.* Oakland: Howell-North Press, 1942.

Brown, Gertrude K. "Initial Monuments for California's Base and Meridian Lines," *Calif. Hist. Soc. Quarterly,* XXXIV (Mar. 1935), 1–17.

Brown, Millard. "Indian Wars in Trinity 1858–1865," *Trinity. Yearbook of the Trinity County Hist. Soc.*, 1969. 36–38.

Brown, William S. *California Northeast*. Oakland: Biobooks, 1951.

Browne, Lina Fergusson, Ed. *J. Ross Browne: His Letters, Journals, and Writings*. Albuquerque: Univ. of New Mexico Press, 1969.

Bryarly, Wakeman and Vincent Geiger. David M. Potter, Ed. *Trail to California*. New Haven: Yale Univ. Press, 1945.

Carranco, Lynwood and Estele Beard, *Genocide and Vendetta. The Round Valley Wars of Northern California*. Norman: Univ. of Oklahoma Press, 1981.

Carson, James F. "California Gold to Help Finance the War," *Journal of the West*, XIV (Jan. 1975), 25–41.

Chandler, Robert. "The Failure of Reform: White Attitudes and Indian Response in California During the Civil War Era," *The Pacific Historian*, Vol. 24, No. 3 (Fall 1980), 284–94.

Cook, Sherburne F. *The Conflict Between the California Indian and White Civilization*. Berkeley: Univ. of California Press, 1976.

Crist, Lynda Laswell. *The Papers of Jefferson Davis*, Vol. 5. Baton Rouge: Louisiana State Univ. Press, 1985.

Crouter, Richard E. and Andrew F. Rolle. "Edward Fitzgerald Beale and the Indian Peace Commissioners in California, 1851–1854," *Southern California Quarterly*, XLII (June 1960), 107–32.

Egan, Ferol. *Sand in a Whirlwind. The Paiute Indian War of 1860*. Reno: Univ. of Nevada Press, 1985.

Ellington, Charles G. "Charles Peter Deyerle at Fort Humboldt," *Journal of the West*, XX (Oct. 1981), 26–34.

————*The Trial of U.S. Grant. The Pacific Coast Years 1852–1854*. Glendale: The Arthur H. Clark Co., 1987.

Ellison, W. H. "The Federal Indian Policy in California," *Mississippi Valley Historical Review*, IX (June 1922), 37–67.

Fairfield, Asa Merrill. *Fairfield's Pioneer History of Lassen County California*. San Francisco: H. S. Crocker Co., 1916.

Frazer, Robert W. *Mansfield on the Condition of the Western Forts 1853–54*. Norman: Univ. of Oklahoma Press, 1963.

Giles, Rosena A. *Shasta County California: A History*. Oakland: Biobooks, 1949.

Goetzmann, William H. *Army Exploration in the American West, 1803–1863*. Lincoln: Univ. of Nebraska Press, 1979.

Goodman, David M. *J. Ross Browne*. Glendale: The Arthur H. Clark Company, 1966.

Grant, Ulysses S. *Personal Memoirs of U. S. Grant*. New York: Charles L. Webster & Co., 1885.

Gudde, Erwin G. *California Place Names*. Berkeley: Univ. of California Press, 1974.

Heitman, Francis B. *Historical Register and Dictionary of the United States Army*. Urbana: Univ. of Illinois Press, 1965.

Heizer, Robert F. and Alan J. Almquist. *The Other Californians*. Berkeley: Univ. of California Press, 1977.

Heizer, Robert F., Editor. *Handbook of North American Indians*. Vol. 8, *California*. Washington: Smithsonian Institution, 1978.

Hill, Edward H. *The Office of Indian Affairs, 1824–1880: Historical Sketches*. New York: Clearwater Pub. Co., Inc., 1974.

Hislop, Donald L. *The Nome Lackee Indian Reservation 1854–1870*. Chico, Calif.: Assoc. for Northern California Records and Research, 1978.

Hood, J. B. *Advance and Retreat*. New Orleans: Hood Orphan Memorial Fund, 1880.

Hoopes, Alban W. *Indian Affairs and Their Administration, with Special Reference to the Far West, 1849–1860*. New York: Kraus Reprint Company, 1972.

Hoopes, Chad L. *Fort Humboldt. Exploration of the Humboldt Bay Region and the Founding of the Military Post*. Provo: Brigham Young Univ., 1964.

Hulse, James W. "The California-Nevada Boundary: History of Conflict." *Nevada Hist. Soc. Quarterly,* XXIII (Summer 1980), 87–109.

Hunt, Aurora. *The Army of the Pacific.* Glendale: The Arthur H. Clark Co., 1951.

———"The Far West Volunteers," *Montana,* Vol. 12 (Apr. 1962), 49–61.

Hurtado, Albert L. *Indian Survival on the California Frontier.* New Haven: Yale Univ. Press, 1988.

Irvine, Leigh H. *History of Humboldt County California.* Los Angeles: Historic Record Co., 1915.

Jackson, W. Turrentine. *Wagon Roads West.* Lincoln: Univ. of Nebraska Press, 1979.

Kelsey, Harry. "The California Indian Treaty Myth," *Southern California Quarterly,* LV (Fall 1973), 225–38.

Keyes, E. D. *From West Point to California.* Oakland: Biobooks, 1950.

Kibby, Leo P. *California, The Civil War, and the Indian Problem.* Los Angeles: Lorrin L. Morrison, 1968.

Kip, William I. *The Early Days of My Episcopate.* New York: Thomas Whittaker, 1892.

Kroekr, Marvin E. *Great Plains Command: William B. Hazen in the Frontier West.* Norman: Univ. of Oklahoma Press, 1976.

Kvasnicka, Robert M. and Herman J. Viola. *The Commissioners of Indian Affairs 1824–1977.* Lincoln: Univ. of Nebraska Press, 1979.

Lacour-Gayet, Robert. *Everyday Life in the United States Before the Civil War 1830–1860.* New York: Frederick Ungar Publishing Co., 1983.

Lewis, E. Raymond. *Seacoast Fortifications of the United States.* Annapolis: Leeward Pubns., 1979.

Lewis, Lloyd. *Captain Sam Grant*. Boston: Little, Brown and Co., 1950.

Lingenfelter, Keith. "Supervisors of the Nome Lackee Indian Reservation," *Wagon Wheels*, XXVII (Feb. 1977), 20–24.

Lowe, Percival G. *Five Years a Dragoon*. Norman: Univ. of Oklahoma Press, 1965.

Madden, Henry Miller. *Xantus: Hungarian Naturalist in the Pioneer West*. Palo Alto: Books of the West, 1949.

McLetch, Larry. "Fort Weller, Mendocino County, 1859," *The Far Westerner*, Vol. 15 (Oct. 1974).

Miller, Joaquin. *His California Diary Beginning in 1855 & Ending in 1857*. Edited with an introduction by John S. Richards. Seattle: Dogwood Press, 1936.

Millet, Allan R. and Peter Maslowski. *For the Common Defense*. New York: The Free Press, 1984.

Murray, Keith A. *The Modocs and Their War*. Norman: Univ. of Oklahoma Press, 1984.

Olmstead, Roger R. *Scenes of Wonder & Curiosity*. Berkeley: Howell-North, 1962.

Palmer, Lyman L. *History of Mendocino County*. San Francisco: Alley, Bowen & Co., 1880.

Pitt, Leonard. *The Decline of the Californios*. Berkeley: Univ. of California Press, 1971.

Powers, Stephen. *California Indian Characteristics*. Berkeley: The Friends of the Bancroft Library, 1975.

Prucha, Francis Paul. *Guide to the Military Posts of the United States*. Milwaukee: The State Hist. Soc. of Wisconsin, 1964.

———*The Sword of the Republic*. Bloomington: Indiana Univ. Press, 1977.

———*The Great White Father: The United States Government and the American Indians*, Vol. I. Lincoln: Univ. of Nebraska Press, 1984.

Ramirez, Salvador A. *Fort Gaston, California: A Brief Historical Sketch*. Encinitas, Calif.: Mustang Press Club, 1985.

Rawls, James J. *Indians of California: The Changing Image*. Norman: Univ. of Oklahoma Press, 1984.

Rodenbough, T. F. and W. L. Haskins, Eds. *The Army of the United States*. New York: Maynard, Merrill & Company, 1896.

Rogers, Fred B. "Early Military Posts of Del Norte County," *California Hist. Soc. Quarterly*, XXVI (Mar. 1974), 1–11.

————"Early Military Posts of Mendocino County," *California Hist. Soc. Quarterly*, XXVII (Sept. 1948), 215–28.

————"Bear Flag Lieutenant," *California Hist. Soc. Quarterly*, XXX (June 1951), 157–75.

Roland, Charles P. *Albert Sidney Johnston: Soldier of Three Republics*. Austin: Univ. of Texas Press, 1964.

Rosborough, Alex J. "A. M. Rosborough: Special Indian Agent," *California Hist. Soc. Quarterly*, XXVI (Sept. 1947), 201–07.

Salley, H. E. *History of California Post Offices*. La Mesa, Calif.: Postal History Associates, 1971.

Sawyer, Robert W. *Henry Larcom Abbot and the Pacific Railroad Surveys in Oregon, 1855*. NP.

Schlicke, Carl P. *General George Wright: Guardian of the Pacific Coast*. Norman: Univ. of Oklahoma Press, 1988.

Schmitt, Martin F. *General George Crook: His Autobiography*. Norman: Univ. of Oklahoma Press, 1946.

Schubert, Frank N. *Vanguard of Expansion: Army Engineers in the Trans-Mississippi West, 1819–1879*. Washington, D.C.: Hist. Div., Office of the Chief of Engineers, 1980.

Sheridan, Philip H. *Personal Memoirs of P. H. Sheridan*. New York: Charles L. Webster & Co., 1888.

Simon, John Y., Editor. *The Papers of Ulysses S. Grant*, Vol. 1, 1837–1861. Carbondale: Southern Illinois Univ. Press, 1967.

Smith, Donald K. *Sergeant Feiler's Furlough*. Chico, Calif.: Assoc. for Northern California Records and Research, 1977.

Sparks, V. K. "Barbs Exchanged by Early Day Editors." *The Humboldt Historian*, 35 (Nov. 1987, Dec. 1987), 3–5, 10–11.

Stewart, George R. *John Phoenix, Esq.* New York: De Capo Press, 1969.

———*The California Trail*. New York: McGraw-Hill Book Co., 1971.

Sweeney, Thomas W. *Journal of Lt. Thomas W. Sweeney, 1849–1853*. Ed. by Arthur Woodward. Los Angeles: Westernlore Press, 1956.

Thompson, Gerald. *Edward F. Beale & The American West*. Albuquerque: Univ. of New Mexico Press, 1983.

Todd, Frederick P. *American Military Equipage, 1851–1872*. New York: Charles Scribner's Sons, 1980.

Utley, Robert M. *Frontiersmen in Blue: The United States Army and the Indian, 1848–1865*. New York: Macmillan Pub. Co., Inc., 1967.

———*The Indian Frontier of the American West, 1846–1890*. Albuquerque: Univ. of New Mexico Press, 1985.

Uzes, Francois D. *Chaining the Land: A History of Surveying in California*. Sacramento: Landmark Enterprises, 1977.

Wells, Henry L. *History of Sikiyou County, California*. Oakland: D. J. Stewart & Co., 1881.

Winn, Robert. "The Mendocino Indian Reservation," *Mendocino Hist. Rev.*, XII (Fall/Winter 1986), 1–38.

Wooster, Robert. *Soldiers, Sutlers, and Settlers: Garrison Life on the Texas Frontier*. College Station, Texas: Texas A & M Univ. Press, 1987.

Zwinger, Ann H. *The Letters of John Xantus to Spencer Fullerton Baird from San Francisco and Cabo San Lucas, 1859–1861*. Los Angeles: Dawson's Book Shop, 1986.

NEWSPAPERS

Crescent City. *Herald*.

Eureka. *Humboldt Times*.

Gardiner, Maine. *Home Journal*.

San Francisco. *Alta California*.

Shasta. *Courier*.

Ukiah. *Mendocino Herald*.

Index